The Reagan Presidency

The Reagan Presidency

Assessing the Man and His Legacy

Edited by Paul Kengor
& Peter Schweizer

ROWMAN & LITTLEFIELD PUBLISHERS, INC.
Lanham • Boulder • New York • Toronto • Oxford

ROWMAN & LITTLEFIELD PUBLISHERS, INC.

Published in the United States of America
by Rowman & Littlefield Publishers, Inc.
A wholly owned subsidiary of The Rowman & Littlefield Publishing Group, Inc.
4501 Forbes Boulevard, Suite 200, Lanham, Maryland 20706
www.rowmanlittlefield.com

PO Box 317
Oxford
OX2 9RU, UK

British Library Cataloguing in Publication Information Available

Library of Congress Cataloging-in-Publication Data

The Reagan presidency : assessing the man and his legacy / edited By Paul Kengor &
Peter Schweizer.
    p. cm.
  Includes bibliographical references and index.
  ISBN 0-7425-3414-6 (cloth : alk. paper) – ISBN 0-7425-3415-4 (pbk. : alk. paper)
  1. United States—Politics and government—1981-1989. 2. Reagan, Ronald. 3. Reagan, Ronald—Political and social views. 4. Reagan, Ronald—Influence. I. Kengor,
Paul, 1966– II. Schweizer, Peter, 1964-

E876.R41164 2005   2004029779
973.927'092—dc22

Printed in the United States of America

∞™ The paper used in this publication meets the minimum requirements of American
National Standard for Information Sciences—Permanence of Paper for Printed Library
Materials, ANSI/NISO Z39.48-1992.

Contents

Acknowledgments

In addition to the impressive group of authors who contributed to this volume, we would like to thank the Hoover Institution and director John Raisian; the Earhart Foundation; and Barton A. Stebbins and his trustee, Donald W. Crowell. Without their support this project would not have been completed. We also thank Erin Kinnen for her excellent editorial assistance. Paul Kengor is particularly grateful to Grove City College, its president, Dick Jewell, Provost Bill Anderson, Dean John Sparks, and all of the college's trustees and administration for creating the sabbatical program that made it possible for him to finish this project in a timely manner. Finally, we most appreciate our wives and families for the continued patience as we take on these writing chores.

Paul Kengor
Peter Schweizer

December 2004

Introduction

On June 5, 2004, Ronald Wilson Reagan, the nation's 40th president, died at the age of 93. In the week that followed, he was eulogized as everything from the man who won the Cold War to the president who restored morale and economic growth at home and respect for America abroad. On the negative side, Reagan left behind huge deficits, a record-high national debt, and a controversial scandal called Iran-Contra; he was criticized as a detached chief executive. What was the real Reagan record? What will history say about the man? What was Ronald Reagan's legacy?

Ever since Ronald Reagan left office in January 1989 there has been intense debate over what the Reagan years meant for the country and the world. In the early years that followed, much of the academic community was largely negative toward Reagan. How much of this reflected historical realities or ideological bias is open to debate. But in recent years the view within academe has changed considerably. As evidenced by certain polls, scholarly opinion (and elite opinion generally) may have undergone a reappraisal of Reagan and his legacy. An April 2002 article in the *New York Times* with the title, "Rethinking Reagan: Was He a Man of Ideas After All?" captured the shifting elite opinion. The reevaluation was seen in two major polls of mainstream presidential scholars, which ranked Reagan near the upper echelon of presidents. One was C-SPAN's 1999 survey of American presidents, which rated Reagan the 11th best president ever. Using *Political Science Quarterly*'s categories, an 11th place finish would mark Reagan a "high average" president only two spots away from the "near great" designation. The historians in the C-SPAN poll also ranked Reagan fourth best among all chief executives in the category of "public persuasion," behind only FDR, TR, and Lincoln. Another poll was done in 2000 by a group of academics selected for a *Wall Street Journal—Federalist Society* poll. Editorially, the *Wall Street Journal* is a conservative newspaper. Nonetheless, the list of academics surveyed was not a conservative group. A total of 78 historians, political scientists, and even legal scholars were surveyed (compared to 58 in the C-SPAN poll). Reagan placed as the eighth best president in history in this poll, putting him in the "near great" category.

Precisely where Reagan should be ranked will continue to be hotly contested. But there seems to be little doubt about Reagan's influence on America and the world. Regardless of whether one liked Reagan or his beliefs, it seems fair to conclude that the country and world changed rather dramatically during the Reagan years; where we are now certainly has something to do with Reagan.

Ronald Reagan was a son of the American Midwest. Born in Tampico, Illinois on February 6, 1911, he was the son of a heavy-drinking shoe salesman (Jack) and a devoutly religious mother (Nelle). Nelle inculcated in Reagan the values, particularly spiritual values, he would carry throughout his life. He was raised in nearby Dixon, Illinois, a town that provided him with (in his words) his "inheritance." Dixon shaped Ronald Reagan.

Reagan attended college at nearby Eureka College where he majored in economics, was active in sports and a member of the drama club. Like many young and ambitious performers of the stage, he dreamed of a life in Hollywood, and moved there in 1937 after a successful stint as a radio broadcaster in Iowa. Reagan signed on with Warner Brothers and performed in dozens of films, including *King's Row* and *Knute Rockne*, as well as forgettable films like *Cattle Queen of Montana* and *Bedtime for Bonzo*, meaning his co-stars ranged from Humphrey Bogart to Bette Davis to a chimpanzee. He would serve several terms as head of the Screen Actors Guild and then as a pitchman for General Electric. He was the host of *GE Theatre* from 1954 to 1962, a very popular weekly television program that reached #1 within just weeks of its debut, immediately eclipsing *I Love Lucy*. The *GE*

Theatre exposure literally made Reagan one of the most recognized male names in America. He ended his performing career in the early 1960s.

During his Hollywood years, Reagan was married first to actress Jane Wyman, who divorced him in 1947, and then to actress Nancy Davis in 1952. With Wyman he had two children, Maureen and Michael, the latter of whom was adopted. With Nancy he had Ron and Patti. Reagan's relationship with his children was friendly but at times rocky, though his relationship with Nancy seemed the thing of storybooks.

Reagan's interest in politics was sparked in his youth, when his father spoke fondly of the policies of FDR. Reagan considered himself an FDR admirer and a New Deal Democrat for many of his adult years. But a series of violent strikes in Hollywood, the high progressive income tax rates he experienced (91%) while making money in the film business, and his response to the communist threat from Moscow, slowly transformed him into a political conservative. Soon, he was a Democrat for Eisenhower, and then became a Republican for Nixon. When he entered elective politics in 1966 to run as governor of California, Reagan was a full-fledged conservative Republican.

Reagan served two terms as governor, leaving office in 1974, winning twice in landslides, including (initially) against a popular incumbent. In 1976 he challenged President Gerald R. Ford for the Republican Party nomination, but lost narrowly. When he ran again in 1980, he won the Republican Party nomination and defeated Democratic President Jimmy Carter in the general election. He won 44 of 50 states against Carter. In 1984, he defeated Carter's vice president, Walter Mondale, by sweeping 49 of 50 states and winning the Electoral College by 525 to 13 votes.

Reagan left the presidency in 1989. By the end of that year, communism was finished in the Soviet bloc: Solidarity had been elected in Poland, the Berlin Wall fell, and vicious dictator Nicolae Ceausescu was executed by the citizens of Romania. Two years later, the USSR disintegrated. Reagan's mind lasted long enough to comprehend this momentous development—which he had both hoped for and predicted—before Alzheimer's overtook him. On November 5, 1994, he informed the world of his disease. Blessed by a remarkably healthy body—soon his worst enemy—the disease needed 10 years to take his life.

In the essays below, scholars analyze Reagan the man and his presidency from a variety of angles, in an effort to answer the fundamental question: What was Reagan's legacy? In a very real sense, this question cannot be fully answered because his legacy is still not completely visible. History is still being written and Reagan's two terms in office, the policies he adopted, and the ideas he championed still influence us to this day. Nonetheless, certain things can be said. It is our hope that the following essays provide a fair and objective analysis of Ronald Reagan; their goal is to inform, to enlighten, and to bring us closer to the real Reagan and his presidency.

Paul Kengor
Peter Schweizer

1

Elections and Achievement: Campaigning and Governing in the Reagan Era

Michael Nelson

When Ronald Reagan swore the oath of office as president for the first time on January 20, 1981, the prevailing wisdom among pundits, politicians, and political scientists was that the American presidency was a weak, even endangered institution. Former president Gerald R. Ford wrote an essay for *Time* magazine whose title described the office as "Imperiled, Not Imperial." Others used more vivid imagery— the "tethered presidency," the "revolving-door presidency," the "no-win presidency."[1] Whatever the term, the agreed-upon explanation for presidential weakness was the same: public expectations of the office had risen precipitously, even as the institutional capacity to meet them had declined.[2] Presidents, consequently, were pro-grammed for failure, doomed to disappoint. Reagan's immediate predecessors, Ford and Jimmy Carter, had been worn down by the hopelessness of their situation. The consensus was that Reagan, the sixth president to be inaugurated in the past twenty years, was destined to join them on the roster of undistinguished, one-term pres-idents.

Four years later, the prevailing wisdom could not have been more different. In the aftermath of Reagan's forty-nine state landslide re-election against former vice president Walter F. Mondale, the chorus of experts sang a different tune: the presidency is strong again. Some found this a cause for celebration, others for lamentation. Former Reagan aide David Gergen spoke for the first group when he trum-peted that Reagan had "restore[ed] the strength of the institutionalized

5

presidency."[3] In stark contrast, *New York Times* columnist Anthony
Lewis warned, "The imperial presidency is on the rise again."[4]

Such wild oscillations of opinion are all too common among students
of the presidency. They result from widespread overreactions to the nation's experience with whoever has just been president. During the administrations of Lyndon B. Johnson and Richard Nixon, a different kind
of scholarly swing had taken place, from consensus that the presidency
was a benign institution to concern that it was dangerous. (No one
doubted then that it was a powerful office, however.) In truth, the presidency is best regarded as neither strong nor weak, benign nor malignant, but rather as empowered for different purposes at different times,
primarily by the national will as expressed in presidential elections.
Viewed in this light, the forecast for Reagan's first term should have
been for dramatic domestic policy change initiated by the president—
that is, for a Presidency of Achievement in the manner of three of the
new president's twentieth century predecessors: Woodrow Wilson,
Franklin D. Roosevelt, and Lyndon Johnson.[5]

PRESIDENTS OF ACHIEVEMENT

A President of Achievement is one who spurs Congress to great bursts
of legislative activity that significantly alter the role of the federal government in American society. These changes are grounded in American
political culture, the nation's widely shared and deeply rooted beliefs
concerning how the political system ought to work and the ends it ought
to advance. Presidencies of Achievement manifest new, intensely felt
definitions of liberty and equality—Americans' two main values concerning the ultimate purposes of government. Public optimism runs
high at the outset of such presidencies, fostering a sense that the government can solve any problem. The voters' usual ambivalence toward
political authority resolves temporarily into faith in government, especially the president, to act as the embodiment of national purpose.

Three Presidents of Achievement: Wilson, Roosevelt, and Johnson

Woodrow Wilson was the century's first President of Achievement.
During the early 1910s, Wilson persuaded Congress to enact his "New

Freedom" agenda: the Clayton Act, which strengthened the federal government's antitrust policies; the Federal Trade Commission Act, which created a new commission with authority to punish unfair business competition; the Underwood Tariff Act, which fostered international trade and provided for an income tax; and the Federal Reserve Act, which created the Federal Reserve Board and assigned it control over the nation's credit system. Taken as a whole, Wilson inaugurated a new role for the federal government as a national umpire that would regulate the excesses of private economic power in defense of personal liberty.

Franklin Roosevelt's Presidency of Achievement began in 1933 with the celebrated "first hundred days." An emergency banking bill, completed by the newly-inaugurated president and his advisers at 2:00 A.M. on March 9, was passed unanimously by the House that same day after thirty-eight minutes of debate; it became law within hours when the Senate followed suit.[6] Other bills followed in rapid succession:

- March 26: Economy Act
- March 31: Civilian Conservation Corps
- April 19: Gold standard abandoned (ratified by Congress on June 5)
- May 12: Federal Emergency Relief Act
  Agricultural Adjustment Act (AAA)
  Emergency Farm Mortgage Act
- May 18: Tennessee Valley Authority (TVA) Act
- May 27: Truth-in-Securities Act
- June 13: Home Owners Loan Act
- June 16: National Industrial Recovery Act
  Glass-Steagall Banking Act
  Farm Credit Act

A "second hundred days" occurred in early 1935, when Congress passed the National Labor Relations Act, the Social Security Act, acts to strengthen the previous banking and TVA laws, and a tax bill that increased the responsibility of the wealthy. The legislation of the second hundred days was aimed more at restructuring the economy than was the legislation of the first hundred days, which was preoccupied with the need to revive it. But the public philosophy of the New Deal was fairly consistent throughout: the federal government is ultimately responsible for securing the foundations of the people's liberty, which Roosevelt reconceived to include welfare, security, and employment.

Lyndon Johnson, the century's third President of Achievement, invoked the nation's cultural commitment to equality in extending the helping hand of government to economically deprived minorities who had been generally untouched by the New Deal. He also addressed quality-of-life concerns such as education, the arts, and the environment in pursuit of his Great Society agenda. As the political scientist Roger Davidson points out, "The legislative record of the 89th Congress (1965–1967) reads like a roll call of contemporary government programs: Medicare/Medicaid, Voting Rights Act of 1965, Older Americans Act, Freedom of Information Act, National Foundation on the Arts and Humanities, highway beautification, urban mass transit, clean water, and the Departments of Transportation and Housing and Urban Development, among others."[7]

Elements of a Presidency of Achievement

Presidencies of Achievement are rare occurrences in American politics. They occur only when three conditions are met: an empowering election, a politically skillful president, and a fount of suitable policy ideas.

Election. A president is empowered for achievement if he campaigns for the office with promises, however general, of significant policy change; is elected by a landslide majority; and has long "coattails" (that is, helps to foster large gains for his party) in the accompanying congressional elections.[8] In 1912, Wilson defeated his nearest rival by a margin of 14.4 percentage points and 347 electoral votes, while his party gained sixty-two seats in the House of Representatives and nine in the Senate. Twenty years later, Roosevelt won by 17.7 points and 413 electoral votes; his party secured ninety-seven new House seats and twelve new seats in the Senate. In 1964, Johnson won by a margin of 22.6 percentage points and 434 electoral votes as his party gained a new senator and thirty-seven new representatives. All three ran change-oriented campaigns in securing these victories.

The first two characteristics of an empowering election—a landslide victory in response to a campaign for change—seem obvious, the third perhaps less so. The reason that the length of the president's coattails in the accompanying congressional elections matters more than the overall size of his party's majority in Congress is that the gains invariably are attributed, accurately or not, to the president. Such gains create a heightened disposition among legislators of both parties to support the president's initiatives whenever they can: members of his own party because they want to ride his bandwagon, members of the opposition (especially those representing states or districts that the president carried) because they want to avoid being flattened by it. A president whose election is not accompanied by long coattails is more likely to be regarded by legislators as tangential to their own political fortunes. Franklin Roosevelt had an easier time with the Congress that was elected in 1932, which contained many new Democrats, than with the Congress that was chosen in the 1936 elections, in which the Democrats made only small gains. This was so even though the total Democratic membership in the latter Congress was larger.

Skill. Winning an empowering election makes a Presidency of Achievement possible, even likely—but not inevitable. The president must still convert opportunity into accomplishment. A crucial ingredient in meeting this challenge is the effective deployment of leadership skills.

What skills do Presidents of Achievement require? The skill they need most is a strong strategic sense of the grain of history—an ability to understand the public mood and to shape and fulfill the historical possibilities of the time.[9] They also should be able to present themselves and their policies to the general public through effective rhetoric and symbolic action and to deal in a tactically skillful way with the rest of the Washington community (especially members of Congress) through negotiation, persuasion, and other forms of bargaining. Finally, Presidents of Achievement must be able to manage their lieutenants in the White House staff and the executive departments to help them translate campaign promises into specific, appealing public policies.

Not all Presidents of Achievement will have all of these skills, nor do they need to as long as they have most of them. Wilson, for example, was a brilliant rhetorical president but awkward in his personal dealings with legislators. Johnson was the opposite. Only Roosevelt had them all.

   Ideas. Few of the ideas that historians associate with the New Freedom, the New Deal, and the Great Society were first conceived during the Presidencies of Achievement that brought these ideas to fruition. Wilson drew his broad philosophy and specific policies from the Progressive movement of the 1890s and 1900s, especially the movement's Louis Brandeis–led, corporate-smallness wing. Roosevelt drew on an eclectic mix of ideas that had been propounded during the 1920s. As the political scientist James MacGregor Burns notes, Roosevelt "had grasped the standard of Wilsonian reform in his measures for federal supervision of securities, friendliness to labor, business regulation. He had trod Cousin Theodore's old path in conservation and in the elements of planning in the AAA. He had filched a plank from American socialism in the public ownership features of TVA," and later, in the social security and tax bills.[10] Johnson drew primarily on the ideas for new programs that liberal Democratic legislators and intellectuals had developed during the 1950s.

   Presidents of Achievement cannot assume that a deep inventory of policy ideas that are suitable to their purposes will be available when they take office. The reason is that successful ideas are more than just substantively sound, although that standard alone is a high one. They must also be politically appealing. Successful ideas are syntheses of expert knowledge, values grounded in the political culture, and short-term political reality. They are not only accepted as workable by policy experts, but also respond in culturally acceptable terms to the concerns of the American people.

The Postachievement Phase of a Presidency of Achievement

The essence of a Presidency of Achievement is the dramatic change in the role of the federal government in American society that the president engineers. Historically, the period of achievement within such presidencies has been relatively brief, usually the first two to four years. Momentum slows when administrative difficulties arise from the attempt to attain major social and economic change through governmental action so quickly, when more traditional meanings of values in the political culture are reasserted, and when the anti-government strain in the public's ambivalence toward authority reemerges. This presents a problem of governance. The grateful citizenry, voting retrospectively, is likely to reward the President of Achievement with reelection. But it may no longer support his basic temperamental and philosophical ambition, which is to continue to make his mark on government and society through legislative action.

For the President of Achievement, who is unlikely to change his spots even when the voters change theirs, two strategies present themselves. The first is to throw caution to the wind and seek another empowering election when he runs for a second term. Yet no President of Achievement has ever attempted to do this. One reason is that a change-oriented campaign is the natural strategy of a challenger seeking to evict the current tenant from the White House, not an incumbent trying to remain there. Another is that, almost by definition, a President of Achievement's best strategy for getting reelected is to remind the voters how much he has accomplished rather than dwell on all the problems that remain, presumably because he has failed to solve them.

The second strategy for the President of Achievement who wants to keep achieving is to emphasize foreign policy during the second term. On the world stage, the constraints that typically bring the brief period of domestic achievement to an end bind the president less closely. The public is more consistent in its support of strong presidential leadership in foreign policy. The problems of bureaucratic implementation are generally less severe. One cannot help but note the coincidence of Presidencies of Achievement and war: Wilson and World War I, Roosevelt and World War II, Johnson and Vietnam. In every case, these were wars that the United States, led by a president who invoked the highest values in American political culture, chose to enter. One need not draw a deterministic connection between war and Presidents of Achievement, however. What is common to both is a high tide of cultural optimism, the belief that Americans have the power to transform the system, at home or abroad, for the better. Thus, one might just as logically expect a President of Achievement to try to forge a different kind of dramatic foreign policy success, such as nuclear disarmament or universal free trade.

ELECTIONS IN THE 1980S AND
REAGAN'S PRESIDENCY OF ACHIEVEMENT

Ronald Reagan was the twentieth century's fourth President of Achievement and its first conservative one. The turn from liberalism to conservatism as the dominant political ideology during the Reagan era originated in the last years of the Nixon presidency. This was an unusual period for all sorts of reasons, including not just Watergate but one that is sometimes overlooked: the nature of the intellectual ferment and social discontent that was developing around the country. New problems seemed less tractable than older ones had been: in the economy, "stagflation," a condition of simultaneously high inflation and unemployment; in social policy, the development of a seemingly permanent underclass; in foreign policy, disorientation about the post-Vietnam role of the United States in the world. Many liberal thinkers lost confidence in their ability to define the appropriate direction of policy change and to develop suitable programs to achieve it. Some of them joined ranks with increasingly confident conservative intellectuals, whose ideas on supply-side economics, corporate deregulation, administrative decentralization, moral conservatism, nuclear strategy, and a hawkish foreign policy toward the Soviet Union were percolating in conservative think tanks like the Heritage Foundation, the Hoover Institution, and the American Enterprise Institute, as well as in journals of opinion such as *The Public Interest* and *Commentary* and in groups of legislators led by Rep. Jack Kemp of New York, Rep. David Stockman of Michigan, and others.

The Ford presidency, nominally a corruption-free continuation of the Nixon administration, inherited the intellectual and social confusion that accompanied this shift from left to right. Ford's misfortune was to govern at a time of uncertainty about how government can accomplish even widely shared goals such as prosperity and peace. Neither Ford nor his rivals in the heavily Democratic Congress had confident answers to the new problems of stagflation at home and post-Vietnam tentativeness abroad.

The Carter Years: Preparing the Way

Ford was defeated in his bid for a full term in 1976, but the results of the election allowed his opponent, former governor Jimmy Carter of Georgia, no room to claim a mandate from the voters. Carter's margin of victory over Ford was tiny and his party gained only one new seat in Congress. Worse, Carter was the first Democratic president in nearly a century to be forced to confront policy problems that were not amenable to the liberal programmatic impulses of his party's governing coalition. Stagflation seemed chronic, with the "misery index" of inflation plus unemployment at 12 percent when Carter took office in January 1977. The federal budget deficit was rising steeply, largely because of rapid increases in the cost of Great Society entitlement programs such as Medicare, Medicaid, and food stamps. Industrial productivity was declining. To complicate matters, Carter had played to the public's disenchantment with government in his campaign, lavishing particular disdain on bureaucratic inefficiency and moral laxity. This was not a good platform from which to rouse confidence in an activist reform administration.

Carter came to the presidency with a coherent philosophy of domestic policy, one grounded in an approach of comprehensive solutions based on sound and dispassionate analysis. He was a fiscal conservative and social liberal who thought it possible to pursue humane social goals through restrained budgetary policies and efficient management.[11] Conservative but tolerant on moral issues, Carter preached conscience and traditional values while scorning the demands of the Moral Majority and other organizations of the newly mobilized Religious Right to write into law their positions on issues such as school prayer and abortion.

Unfortunately, Carter found that there was no organized political constituency for his centrist approach. For example, his welfare reform proposal, which sought to provide greater security for the poor at no additional cost through more efficient design and administration was opposed by liberals because it was fiscally austere and conservatives because it was not austere enough. Similarly, Carter vacillated for three years on health policy because he could not persuade Massachusetts senator Edward M. Kennedy, the unions, and other liberal advocates of national health insurance to accept his own less comprehensive but more economically sound proposal. Kennedy's bill could not pass Congress, but without the liberal senator's support Carter's plan could not pass either. Ultimately, the public became convinced that a president who could not lead his own party must be incapable of leading the nation.

Carter's problems were complicated by his limited repertoire of leadership skills. As a former naval engineer who felt that, once elected, his main task was to make "correct" decisions and simply explain them, Carter gave little attention to the challenge of persuasively presenting to the nation his policies and himself as leader. In dealing with other Washington politicians, he showed even less interest in offering political incentives as a means of tactical leadership. As for Carter's management of lieutenants for policy formation, it oscillated between drowning himself in the technical details of some issues, often losing sight of larger political realities in the process, and freely delegating responsibility for the remaining issues to others, usually with little guidance about what he wanted. Finally, Carter's strategic sense of the historical possibilities of his time was limited. Unlike other presidents who were narrowly elected, such as John F. Kennedy, Carter did not see the need for a preparation stage in which he would select a few crucial goals, nurture public support for them, and tie their enactment to a clear sense of where he wanted to lead the country. Bucking the liberal interests in his own party and with no other base of support to take their place, Carter tried unsuccessfully to be a President of Achievement without meeting any of the requisites.

Despite his woes in office and his humiliating defeat by Ronald Reagan in the 1980 election, Carter inadvertently helped to prepare the way for Reagan and his policies. The themes of Carter's administration, the most conservative of any twentieth century Democratic president, foreshadowed those of his successor: moral conservatism, by example and exhortation if not by law; a preoccupation with inflation, growth, and deregulation in economic policy (Carter's success in securing legislative deregulation of the airline and trucking industries was unparalleled); and an anti-bureaucratic, anti-Washington posture that more than anything else accounted for his rise from the obscure status of a former southern governor to the presidential nomination of the Democratic party.

In foreign policy, too, Carter helped prepare the way (again, unwittingly) for his successor. Although he had called for reductions in defense spending during the 1976 campaign, Carter reversed course as president and increased appropriations for the armed services every year. Equally important, he altered the basis of American foreign policy from Nixon- and Ford-style realism to moralism in the service of human rights.

The Reagan Years: Achievement and Its Aftermath

Carter's actions as president reflected his rhetoric but were unable to fulfill it. In 1980, voters' concerns about inflation, high interest rates, slow economic growth, and big government created a climate in which a candidate who promised great and sudden change in the role of the federal government in American society could thrive. Ronald Reagan's campaign and election clearly set the stage for a Presidency of Achievement. Reagan ran a change-oriented campaign, pledging enormous tax cuts, serious reductions in social spending, and an unprecedented peacetime defense buildup. He won a landslide victory, securing the largest electoral vote in history against an incumbent president, 489 to 49. Finally, he extended long coattails to his party's candidates for Congress: Republicans gained thirty-three seats in the House and twelve in the Senate, taking control of the Senate for the first time since 1955. Public confidence in government rose.[12]

Seizing the moment, Reagan moved simultaneously on almost all political fronts during his first months in office. For domestic policy ideas, he drew from the ranks of supply-side economists and other conservative intellectuals, including his own Office of Management and Budget (OMB) director, former representative David Stockman. Reagan's initial budget included eighty-four proposals to reduce or eliminate federal programs. A *New York Times* survey found that he won on 60 percent of them, including assaults on political "untouchables" such as housing assistance, public service employment, food stamps, child nutrition, and aid to working welfare mothers. (Even more important, these victories involved "85 to 90 percent of the dollar savings he wanted.")[13] Reagan also was able to reduce the number of federal categorical grant programs from 361 to 259 by eliminating some and consolidating others into block grants. At the same time, the money for these programs was substantially reduced. His Task Force on Regulatory Relief, with Vice President George H. W. Bush as chair, checked the historical increase in new federal regulations, and his reductions in the enforcement divisions of agencies such as the Federal Trade Commission and the Occupational Safety and Health Administration diminished the effectiveness of existing regulations. Reagan secured the enactment of a 25 percent cut in the federal income tax on individuals, along with the permanent indexing of the tax brackets to changes in the cost of living. Corporations benefited from the new tax law even more.

Congress's acquiescence in all this was nearly complete. In 1981, Republican senators and representatives gave Reagan the highest "index of loyalty" any party had given to its president since Congressional Quarterly began keeping track in 1953. The conservative coalition also had its best year ever, winning 92 percent of the votes on which it was active, as Republican legislators were joined by conservative "Boll Weevil" Democrats, who represented districts in which Reagan and his policies were popular.[14] Even the House Democratic leadership initially bowed to Reagan's power, handing over virtual control of the legislative agenda to the president. An aide to Speaker Thomas P. O'Neill Jr. said:

> What the Democrats did, in extraordinary fashion, was to recognize the cataclysmic nature of the 1980 election results. The American public wanted this new president to be given a chance to try out his programs. We weren't going to come across as being obstructionists.[15]

Reagan's mark on security policy was equally distinct. Matching his confidence that the United States could win, not just survive, the Cold War to the new strategic thinking of conservative defense intellectuals in the Heritage Foundation, the Committee on the Present Danger, and the Hoover Institution, Reagan had argued throughout the 1980 campaign that Carter's increases in defense spending were inadequate to match the Soviet arms buildup and that the United States would soon face a "window of vulnerability" to Soviet nuclear superiority. Once in office, he persuaded Congress to enact massive increases in defense spending in general and weapons procurement in particular, downplayed strategic arms negotiations with the Soviet Union pending the restoration of American military might, and let it be known that his administration would seek to roll back communist advances throughout the world, especially in Western Hemisphere nations such as

Nicaragua and Grenada, instead of just trying to contain them. As had Carter, Reagan viewed foreign policy in moral terms. But Reagan defined anti-communism rather than human rights as the paramount moral cause that the United States should pursue. At the first news conference of his presidency, Reagan declared that the Soviets "reserve unto themselves the right to commit any crime, to lie to cheat"; later he described the Soviet Union as "the evil empire."

Reagan saw himself from the start as a president in the mold of Franklin Roosevelt. Like his Democratic predecessor, Reagan exuded optimism that the United States could solve any problem to which it set its mind. Like Roosevelt, too, he wished to bring a new deal to the nation that would form the basis for a new political era. Reagan had all the rhetorical skills required of a President of Achievement: having spent most of his adult life either as a public speaker or before the camera as an actor, he was particularly adept at clarifying complex issues through a simple, straightforward, smoothly delivered message. Reagan's presentational skills supplemented his strategic sense that voters wanted root-and-branch, not incremental approaches to the problems that concerned them. Traditional Republican economic policies, which alternated moderate stimulus with belt-tightening response, would have been no more popular for Reagan than they had been for Nixon and Ford. Reagan also realized that, both as an overall strategy and as a tactical ploy with members of Congress and other Washington politicians, he should set his policy course and stay with it, even in the face of short-term adversity, such as the recession of 1981–1982. Reagan's "stay the course" approach conveyed a strong sense of purpose and self-confidence that reinforced his image as a leader. This belief carried over into his management of policy formation within the executive branch. Reagan reserved fundamental choices to himself and delegated almost everything else to lieutenants who had been appointed to the White House staff, OMB, and the departments primarily because of their political loyalty and ideological purity.

By the end of Reagan's first term, a cascade of numbers testified to the new directions he had imposed on government, both in foreign and domestic affairs. Spending on food stamps and on Aid to Families with Dependent Children, the federal government's main welfare programs, was down 13 percent from what it would have been if the government had simply continued the budget policies that were in place when Reagan became president. Medicaid spending was down 6 percent; housing assistance, 4 percent; compensatory education, 17 percent; child nutrition, 28 percent. Public service employment, a $4.5 billion program, had been eliminated. In all, spending on the non-defense activities of the federal government other than Social Security and Medicare was 12.5 percent lower in real dollars than when Reagan took office, and the proportion of the total economy devoted to social programs was rapidly descending to the level that prevailed prior to the passage of Johnson's Great Society. Meanwhile, defense spending was up 49 percent in real dollars, and the federal work force, which was 10 percent smaller in the domestic bureaucracies, rose in the Department of Defense.[16]

Not all of Reagan's proposals for policy change were adopted, and the exceptions are revealing of the limits encountered even by Presidents of Achievement. His efforts to turn the nation's environmental policies in a conservative direction provoked a hostile and politically overwhelming response, as did his attempts to undo civil rights landmarks such as the Voting Rights Act and the Internal Revenue Service's policy of denying tax-exempt status to racially segregated private schools. Unlike those policies with which Reagan was successful, these were matters that he had not brought before the voters during the 1980 election campaign. Reagan's stance on moral issues was politically shrewder, if no more successful in policy terms. While frequently invoking traditional religious and moral values in speeches, he downplayed proposed constitutional amendments on school prayer and abortion for the sake of pursuing his economic and defense policies without distraction. Finally, there was Reagan's greatest first-term failure: four years of unprecedented twelve-figure federal budget deficits that, taken together, nearly doubled the national debt. Reagan's policies helped to achieve certain macroeconomic wonders—the decline in inflation from 12 percent to 4 percent first among them—but the budgetary effects of his defense increases and tax cuts simply overwhelmed those of his domestic spending reductions.

Reagan's status as a President of Achievement rests on a firmer foundation than a tally sheet of specific successes and failures. His policies, in addition to being dramatic, involved a sufficiently clear change in the direction of federal activity to make them heroically incremental in the tradition of other Presidents of Achievement. Although conservative in substance, they were imbued with a familiar cultural optimism about the capacity of determined political leaders to bring about desired changes: prosperity through tax cuts, the defeat of leftist revolutionaries abroad through American military aid and advice, and so on. Finally, more than anything else, Reagan transformed the agenda of political discussion. He "redefined the terms of the national debate," lamented the historian Arthur M. Schlesinger Jr., a longtime adviser to liberal Democratic presidents and politicians. "In domestic affairs, he placed a stigma on 'big government' and exalted the capacity of the unregulated marketplace to solve all our problems. In foreign affairs, he placed a stigma on détente and exalted large military budgets and an indefinitely escalating arms race."[17] The best evidence that Schlesinger's backhanded tribute to Reagan was accurate came in 1996, when Democratic president Bill Clinton began his inaugural address by declaring, "The era of big government is over."

Like previous Presidents of Achievement, Reagan ran a reelection campaign in 1984 that pointed with pride to his first-term successes but said little about his plans for the second term. Although he won an overwhelming personal landslide from the grateful voters (Mondale carried only one state), his coattails were short. Bereft therefore of both a mandate and a domestic agenda for the second term, Reagan turned to foreign affairs in pursuit of further dramatic achievement. One secret and partially illegal venture, to sell arms to Iran, a notorious sponsor of terrorism, and divert the proceeds of the sales to the anticommunist contra rebels in Nicaragua, blew up in the president's face when it became public in 1986 as the notorious "Iran-Contra" scandal. A second initiative, however, was considerably more successful. In 1987 Reagan held out the olive branch to his age-old nemesis, the Soviet Union. He and the new Soviet leader, Mikhail Gorbachev, negotiated the Intermediate-range Nuclear Force (INF) treaty, the first treaty in history to bring about the destruction of an entire class of nuclear weapons. The same optimism about Reagan's ability to roll back communism through accelerated defense spending that had characterized the first term marked his equally successful steps toward nuclear disarmament during the second term. Ultimately, of course, his policies helped roll back communism as well. Within two years of Reagan's leaving office, the Soviet Union ceased to exist.

The George H. W. Bush Presidency:
Consolidating Reagan's Presidency of Achievement

Historically, each President of Achievement has been followed in office by one or more presidents who consolidated the dramatic changes his predecessor had wrought in the federal government's role in American society, weaving them into the administrative fabric of government and retiring them from the roster of divisive political issues. The presidencies of Warren G. Harding, Calvin Coolidge, and Herbert Hoover helped consolidate Wilson's achievements. Eisenhower did the same for Roosevelt's New Deal, as Nixon did for Johnson's Great Society. Although some of these consolidating presidents were elected in landslide victories with long coattails, they based their campaigns on continuity and quiescence. Their mandate was to ease off the throttle by not pushing aggressively for a new round of dramatic change.

Because of the 22nd Amendment, which entered the Constitution in 1951, Reagan's second term as president was by definition his last term. (He would have liked to run again.) In 1988, for the first time in twenty years, both major party presidential nominees, Vice President Bush and his Democratic rival, Gov. Michael S. Dukakis of Massachusetts, were nonincumbents. Both, too, presented themselves to the voters as candidates for president who were less interested in repealing Reagan's achievements than in dealing with some of their unpleasant political and administrative side-effects, especially the enormous annual budget deficits that, by the end of Reagan's second term, had tripled the national debt from $1 billion to $3 billion. In his acceptance speech to the Democratic convention, Dukakis described the election as being "about competence, not ideology" and claimed that his experience as the two-term governor of a large industrial state had equipped him to run the federal government effectively and economically. Bush portrayed himself as the true heir to Reagan, albeit a "kinder and gentler" version of the president in whose administration he had served for eight years. Bush's famous "Read my lips: No new taxes" pledge was joined to a promise to be the "education president" and the "environmental president."

Politically, Bush's argument was the more persuasive. On election day he won the support of 83 percent of the voters who approved of the highly popular Reagan's performance as president.[18] His victory margin was convincing: 53 percent to 46 percent in the popular vote, 426 to 111 in the electoral college. Bush's pollster and political strategist, Robert Teeter, placed the election into historical context:

> We've only had fundamental changes five or six times in our two-hundred-year history. In 1980 there was this fundamental change. In 1984, people said, "We like the change." So by 1988 there was no desire to make a 180-degree turn. They said, "What is needed to be done is modify it, build on it."[19]

Bush carried the theme of continuity and consolidation past the election. His inaugural address thanked Reagan "for the wonderful things that you have done for America" and was laden with repeated invocations of "continuity," "continuance," and "continuum." In April 1989, Bush reaffirmed his status as Reagan's heir by telling reporters, "We didn't come in here throwing the rascals out."[20] Unwittingly, his assessment was a testimony to his predecessor's Presidency of Achievement.

NOTES

1. Gerald Ford, "Imperiled, Not Imperial," *Time* (November 10, 1980): 30–1; Thomas Frank, ed., *The Tethered Presidency* (New York: New York University Press, 1981); Michael Nelson, "The Revolving Door Presidency," *Miami Herald*, November 9, 1980; and Paul C. Light, *The President's Agenda* (Baltimore: Johns Hopkins University Press, 1982).

2. See, for example, Godfrey Hodgson, *All Things to All Men* (New York: Simon and Schuster, 1980).

3. Quoted in Lou Cannon, "Reagan Looks Ahead to Unfinished Business," *Washington Post National Weekly Edition*, February 6, 1984, 11.

4. Anthony Lewis, "Imperial Presidency on the Rise," *New York Times*, January 10, 1984.

5. A fuller treatment of the concept of Presidents of Achievement may be found in Erwin C. Hargrove and Michael Nelson, *Presidents, Politics, and Policy* (Baltimore: Johns Hopkins University Press, 1984). The theory applies to the

twentieth century because only then did the federal government, in particular the presidency, become the main object of the public's domestic policy demands.

6. Roosevelt was inaugurated on March 4, 1933, the date fixed for the start of presidential terms until the 20th Amendment changed it to January 20 in time for Roosevelt's second inaugural.

7. Roger Davidson, "The Presidency and Congress," in *The Presidency and the Political System*, ed. Michael Nelson (Washington, D.C.: CQ Press, 1984), 385.

8. A great deal of scholarly research suggests that the "coattails effect" is lesser in magnitude and greater in subtlety than most political observers believe. But, as Gary C. Jacobson has pointed out, as long as politicians—especially members of Congress—believe in it, the coattails effect will matter as much as if it were real. See Jacobson, *The Politics of Congressional Elections*, 3rd ed. (New York: HarperCollins, 1992), ch. 8.

9. "Strategic sense" strongly resembles Woodrow Wilson's idea of "interpretation." See Jeffrey K. Tulis, "The Two Constitution Presidencies," in *The Presidency and the Political System*, 7th ed. (Washington, D.C.: CQ Press, 2003), 79–110.

10. James MacGregor Burns, *Roosevelt: The Lion and the Fox*, Harvest ed. (New York: Harcourt, Brace and World, 1956), 179.

11. Erwin C. Hargrove, *Jimmy Carter as President: Leadership and the Politics of the Public Good* (Baton Rouge: Louisiana State University Press, 1988).

12. Seymour Martin Lipset and William Schneider, *The Confidence Gap: Business, Labor, and Government* (New York: Free Press, 1983), 21–2.

13. Robert Pear, "The Reagan Revolution," *New York Times*, January 31, 1984.

14. Bill Keller, "Voting Record of '81 Shows the Romance and Fidelity of Reagan Honeymoon on Hill," *Congressional Quarterly Weekly Report*, January 2, 1982, 19; and Irwin P. Arieff, "Conservatives Hit New High in Showdown Vote Victories," *Congressional Quarterly Weekly Report*, January 9, 1982, 50.

15. Quoted in Michael Nelson, "The Presidency: Clinton and the Cycle of Politics and Policy," in *The Elections of 1992*, ed. Michael Nelson (Washington, D.C.: CQ Press, 1993), 125–52.

16. These figures are drawn from Nicholas Lemann, "The Culture of Poverty," *Atlantic Monthly* (September 1984): 25; David Gergen, "Is Ronald Reagan Really Ready for the Future?" *Washington Post National Weekly Edition*, March 5, 1984, 23; and Nicholas Lemann, "The Peacetime War," *Atlantic Monthly* (October 1984): 71.

17. Arthur M. Schlesinger Jr., "The Democratic Party after Ted Kennedy," *Wall Street Journal*, December 7, 1982.

18. William Schneider, "Solidarity's Not Enough," *National Journal* (November 12, 1988): 2853–5.

19. Quoted in Michael Duffy and Dan Goodgame, *Marching in Place: The Status Quo Presidency of George Bush* (New York: Simon and Schuster, 1992), 19.

20. Duffy and Goodgame, *Marching in Place*, 37.

2

Ronald Reagan and Economic Policy

Andrew E. Busch

Of all of Ronald Reagan's policy departures, none were more controversial or more remarked upon than the new direction he promoted in economic policy. Inheriting a catastrophic economic situation, Reagan offered a diagnosis and a prescription. The diagnosis was that steadily increasing federal taxes, spending, and regulation had sapped the American economy of its vitality. The prescription was that government had to be re-limited. A decade and a half after its namesake left office, "Reaganomics" remains controversial, but has also exhibited greater staying power than many of its critics had thought possible.

THE ECONOMIC CRISIS OF THE 1970s

The first step to understanding the development and significance of the Reagan economic policy is to review the economic crisis of the 1970s. Following a period of non-inflationary prosperity in the 1960s, the nation began experiencing serious economic difficulties in the early 1970s. The annual rate of inflation grew from 3.0 percent in 1967 to 5.6 percent in 1970, before President Richard Nixon imposed temporary federal wage and price controls. Inflation quickly resumed its upward course, averaging 8.1 percent from 1973 through 1978; in 1979 the inflation rate reached 13.5 percent. At the same time, productivity foundered, unemployment rose, and the United States suffered recessions in 1974–1975 and 1979–1980. Real household incomes fell from

1973 to 1980. Not helping matters was a persistent energy crisis, including oil shortages in 1973–1974 (caused by an OPEC oil embargo) and 1979–1980 (caused by loss of oil from revolutionary Iran).

These conditions became known as "stagflation," an unprecedented combination of stagnation and inflation. In 1980, inflation was 12.5 percent, unemployment peaked at 7.5 percent, mortgage rates were at 15 percent, the prime interest rate approached 20 percent, and the nation saw its worst year in real family income since World War II. Stagflation was, of course, disastrous for American workers, businesses, and consumers, but it also wreaked havoc on the purveyors of economic conventional wisdom. For decades, economic thinking and policy was guided by the theory of Keynesianism, which advocated an activist government manipulating aggregate demand through fiscal policies of taxing and spending. Constructed to deal with the problems of deflation and unemployment, Keynesianism was not well suited to address a combination of inflation and unemployment. Indeed, a key corollary of Keynesian thinking (the "Phillips Curve") held that there was a mathematical trade-off between the two, that when one went up the other should go down.

This two-edged crisis—in both economic reality and economic theory—led a number of observers to wonder whether free-market capitalism was on the verge of destruction. A *Time* magazine cover story trumpeted the question "Can Capitalism Survive?" while noted economist Robert Heilbroner asked in the *New York Times Magazine* "Does Capitalism Have a Future?"[1] It was clear that the moment had arrived for a reappraisal of economic theory and policy.

ALTERNATIVES TO KEYNESIANISM

In this environment, there was a revival of classical free-market economic thinking for the first time since the Great Depression. This thinking took two major forms. One was monetarism, championed by Nobel Prize–winning economist Milton Friedman. Friedman argued that inflation should be suppressed with monetary policy focusing on a stable money supply and that the economy could grow as long as government intervention was limited. Another came to be known as "supply side" economics. In this view, the way to defeat stagflation was to concentrate not on aggregate demand but on market in-centives to increase supply. Greater production resulting from these incentives could bring both employment gains and falling inflation. The supply-siders held that lower marginal income tax rates were the key to the economy.[2]

To these variants one could add the more general economic position held by political conservatives—namely, that overtaxation, overspending, and overregulation with roots in the New Deal and Great Society were coming home to roost. This interpretation was viewed by the public with increasing sympathy as the 1970s wore on, and it is not difficult to see why. For example, the *Federal Register*, which includes a listing of federal regulations, grew from approximately 20,000 pages in 1970 to 87,000 pages in 1980. Because income taxes were not indexed to inflation, "bracket creep" pushed families into higher tax brackets even though their real (inflation-adjusted income) was falling. A family of four with an income of $25,000 in 1978 would have seen the rate on its last dollar of income rise from 19 percent in 1965 to 28 percent in 1978.[3]

The new climate could be seen in a variety of ways. In 1978, California voters began a national tax revolt by passing Proposition 13, a measure cutting skyrocketing property taxes. At the same time, two congressional bills signaled that change was in the air: the Steiger Amendment (introduced by Rep. William Steiger, R-Wisc.) cutting capital gains tax rates was passed in 1978; and the Kemp-Roth bill, based on supply-side logic, proposed cutting individual income tax rates by 30 percent across-the-board over three years. Kemp-Roth (sponsored by Rep. Jack Kemp, R-N.Y., and Sen. William Roth, R-Del.) actually passed the Senate in modified form in 1978, though it died in the House. Even president Jimmy Carter felt compelled to support some tax cuts and spending limitations. Carter also embraced some early deregulation measures, such as deregulation of the airline industry.

THE ECONOMIC RONALD REAGAN

Into this situation stepped Ronald Reagan. His views on economics were shaped by at least four experiences. First, he was an economics major at

Eureka College in the 1920s, before Keynesianism had begun to dominate the teaching of economics. Consequently, he was exposed to a
canon consisting of a wide range of classical economists like Adam
Smith, Alfred Marshall, Irving Fisher, Eugene Boem-Barwek, David Ri-
cardo, and Jean-Baptiste Say. Reagan's economic adviser Martin Anderson would later say that, "The essence of the comprehensive economic
program Reagan pursued in the 1980s was derived from the classical
economic principles he learned almost sixty years ago as a young man."[4]
Next, as an actor, he found himself in Franklin Roosevelt's 91 percent
top income tax bracket. According to several reports, this experience led
Reagan both to dislike high taxes and to come to a practical understanding of the disincentives inherent within very high marginal rates. Indeed,
Reagan himself said:

> I think my own experience with our tax laws in Hollywood probably
> taught me more about practical economic theory than I ever learned in a
> classroom or from an economist. . . . I began asking myself whether it
> was worth it to keep taking on work. . . . The same principle that affected
> my thinking applied to people in all tax brackets: The more government
> takes in taxes, the less incentive people have to work.[5]

Third, Reagan spent eight years, from 1954–1962, speaking for General
Electric, during which he extolled free enterprise and warned of the
dangers of overweening government. He traveled to 139 GE plants,
spoke to 250,000 employees, and often made addresses to other groups
in conjunction with his plant visits. Like his personal exposure to the 91
percent tax rate, his experience on these speaking tours proved cat-
alytic. In his words, "Those GE tours became almost a postgraduate
course in political science for me. . . . From hundreds of people in every
part of the country, I heard complaints about how the ever-expanding
federal government was encroaching on the liberties we'd always taken
for granted. . . . I'd listen and they'd cite examples of government in-
terference and snafus and complain about how bureaucrats, through
overregulation, were telling them how to run their business."[6] Finally,
Reagan was influenced by his own reading of noted free-market economists like Friedman, Ludwig von Mises, and Friedrich Hayek.[7]

    As Reagan began his 1980 presidential run, Jimmy Carter's eco-
nomic record became a key target. Reagan frequently joked that, "A re-

cession is when your neighbor is out of work; a depression is when you are out of work; and a recovery is when Jimmy Carter is out of work." Reagan succeeded in making the election a retrospective judgment on Carter's stewardship of the economy and foreign policy. In a moment that may have done more to seal his victory than any other, Reagan asked in his sole debate with Carter, "Are you better off than you were four years ago?" Few Americans could answer yes.

The economic plan Reagan offered as an alternative consisted of four essential pillars: Tax cuts, reducing the rate of growth of government spending, deregulation, and slow, stable growth of the money supply. Each of these prongs will be examined in turn.[8]

Tax cuts. In the 1980 campaign, Reagan embraced the Kemp-Roth 30 percent/three year tax cut (10–10–10), along with faster business depreciation to spur investment. Once in office, he secured a modified version of Kemp-Roth containing a 25 percent/three year income tax cut (5–10–10), starting in October 1981. The top rate was reduced from 70 percent to 50 percent. An amendment to the tax cut added a provision indexing tax rates to inflation after the third tax-cut installment; this was intended to prevent "bracket creep," a reform praised by the *New York Times* as "one of the fairest pieces of tax law in many a year."[9] Capital gains taxes were cut, and businesses saved an estimated $400 billion in depreciation allowances through 1990. A large part of the 1984 presidential election was fought over the issue of taxes, as Reagan pledged to maintain his 1981 tax cuts and Democratic challenger Walter Mondale vowed to roll them back.

In keeping with the aim of lower rates and less government management of the economy, Reagan also proposed major income tax reform and simplification in his January 1984 State of the Union address. Congress began deliberating plans advanced by the Treasury Department in 1985, and in 1986 passed a sweeping tax reform bill which reduced 14 brackets to two, cut the top rate to 28 percent, took four million working poor off the tax rolls, and eliminated scores of special-interest tax deductions.[10]

In pursuit of deficit reduction, Reagan did agree to a significant excise tax increase in 1982, a significant Social Security payroll tax increase in 1983 (actually an acceleration of the phased-in payroll tax increase passed in 1977), and smaller tax hikes in 1984 and 1987.

These tax increases often stirred conservative resentment, as in 1982, when Jack Kemp publicly broke with the White House. However, Reagan always refused to trim the centerpiece of his tax cuts—the personal rate reductions and indexing to inflation.

Slowing the growth of government spending. Reagan's most notable effort to tackle federal spending came in 1981, when Congress passed a budget reconciliation bill achieving savings of $38 billion in one year and $140 billion over three years compared with the current services baseline. By one estimate, $500 billion in domestic spending was saved over the course of the decade (relative to the 1980 baseline).[11] Measured another way, discretionary domestic spending fell from 4.7 percent of Gross Domestic Product (GDP) in 1980 to 3.1 percent in 1989, approaching pre–Great Society levels. In real dollars, such spending was cut by 14 percent. Entitlement spending was a much tougher nut, and continued exploding in real dollars. However, even there, so-called mandatory spending (excluding interest) was 10.3 percent of GDP in 1980 and 9.8 percent of GDP in 1989.

There were several keys to Reagan's successes in this area. He used the window of opportunity that opened in 1981 to maximum effect, forging a coalition with conservative Democrats to pass his reconciliation bill. Furthermore, his refusal to cancel the 1981 tax cuts imposed continuing pressure for spending restraint. As economist June O'Neill argued, "By accommodating higher levels of spending with tax increases, pressure to restrain spending growth . . . would have been diminished."[12] Many Democrats long suspected that the tax cuts were meant to stifle the growth of government generally, and Reagan himself declared that, "I have always thought of government as a kind of organism with an insatiable appetite for money, whose natural state is to grow forever unless you do something to starve it. By cutting taxes, I not only wanted to stimulate the economy but to curb the growth of government and reduce its intrusion into the economic life of the country."[13]

The President's Private Sector Survey on Cost Control (or Grace Commission, after its chairman, Peter Grace) was charged with improving government efficiency, and its recommendations saved an estimated $100 billion from 1985 through 1991, according to a Bush administration study.[14] Throughout his presidency, Reagan also made a major rhetorical effort to restore at least the metaphor of enumerated powers, the doctrine that the authority of the federal government is limited to the objects specified in Article I, Section 8 of the Constitution. This rhetorical defense of limited government, which was so central to Reagan's public discourse, called for a hardheaded evaluation and prioritization of current programs, skepticism of future programs, and a willingness to consider federal inactivity as a legitimate policy option.

Finally, Reagan ultimately supported—though he had reservations—the Gramm-Rudman-Hollings amendment of 1985 (GRH I) and its subsequent revision in 1987 (GRH II). GRH set deficit targets that declined each year until a zero deficit in year five. Failure to reach those targets would trigger automatic across-the-board spending cuts ("sequestrations")—half in defense and half in domestic spending. GRH also required zero-sum budgeting; any new programs had to be paid for by reduced spending (or increased revenue) elsewhere. In one sense, GRH was a clear failure, as it never came close to reaching its targets. Congress became quite adept at using accounting gimmickry to avoid sequestrations. On the other hand, if taken less literally, GRH did serve as a powerful instrument to encourage spending limitation. In the period 1986–1989, federal spending increased an average of 1.4 percent a year over inflation, the slowest rate in thirty years. As important as its effect on existing program spending, GRH made it nearly impossible to establish new federal spending programs. Altogether, real federal spending from 1980–1989 grew at a slower rate than in any decade in half a century.

Despite these successes, the Reagan record on government spending can only be considered mixed. To some extent, this was the result of congressional reluctance to limit domestic spending. Administration proposals in late 1981 to slow Social Security spending (which would have saved an estimated $50 billion in 1982–1986 alone) and to impose additional discretionary domestic spending cuts (which would have saved an estimated $200 billion through the decade) were killed by Congress.[15] Looking only at annual budget messages, federal outlays from 1981 through 1989 exceeded the president's spending requests in eight of nine years, by an average of nearly $29 billion.

Reagan, himself, contributed to the deficits by both action and inaction. The rapid Reagan defense buildup, while an essential part of the administration's successful Cold War strategy against the Soviet Union, contributed to increased federal spending. In real terms, defense spending increased by 35 percent from 1980 to 1985 before stabilizing in the last half of the decade. Former Reagan budget director David Stockman argued that part of the first-year defense spending increase, which created the baseline for the remainder of the Reagan presidency, was inflated on the basis of a misunderstanding of the numbers.[16] In any case, Reagan saw defense spending as first and foremost a national security issue that took precedence over domestic-budget concerns, and he was never willing to compromise on it. This exerted upward pressure on spending in two ways. Directly, defense was mostly off the table as a source of budget savings. Indirectly, Reagan's unflinching position on defense made it possible for congressional Democrats to hold defense spending hostage in order to win higher domestic spending than Reagan would have preferred. Given the stakes in the Cold War, it is far from clear that Reagan was wrong to accept this compromise, but its effect was to elevate the overall level of federal spending. Furthermore, after the political drubbing Reagan received for proposing Social Security savings in 1981, he never again sought significant reform of entitlement spending, the largest component of the federal budget, and he rarely used his veto on appropriations bills.

Deregulation. Reagan continued and accelerated industry-specific deregulation begun under Carter, including airlines, trucking, and oil. Reagan ended oil price controls, added banking and telecommunications to the list of deregulated industries, and sought a more general trimming of government regulation of the economy. Within ten days of his inauguration, Reagan froze more than 170 pending regulations. He ultimately imposed stricter cost-benefit analysis and subjected new regulations to "central clearance" by the Office of Management and Budget. Overall, the administration promulgated 6,000 fewer rules in its first four years than had the Carter administration, and the White House estimated that time devoted by the public to regulatory paperwork was cut by 600 million hours from 1981–1987.[17] Indeed, pages in the *Federal Register* declined from nearly 87,000 in 1980 to about 47,000 in mid-decade, though they crept back up to 53,000 by 1988.

Stable money supply to fight inflation. In this, the Federal Reserve Board was crucial, and there was not much the president could do directly and immediately to attain his preferred policy. However, Reagan could appoint individuals to the Board who shared his views on the preeminence of fighting inflation. He reappointed Paul Volcker to a new four-year term as chairman of the Fed in 1983 and then appointed Alan Greenspan chairman in 1987, a position to which he was reappointed by presidents George H. W. Bush, Bill Clinton (twice), and George W. Bush. Reagan also refrained from criticizing the Federal Reserve Board when it might have been politically expedient to do so, especially during the hard year of 1982. As Reagan biographer Lou Cannon pointed out, "Reagan stuck by the Fed chairman when it counted."[18] What the Federal Reserve Board helped to accomplish though anti-inflationary monetary policy was not, however, achieved through strict adherence to Milton Friedman's money-supply theories, which it abandoned when it became clear that it was too difficult to successfully calibrate money-supply targets.[19]

To these four pillars might be added support for free trade, a free market labor policy, and encouragement of a small-investor class. In 1981, Reagan's Council of Economic Advisers announced a free-trade framework consisting of deregulation for the sake of competitiveness, reliance on market forces to deal with the dislocation produced by trade, and reduction of trade barriers.[20] Reagan promoted regional free trade initiatives like the Caribbean Basin Initiative and the U.S.-Canada free trade agreement, precursor to the North American Free Trade Agreement (NAFTA). He also opened a new round of the General Agreement on Tariffs and Trade (GATT) talks in 1986 aimed at reducing global agricultural subsidies. More generally, he fought against growing protectionist pressures throughout the 1980s, most importantly killing the protectionist Gephardt Amendment with a well-timed veto threat in 1987. In general, Reagan envisioned a high-tech, trade-oriented future for the American economy. *Washington Post* political correspondent David Broder observed that Reagan believed "that government policy must assist—and not resist—the great transition of the American manufacturing base from heavy industry to high technology. And it comes at a time when the Democratic Party and most of its leading presidential hopefuls are lashing themselves ever more tightly to the very protectionist measures Reagan has rejected."[21] Despite Reagan's free trade inclinations, he was not

immune to protectionist pressures: One of his earliest trade accom-
plishments was a deal in which Japan agreed to "voluntary" automo-
bile import quotas, among other protectionist measures.

Reagan's labor policies generally sought to reduce government
mandates and reduce the relative power of labor unions. For example,
the minimum wage was not increased at any time during the eight
years of the Reagan presidency—meaning that its value declined significantly in real terms—consistent with a desire to not interfere with
the free workings of the labor market. And when Reagan fired the
striking members of the air traffic controllers' union (PATCO) in August 1981, he sent a powerful signal that excessive union demands
would not find favor or comfort in his White House.

Finally, the Reagan administration made a concerted effort to expand
investment by private individuals. Most notably, Reagan's 1981 tax cut
bill included creation of Individual Retirement Accounts (IRAs) in the
tax code, and it was Reagan's Internal Revenue Service that ruled in
1981 that employees' income could be tax-free if matched by employ-
ers and put into private retirement accounts, thus leading to the explosion of 401(k) plans. Two decades later, over 40 percent of American
households held shares in corporate or equity mutual funds, and more
than half of all shareholders had incomes below $50,000 a year. To this
extent, Reagan could be considered the father of the "small investor
class" that is now so much a part of the nation's economic fabric.

The Reagan economic policy consequently represented a synthesis
of varying neo-classical economic strands. While the supply-side
strand was present, it was one strand among many. What the pieces had
in common was a devotion to the notion, famously enunciated in Reagan's first inaugural address, that, "In our current crisis, government is
not the solution; government is the problem."

Reagan's aims were clearly twofold, though intertwined. First, and
most obviously, Reagan hoped to end the economic crisis and restore
American economic vitality. This was crucial, as he understood it, not
only for the economic health of America (and Americans), but for their
security in a dangerous world. Reagan declared that economic policy
was his "most immediate priority" because "without a recovery, we
couldn't afford to do the things necessary to make the country strong
again," including the defense buildup.[22]

Second, Reagan sought to achieve what might be called "political economy." In his view, the increasing concentration of economic power in Washington threatened not only economic wealth but political liberty. Thus, Reagan saw his economic initiatives as a means of preserving and enhancing American freedom by strengthening its economic prerequisites of private property rights and decentralization of power and resources. For example, he referred to his 1981 tax cuts and 1986 tax reform as "the first important steps back to economic liberty."[23] In Reagan's view, "Throughout human history, taxes have been one of the foremost ways that governments intrude on the rights of citizens. . . . Our forefathers knew that if you bind up a man's economic life with taxes, tariffs, and regulations, you deprive him of some of his most basic civil rights."[24] Reagan thus rejected the notion, first introduced by the Progressives and now a central tenet of liberalism, that property rights can be divorced from human rights. Instead, he hewed to the conception of the Founders that property rights and economic freedom were inseparable from political liberty.

Though the thrust of Reagan's economic policy was clear, its principles were not always carried out consistently. Indeed, in each area of economic policy, observers could point to instances in which the administration contradicted those principles—from the tax increases to auto quotas to failure to veto overloaded domestic appropriations. Some of Reagan's conservative supporters considered these contradictions to be betrayals of fundamental principle. Others, however, saw them as tactical compromises necessary to advance the president's broader agenda in a context of divided government.

ASSESSMENTS

For most Americans, the key economic fact of the Reagan presidency was that the economic crisis inherited by Reagan in 1981 was no longer a threat when he left office in 1989. After a severe recession in 1981–1982—which Democrats ascribed to Reagan and Reagan ascribed to Carter and decades of economic liberalism—the nation began what was at that time the longest economic recovery in its history, which ultimately reached ninety-two months (the previous record had been fifty-eight months). What *Wall Street Journal* editor Robert L. Bartley called *The Seven Fat Years* featured robust economic growth, the creation of nearly twenty million jobs, and declining unemployment, inflation, and poverty rates: By 1989, inflation was 3.5 percent and unemployment 5.3 percent. Productivity rates rose again. The burst of entrepreneurship in the 1980s was unprecedented, with record rates of small business formation. Nascent industries like telecommunications and computers began their steep ascent. The Dow Jones Industrial Average, which had fallen 70 percent in real terms from 1967–1982, roughly tripled during the remainder of the 1980s.

Altogether, Reagan was the first president since World War II who presided over a decline in both unemployment and inflation. Harvard economist Robert Barro evaluated all presidents from Truman through George H. W. Bush on economic growth plus changes in inflation, unemployment, and long-term interest rates. On these criteria, Barro determined Reagan I and Reagan II to be the most successful presidential administrations from 1949 to 1992.[25] On key indicators like GDP growth, rates of job creation, and improvements in inflation and unemployment, the 1983–1990 expansion was actually stronger than the much-touted 1992–2000 expansion.[26] This economic turnaround accounted for a significant shift in the issues voters thought most important. In 1980, 43 percent cited either inflation or unemployment; in 1988, only 7 percent said so.[27]

Of course, it is not possible to prove beyond doubt that Reagan's policies were responsible for the expansion of the 1980s, since one cannot go back in time and re-run the decade with, say, Jimmy Carter's or Edward Kennedy's preferred policies. However, such a link is logically plausible. In sum, a good argument can be made that a combination of the Fed's monetary policy, deregulation, and slowed federal spending defeated inflation, while the tax cuts boosted economic growth and employment. (According to the supply-siders, the tax cuts also dampened inflation by boosting real production.) Thus, even many Keynesians credit Reagan's policies for the boom, though they see a different chain of causation than do the supply-siders or other conservative economists.

Four things can be said with certainty. First, the economic crisis—arguably the worst since the Great Depression—ended. Second, consequently, by 1989 the question was no longer being asked whether capitalism could survive. Free market economics was rejuvenated and relegitimized, at home and abroad. China and the Soviet Union reformed their command economies, and welfare state bastions like Germany, France, and even Sweden cut their marginal income tax rates. Third, this development strengthened the position of the United States in the world and almost certainly contributed to the American victory in the Cold War. Materially, the United States was assured of the resources it needed to wage the struggle indefinitely. Furthermore, any hopes the Soviets might have harbored about the imminent economic collapse of capitalism were laid to rest. Secret National Intelligence Estimates prepared in 1984 asserted that the Soviet leadership was "psychologically shaken" by the American economic recovery.[28] Finally, there can be little question that at the end of the Reagan presidency the American people were freer economically than they had been at the beginning; Reagan's hope of decentralizing power had been substantially achieved. It is interesting, and perhaps instructive, to note that the same analysts who praise Franklin Roosevelt for saving capitalism by subduing it seldom praise Reagan for saving capitalism by revivifying it.

Despite these successes, there were also failures, and no shortage of critics. To opponents of the Reagan policies, the economy of the 1980s represented a "silent depression," an "age of diminished expectations," a "fraud from the beginning" that "left the economy in shambles."[29] As a presidential candidate in 1992, Bill Clinton argued that, "For the last twelve years, we have been in the grip of a failed economic theory."[30]

Critics of Reagan's economic policies have generally argued along one of three lines. First, in the view of many, the rise of the federal deficit under Reagan outweighed the benefits of recovery—and may have been the sole cause of the recovery. Indeed, the federal debt roughly tripled under Reagan, and one force driving federal spending upward was the growth of interest payments on the national debt, which grew from $52.5 billion in 1980 to $169.3 billion in 1989. While Reagan consistently argued for a balanced budget in the abstract and called the deficit "one of my biggest disappointments as president,"[31] he made it quite clear that "I did not come here to balance the budget—not at the expense of my tax cutting program and my defense program."[32] As president, Reagan cannot escape a large measure of responsibility for allowing deficits to balloon.

However, it should be pointed out that deficits in the 1980s were actually part of a long pattern of deficit spending, in which every presidential administration from Kennedy/Johnson through George H. W. Bush oversaw higher real annual deficits than the previous administration. Furthermore, in historical terms, taxes under Reagan were higher, and defense spending lower, than they had been in 1960, when there was a small federal surplus. From 1980 to 1990, the rise in defense spending accounted for only $163 billion of the $564 billion increase in total spending excluding interest—less than 30 percent. And, despite (supply-siders might say because of) the tax cuts, real federal revenue increased by 27 percent from 1980–1989, faster than it had grown in the tax-happy 1970s. Altogether, due to spending restraint and (thanks to the recovery) rapidly rising revenues in the last half of the decade, the federal deficit by 1989 had fallen to 2.8 percent of GDP, almost exactly what it had been in 1980.[33]

It is also important to note that many of the most dire predictions about the consequences of the deficits did not materialize. These ranged from hyper-inflation to extremely high interest rates choking off economic growth to a collapse of the American competitive position in the world, none of which happened. Upon Reagan's departure from office, former House Speaker Tip O'Neill predicted that Reagan's deficits would be disastrous: "Within 10 years, West Germany will be the richest nation in the world and Japan will be the strongest economic power. We're losing the economic leadership of the 20th century because of Reaganomics."[34] Instead, Japan stagnated, Germany acquired a chronic unemployment rate approaching 10 percent, and America surged forward after a brief and mild recession in 1990–1991.

The trade balance, which went from a small deficit of $25.5 billion in 1980 to a $159.6 billion deficit in 1987, was a major concern in itself, and fueled protectionist pressures throughout the Reagan years. From one perspective it was, at the least, a pernicious result of Reagan's neglect; at the worst, it was a direct consequence of his economic mismanagement. From another perspective, it was merely a sign that the American economy was growing faster than others. As Robert L. Bartley pointed out, the U.S. ran a trade deficit for most of its history, but a surplus during the Great Depression.[35] One might add that new record trade deficits were recorded in the 1990s, and few claimed then that they were a sign of economic weakness. In reality, U.S. exports grew 73 percent from 1983–1989, and there were numerous signs—ranging from worker productivity to the U.S. share of global manufacturing—that American industry became significantly more, not less, competitive in the 1980s.[36]

Aside from the "twin deficits," the most common concerns about the Reagan economic policy and its aftermath revolve around its side effects, especially having to do with social and economic equity. In one of these intertwining critiques, the tax cuts and free market emphasis of Reaganomics encouraged an ethos of "greed," a "creeping zeitgeist of cold-heartedness and mean-spiritedness," and "a spiritual impoverishment in which the dominant conception of the good life consists of gaining access to power, pleasure, and property, sometimes by any means."[37] More tangibly, critics decried growing income inequality, a declining middle class, poverty and homelessness, and the destructive consequences of deregulation. In short, according to this view, "the rich got richer and the poor got poorer."[38]

There was some truth to these accusations against Reagan and his economic plan. For one thing, it was clear that greater economic freedom supplanted equalized income distribution as the key objective of the Reagan team. Income inequality did indeed grow, the proportion of the population in the "middle class" did indeed shrink, and scandals like the savings and loan collapse, which cost American taxpayers some $150 billion, demonstrated the potential pitfalls of deregulation.

Yet it is also clear that many of these claims were overstated, and sometimes missed key points. For instance, the proportion of Americans making between $15,000 and $50,000 (in 1990 dollars) shrank from 58 percent to 53 percent, but the entire aggregate loss moved up in the income distribution to the over $50,000 category, which grew from 25 percent to 31 percent. Income inequality had been growing since at least 1973, had little to do with Reagan policies, and masked the fact that inequality in consumption expenditures—perhaps a better measure of economic well-being than income—did not grow at all in the 1980s.[39]

Furthermore, economic mobility remained high in the 1980s. A Treasury Department study tracking individuals from 1979–1987 showed that individuals starting in the bottom quintile had a slightly higher likelihood of ending in the top quintile than of still being at the bottom; altogether, 86 percent of those in the bottom fifth and 60 percent of those in the next fifth had moved up by 1987.[40] And, though income inequality did rise, it was not because the "rich got richer and the poor got poorer." Rather, it was because all quintiles showed real household income growth after 1982, but the top quintiles' income grew faster than that at the bottom. When one looked at individuals, who can move from one quintile to another, it was actually the reverse: According to a 1994 Urban Institute study, individuals in the top quintile in 1977 saw their real family incomes rise only 5 percent by 1986; those in the bottom 77 percent.[41] Of course, by then they were not in the bottom quintile any longer. And economic gains among blacks, Hispanics, and women were substantial in areas such as income, business creation, and college enrollment.[42]

Likewise, there was little evidence to support claims that deregulation harmed worker, consumer, and environmental protections. At the end of the 1980s, most measures of environmental health had improved since 1978, such as levels of sulfur dioxide (down 35 percent), airborne lead (down 88 percent), carbon monoxide (reduced by 32 percent), dust, soot, and particulates (reduced 21 percent), and ground level ozone (down 16 percent). Average gallons of oil spills per year were down by one-third in the 1980s, while average annual acres of reforestation were up by 50 percent.[43] Average yearly rates of occupational injuries and illnesses were lower from 1981–1989 than from 1973–1980 by about one-sixth; consumer product related electrocutions were down by one-third.[44]

Altogether, it is clear that assessments of the Reagan economic program depend on both objective facts (like GDP growth, income trends, job creation, and trade and budget deficits) and economic and political principles that exist outside of and prior to specific evidence. Those who believe in limited government as a matter of principle are willing to overlook some of the shortcomings of the economy in the 1980s. Those whose first commitment is to redistribution of income and heavy government intervention in the economy to secure their conception of social justice are predisposed to focus on the flaws and ignore or downplay the benefits.

REAGANOMICS AFTER REAGAN

While Reagan's economic policy changed the economic and political landscape in the 1980s, it was an open question when he left office how much would survive of his experiment. First George H. W. Bush's acceptance of a major tax increase in 1990 and then Bill Clinton's election on a program of overturning Reaganism seemed not to bode well for the future of Reaganomics. However, when Republicans gained control of both houses of Congress in the 1994 midterm elections, running largely against Clinton's tax increase and proposed federal health care takeover, the picture once again changed. Clinton was forced to tack to the right, embracing a balanced budget, cutting capital gains and other taxes, and backing away from major expansions of the entitlement state (indeed, Clinton went so far as to join the Republican Congress in reforming welfare).

A thorough look at the period 1989–2000 shows the fundamental thrust of Reagan's economic policy having been trimmed but not transformed. The key objectives of Reaganomics were slowing the growth of federal spending, cutting marginal income tax rates, reducing regulation, supporting an anti-inflationary monetary policy, and promoting free trade. All five survived largely intact, and some even advanced. Real federal spending grew only 10 percent in the 1990s, compared with 28 percent in the 1980s. Top personal income tax rates rose, but only to a high of 39.6 percent; the pre-Reagan top rate was 70 percent. Pages of the *Federal Register* grew again under Bush I and Clinton but never regained their Carter-era high, and industry deregulation was extended in telecommunications, agriculture, and energy. Bush and Clinton not only retained Reagan's monetary policy but his chairman of the Federal Reserve Board. And Clinton jettisoned his party's protectionist stance in favor of free trade.

When George W. Bush took office, he inaugurated what many observers saw as a new era of Reagan-style economics. The centerpiece of Bush's economic plan was a $1.6 trillion, 10-year income tax cut; despite the controversy surrounding his election, he won from Congress $1.3 trillion of it. He then proceeded to wrest from Congress a new tax cut in each of the next two years. Like Reagan, Bush cut back on regulation; like Reagan, he favored free trade, winning renewal of "fast track authority" for trade agreements, but bowed to political necessity by imposing short-term steel quotas. However, unlike Reagan, Bush in his three years of office seemed completely uninterested in restraining spending, which exploded in both defense (due to the war on terrorism) and domestic areas. Bush's embrace of a federal prescription drug program broke a two-decade moratorium on the creation of major new federal spending programs. Thus, as he prepared for his reelection campaign, it was not clear whether Bush could be said to fully represent the reprise of Reaganomics.

In any event, so much of the general thrust of Reaganomics survived the Reagan presidency that a wide variety of analysts, ranging from the predictable (like conservatives James Glassman, Lawrence Kudlow, and Stephen Moore) to the surprising (including liberal historian Robert Dallek and political scientist John W. Sloan), gave a significant share of the credit to Reagan for the boom of the 1990s.[45] This interpretation was, of course, disputed by Clinton administration spokespersons, but the fact that they felt compelled to address these claims was itself evidence of the ongoing impact of Reagan.

Three quarters of a century after the fact, economists are still debating the causes of the Great Depression and the question of whether Franklin Roosevelt's New Deal made things better or worse. It is only a quarter of a century since Reaganomics took the stage at another moment of national crisis. It should be no surprise, then, that debate continues over its efficacy and justice. Yet there is no question that the New Deal transformed American economic (and political) life forever—or that Reagan's economic policies also produced a long-term change in the American political economy, relegitimizing free market economics and limited government politics, stopping the momentum of the welfare state, and encouraging a more decentralized and entrepreneurial economy.

NOTES

1. See *Time* (July 14, 1975); Robert Heilbroner, "Does Capitalism Have a Future?" *New York Times Magazine,* August 5, 1982.

2. Paul Craig Roberts, *The Supply Side Revolution* (Cambridge, Mass.: Harvard University Press, 1984).

3. James Ring Adams, *Secrets of the Tax Revolt* (New York: Harcourt Brace Jovanovich, 1984), 7.

4. Martin Anderson, *Revolution* (New York: Harcourt Brace Jovanovich, 1988), 171–2.

5. Ronald Reagan, *An American Life* (New York: Simon & Schuster, 1990), 231–2.

6. Reagan, *An American Life*, 129.

7. Anderson, *Revolution*, 164.

8. For extensive discussion of Reagan economic policies from those who helped make them, see Anderson, *Revolution*; Roberts, *The Supply Side Revolution*; Lawrence Lindsey, *The Growth Experiment* (New York: Basic, 1990); William A. Niskanen, *Reaganomics: An Insider's View of the Policies and the People* (New York: Oxford University Press, 1988); Robert Bartley, *The Seven Fat Years . . . And How to Do It Again* (New York: The Free Press, 1992).

9. "Truth in Taxing," *New York Times*, March 10, 1983, 26.

10. For an excellent narrative, see Jeffrey Birnbaum, *Showdown at Gucci Gulch* (New York: Random House, 1987).

11. Bill Archer, "Who's the Fairest of Them All?" *Policy Review* (Summer 1991): 67.

12. June E. O'Neill, "The Story of the Surplus," *Policy Review* (June–July 2000): 8.

13. Reagan, *An American Life*, 232. It should be pointed out that this is not exactly the same line of argument used by some who claim that Reagan deliberately stoked the *deficit* in order to restrain government. There is no evidence that Reagan liked the deficit, only that he was willing to tolerate it in preference to raising income tax rates.

14. The Commission proposed 2,478 recommendations that it claimed could save $424 billion in three years. The General Accounting Office thought the figure was more like $98 billion, and in any event many of the proposals were highly controversial. In the end, Reagan estimated his administration had implemented roughly one-third. Citizens against Government Waste, a private group formed to monitor implementation of the report, claimed on the tenth anniversary of the issuance of the report that nearly two-thirds of recommendations had been adopted at a savings of $250 billion.

15. David Stockman, *The Triumph of Politics: The Inside Story of the Reagan Revolution* (New York: Avon Books, 1987), 169–209; Reagan, *An American Life*, 337.

16. Stockman, *The Triumph of Politics*.

17. "Rolling Back Regulation," *Time* (July 6, 1987): 51; Elizabeth Sanders, "The Presidency and the Bureaucratic State," in *The Presidency and the Political System*, ed. Michael Nelson (Washington, D.C.: CQ Press, 1990), 419; "The Reagan Record: Five Years of Continuous Economic Growth," White House Office of Public Affairs, November 1987, 16.

18. Lou Cannon, *President Reagan: The Role of a Lifetime* (New York: Simon & Schuster, 1991), 277.

19. See William Greider, *Secrets of the Temple: How the Federal Reserve Runs the Country* (New York: Touchstone, 1987).

20. Anthony S. Campagna, *The Economy in the Reagan Years: The Economic Consequences of the Reagan Administrations* (Westport, Conn.: Greenwood Press, 1994), 57.

21. David S. Broder, "The Words Do Mean Something," *Washington Post*, January 30, 1983, C7.

22. Reagan, *An American Life*, 230, 333.

23. Ronald Reagan, "Remarks at a White House Briefing for the American Legislative Exchange Council," December 12, 1986, *Public Papers of the Presidents: Ronald Reagan 1986* (Washington, D.C.: GPO, 1988), 1624.

24. Ronald Reagan, "Radio Address to the Nation on Independence Day and the Centennial of the Statue of Liberty," July 5, 1986, *Public Papers of the Presidents: Ronald Reagan 1986*, 925.

25. Robert J. Barro, "A Gentleman's B– for Bush on Economics," *Wall Street Journal*, September 30, 1992, A16. For a similar appraisals, see Robert M. Dunn Jr., "Don't Knock Reaganomics," *Washington Post*, July 24, 1988, C5. Using a much more complex formula that included 18 economic criteria, Richard J. Carroll ranked Reagan fourth of 10 postwar presidents in "Clinton's Economy in Historical Context, or Why Media Coverage on Economic Issues Is Suspect," *Presidential Studies Quarterly* 26, no. 3 (Summer 1996), 828–34.

26. In the 1980s boom, average GDP growth was 4.3 percent; in the 1990s boom, it was 3.6 percent. Employment increased 17.9 percent in the Reagan expansion, 14.9 percent in the Bush-Clinton expansion. While the average annual unemployment and inflation rates were lower in the 1990s expansion, the 1980s expansion saw much greater improvement from the peak figure recorded to the figure recorded in the last year of the expansion. The 1980s boom saw inflation reduced 7.9 percentage points and unemployment reduced 4.6 percentage points; the 1990s boom saw inflation fall 2.6 percentage points and unemployment fall 3.5 percentage points. Council of Economic Advisers, *2003 Economic Report of the President*, Historical Tables.

27. See Paul R. Abramson, John H. Aldrich, and David W. Rohde, *Change and Continuity in the 1988 Elections*, rev. ed. (Washington, D.C.: CQ Press, 1991), 157.

28. See Peter Schweizer, *Victory* (New York: Atlantic Monthly Press, 1994), 190–1.

29. Wallace Peterson, *Silent Depression* (New York: W. W. Norton, 1994); Paul Krugman, *The Age of Diminished Expectations* (Washington, D.C.: Washington Post, 1990); James Tobin, "Reaganomics in Retrospect," in *The Reagan Revolution*, ed. B. B. Kymlicka and Jean V. Matthews (Chicago: Dorsey, 1988); Campagna, *The Economy in the Reagan Years*.

30. Bill Clinton, "Remarks by Governor Bill Clinton" (remarks, Economic Club of Detroit, Michigan, August 21, 1992), 5.

31. Reagan, *An American Life*, 335.

32. "Goodbye Balanced Budget," *Newsweek*, November 16, 1981, 32.

33. See Andrew E. Busch, *Ronald Reagan and the Politics of Freedom* (Lanham, Md.: Rowman & Littlefield, 2001), ch. 5.

34. "The Long Shadow of the Deficit," *Newsweek*, January 9, 1989, 21.

35. Bartley, *The Seven Fat Years*, 54, also 197–217.

36. See Syvia Nasar, "American Revival in Manufacturing Seen in U.S. Report," *New York Times*, February 5, 1991, 1; "Brave New Economy," *U.S. News & World Report*, March 31, 1986, 42.

37. Cornel West, "The '80s: Market Culture Run Amok," *Newsweek*, January 3, 1994, 48–9.

38. See, for example, Kevin Phillips, *The Politics of Rich and Poor: Wealth and the American Electorate in the Reagan Aftermath* (New York: Random House, 1990); Donald L. Barlett and James B. Steele, *America: What Went Wrong?* (Kansas City, Mo.: Andrews and McMeel, 1992).

39. See, for example, Richard McKenzie, *What Went Right in the 1980s* (San Francisco: Pacific Research Institute for Public Policy, 1994), 157–60.

40. Marvin H. Kosters, "The Rise in Income Inequality," *The American Enterprise* (November–December 1992): 33; see also *By Our Own Bootstraps: Economic Opportunity & The Dynamics of Income Distribution* (Dallas: Federal Reserve Bank of Dallas, 1995).

41. "The Poor Aren't Poorer," *U.S. News & World Report*, July 25, 1994, 36.

42. For a study of the general egalitarian critique of Reaganomics, see Busch, *Ronald Reagan and the Politics of Freedom*, 96–103.

43. Edwin S. Rubenstein, *The Right Data* (New York: National Review, 1994), 180, 286.

44. Consumer Product Safety Commission, "1993 National Estimates of Electrocutions Associated with Consumer Products," report issued September 10, 1996; Occupational Safety and Health Administration website at www .osha.gov.

45. See Lawrence Kudlow and Stephen Moore, "It's the Reagan Economy, Stupid," at www.clubforgrowth.org, accessed February 2000; James F. Glassman, "It's Reagan's Economy, Stupid," *Rising Tide* (Fall 1997); Paul Craig Roberts, "Coasting on the Reagan Boom," *Washington Times National Weekly Edition*, March 13–19, 2000; Robert Dallek, *Ronald Reagan: The Politics of Symbolism with a New Preface* (Cambridge, Mass.: Harvard University Press, 1999), xiii; John W. Sloan, *The Reagan Effect: Economics and Presidential Leadership* (Lawrence: University Press of Kansas, 1999).

3

The Origins and Meaning of Reagan's Cold War

Elizabeth Edwards Spalding

In the field of foreign policy, academics typically argue that presidents are forced to choose between realism and idealism: between power politics and morality politics. Although it is true that some presidents are either realists or idealists, not all presidents fit conveniently into these categories. And neither of these major approaches, nor the notion that they represent all one has to choose from, sits well with the American people. Since the Founding, Americans have been concerned about the health of their regime and take into account how other governments are animated and arranged. They look for moral and intellectual capacities in their statesmen, since it is important to be able to deliberate and choose well in a liberal democracy. Americans want peace in the world but are unwilling to sacrifice freedom for it; a framework of freedom is necessary in order to make moral decisions and enjoy any sort of happy life. While realists put order first in their efforts to establish peace and idealists place justice first in theirs, Americans believe that freedom must precede justice and order in laying the foundation for lasting peace.

Like the majority of Americans, Ronald Reagan was not part of the scholarly debate between realism and idealism, and he rejected the presidential manifestations of power politics and morality politics represented by two of his immediate predecessors, Richard Nixon and Jimmy Carter, respectively. Reagan disagreed with their starting premises and found their policies to be deeply flawed. Instead, by both intellect and instinct, Reagan upheld something closer to the original

American sense of foreign policy and sought to apply American principles to Cold War circumstances. Some would call him lucky, others simplistic; some would call him realist, others idealist or Wilsonian. For his part, Reagan kept his focus on America's first principles of liberty and equality, free and representative government, freedom and independence, and liberal democracy, and pursued a Cold War foreign policy that he believed was based on these principles and appropriate in light of the East-West conflict. Of modern presidents and their foreign policies, he most resembled, even as he went beyond, Harry S Truman.

BEFORE THE PRESIDENCY

Before he ever entered elective office, Reagan had a defined view of politics and the world. His public life as a liberal cold warrior began with his experiences in Hollywood where, elected six times as president of the Screen Actors Guild in the 1940s and 1950s, he fought Communist influence in the union movement. Reagan strongly supported President Harry Truman in 1948 and later wrote that "he and I were in tune on a lot of things about government and I think if he had lived longer he might have come over to the other side like I did."[1] With the war against fascism and Nazi Germany still vivid in his memory and the war against communism of increasing concern to him, Reagan expressed his disdain for all forms of totalitarianism and maintained that the highest dignity of man was found in the freedom of the individual. In May 1947 he used Trumanesque language to argue that "[t]yranny is tyranny and—whether it comes from the Right, Left or Center—it is evil," and concluded that "the only logical way to save our country from both extremes is to remove conditions that supply fuel for the totalitarian fire."[2] In June 1952, he described "the great ideological struggle that we find ourselves engaged in today" as part of "the same old battle. We met it under the name of Hitlerism; we met it under the name of kaiserism; and we have met it back through the ages in the name of every conqueror that has ever set upon a course of establishing his rule over mankind."[3] As president, Reagan would remain true to this understanding of tyranny and of the Cold War as a struggle between good and evil.

Reagan's transformation from New Deal liberal to conservative Republican took place in the 1950s, when he honed his message in patriotic political speeches as a spokesman for General Electric. Although a liberal Democrat who voted his party's ticket through the 1940s, he supported Republican candidates in the 1950s and 1960 and officially changed his party registration to the GOP in 1962.[4] Filled with optimism about America's strengths and confident in its people and principles, he became involved in conservative politics and refined his arguments in defense of freedom of the individual, in support of limited government, and against communism. Especially important to burnishing his credentials as a conservative cold warrior, he began publishing articles in *Human Events* and joined the national board of Young Americans for Freedom (YAF). In 1964, Reagan supported Barry Goldwater for president, speaking before the Republican National Convention, cochairing California Citizens for Goldwater, and giving speeches on the candidate's behalf in California; and he gave "The Speech," an influential address endorsing Goldwater, officially entitled "A Time for Choosing." Many recall "The Speech" as largely pertaining to domestic politics, but Reagan began his remarks by noting that "we are at war with the most dangerous enemy ever known to man." He warned against descending to "the ant heap of totalitarianism" and "selling into permanent slavery our fellow human beings enslaved behind the Iron Curtain" through appeasement, and concluded that the nation's "rendezvous with destiny" was to continue the American experiment in self-government and fight Communist totalitarianism.[5]

Although he was committed to action, ideas clearly mattered to Reagan. In this sense, his temperament was well suited for politics and statesmanship. Many have commented on his background as actor, radio commentator, public speaker, and governor, and how each offered training for the presidency; Reagan often referred to his experiences of having lived through two world wars and the Great Depression. But he also read widely and constantly. Building on his economics major in college, he gravitated to free-market writers such as Friedrich Hayek and Frederic Bastiat. A regular subscriber as well as contributor to *Human Events*, he kept current with major anticommunist writings and was drawn to the works of Whittaker Chambers and Aleksandr Solzhenitsyn. But he also distrusted intellectuals and refused to share their pessimism—even that of an intellectual he admired, like Chambers—about America and its future in the Cold War.[6] Instead, Reagan absorbed observations and examples from authors that he could use in his writing and speaking. His borrowing from and reference to staunch anticommunists is particularly evident from 1975 through 1979, when Reagan gave over a thousand radio addresses—two-thirds of which he wrote in his own hand—and put out a regular newspaper column.[7]

Reagan's key opinions during this period in the 1970s—when much of the political world embraced détente and the Soviets were enjoying gains in both territory and influence in Africa, Latin America, and Asia—merit special attention.[8] Rejecting the moral equivalence of realism, he placed regime distinctions at the heart of his understanding of the Cold War. Reagan referred to communism as a "disease" and—similar to Truman—saw two worlds at war in the ideological struggle between communism and "our belief in freedom to the greatest extent possible consistent with an orderly society." In fact, he read and talked publicly about the strategy and lasting insights of NSC 68, which had been approved by Truman in 1950, not long after the document was declassified and published in 1975. Also in the 1970s, Reagan called for reductions—not limitations—in armaments by the Soviet Union and the United States through verifiable agreements, and he lamented that the United States had bargained away the beginnings of antiballistic missile defense "in exchange for nothing" and settled for the doctrine of mutually assured destruction (MAD), whose acronym he frequently said was all too true. Identifying two of the central weaknesses in the Soviet bloc as the denial of religious freedom and of consumer goods, he stressed that Pope John Paul II's 1979 trip to Poland revealed that Communist atheism—ruthlessly imposed for decades—had failed to stop people from believing in God. All of these convictions on his part informed one of his main campaign themes: that real peace would come through the West's strength and political and economic freedom.[9] Reagan's corollary was that the Cold War had been caused and sustained by the Kremlin's regime and not by the peoples ruled by Communist governments; the peoples under Communist domination should be seen as allies, since many of them were defying and thus wearing down their suppressors from the inside.

Reagan's critique of détente was striking. In 1978—after he had come close to winning the GOP nomination for president in 1976 and was expected to try again in 1980—Reagan made clear that his anti-communism was based on a concept of universal human rights. While acknowledging that the Carter administration meant to achieve good, he faulted its policies for overlooking the "pattern of Communist violations of human rights" that he said should have been evident to all. Reagan saw Vietnam and Cambodia as the latest in a long line of Marxist regimes that were committing human rights abuses. To Reagan, the Soviet Union was using détente as "an opportunity to expand its sphere of influence around the world," while many in the Carter administration knew too little of history and had "lost faith in their own country's past and traditions." Aiming to reconnect the United States with its founding principles, he held that "America is still the abiding alternative to tyranny" and added that the fundamental aim of U.S. foreign policy must be "to insure our own survival and to protect those others who share our values." Reagan concluded that the United States must always be open to the "willingness to change" but also know when to say "no" to change—in the right proportions and according to the circumstances; he hinted that the circumstances would have to be changed before he would adjust his Cold War foreign policy.[10]

Although encouraged by some of his advisors to tone down his hawkish language, Reagan continued to develop his own strategy of "peace through strength" and had his view reinforced after seeing East Berlin in late 1978 on his first trip behind the Iron Curtain. In 1979 he made his well-known visit to North American Aerospace Defense Command (NORAD) in Colorado and included in his radio addresses a critique of MAD and a call for defense against Soviet missiles.[11] A growing minority in political and national security circles criticized détente; Reagan had similar concerns and voiced them clearly and bluntly. And while Reagan may have been ahead of public opinion in 1978, Americans were in sync with him by 1980: In December 1979, a significant 45 percent of Americans judged that "too little" was being spent on defense while only 18 percent said "too much"; by March 1980, Americans who felt that the country was "in deep and serious trouble" reached 84 percent. Although voters thought that Carter was more likely than Reagan to keep the nation out of war, 59 to 28 percent

in September 1980 favored Reagan over Carter for "keeping our defenses strong" and 57 to 25 percent chose Reagan over Carter for
"standing up to the Russians."[12]

Before he was elected in 1980, Reagan had already set forth the main
goals of his administration with respect to foreign policy: telling the
truth as he saw it about the nature of the Cold War; strengthening and rethinking America's defenses across the board; and overhauling containment in order to put pressure on the USSR, to reverse the Brezhnev
Doctrine, and to shape conditions for a future that could move past the
Cold War on terms consonant with freedom and democracy. Even
though global circumstances did not look promising in 1980, Reagan
perceived prospects for a free and democratic post–Cold War world.
Even though there were some ambiguities in public opinion polls, he believed that his base lay in Americans' strong endorsement of rebuilding
U.S. defenses and using strength against the Soviets. Reagan was not
afraid to lead and had faith in America, its citizens, and in the principles
of liberal democracy. Further, he saw a pervasive decay—politically,
morally and spiritually, and economically—in a world that allowed the
Soviet empire to continue to expand without consideration of the costs.

PRESIDENT REAGAN AND THE COLD WAR

From martial law in Poland and the Soviet invasion of Afghanistan to the
Sandinistas in Nicaragua to Communist rule from Vietnam to Angola,
Soviet Premier Leonid Brezhnev could claim a "correlation of forces" in
favor of Marxism-Leninism during the 1970s.[13] President Carter, in response, saw a "crisis of confidence" in his fellow Americans, stood by
his détente policies, and, after the invasion of Afghanistan, was awaken-
ing to Soviet aggression. Tentative about the use of force—to the point
of describing the failed attempt to rescue the hostages in Iran as a hu-
manitarian rather than an armed forces operation—Carter said that his
view of the Soviet Union and his foreign policy remained the same.[14]
Americans were suffering from inflation, a stagnant economy, and high
unemployment at home and believed that Reagan, much more than
Carter, would speak and act from a position of strength toward the
USSR.

Within the free world, the Atlantic Alliance was strained and, some said, broken. To counter the deployment of Soviet SS-20s, which were armed with warheads that could strike any city in Europe, NATO allies issued the 1979 dual track decision: Negotiations seeking the removal of the SS-20s would be pursued with the Kremlin, but the West would deploy intermediate range Pershing II's and ground-launched cruise missiles in countries where they could reach Soviet targets if these negotiations came to naught. At the same time, the nuclear freeze movement gained in numbers and popularity, especially throughout Western Europe but also at home. While many nuclear freeze supporters were sincere in their wishes for a world freed from nuclear terror, the Kremlin and its sympathizers aimed to influence the movement—including the specific anti-Euromissile deployment campaign in Western Europe—through funding, infiltration, and a propaganda campaign against the United States (the scope of which had not been seen since the late 1940s and early 1950s during the Marshall Plan and the establishment of the North Atlantic Treaty Organization).

America was at a turning point by the time Reagan was sworn in as president in January 1981. Vietnam and Watergate were still vivid in people's memories. Although the realist and idealist versions of détente that had been followed by Nixon and Carter had been cast in doubt, Americans did not quite know what to seek as a replacement—except for being sure that they wanted no more Irans or Afghanistans and that Reagan promised an alternative. In this climate, President Reagan sought to help America rediscover its greatness, restore its economy, and meet the challenges of the Cold War. He would succeed to some extent in all three goals and arguably excelled at the last. Reagan had unique credentials to fight the Cold War—at least from the American view of the matter. Alone among postwar presidents, he had been both liberal and conservative politically. In terms of anticommunism, this meant he united liberal and conservative cold warriors, because he understood and agreed with both. Conservatives, neoconservatives who had been liberal or socialist in their younger days, "Reagan Democrats," liberal cold warriors who had been marginalized by their Democratic Party, and many others without titles supported Reagan when it came to Cold War foreign policy. Reagan knit together an American countercoalition that believed in what he called a "forward strategy of freedom," "peace through

strength," and future negotiations with the Communists only from a position of strength.

ON THE RHETORICAL OFFENSIVE

To Reagan, the gravest threat to the United States and the free world
came from the Soviet Union. As president, he expressed this view on
many occasions and was nowhere clearer than in his address to the
members of the British Parliament in June 1982. In these remarks he
painted a picture of the twentieth century and the outlines of the future
he envisioned, all the while invoking and updating Winston Churchill's
message of the "iron curtain" speech.[15] Like Truman, Reagan's analysis of the world started with his perception of an ideal government, and
he was convinced that a free constitutional and representative government was the best form to secure the "inalienable and universal right"
of freedom endowed to all human beings. Everything he believed
about politics flowed from this understanding of the regime distinction. Consequently for him, totalitarianism was the worst form of
dictatorship and therefore the worst form of government, because it
denied each and every person's fundamental right of freedom. All totalitarian regimes were anathema to Reagan—from, as he put it, the
great purge to Auschwitz and Dachau, from the Gulag to Cambodia—
and the Soviet Union was the archetype that, since 1917, had been
spreading Communist ideology, violence, and subversion, and giving
"covert political training and assistance to Marxist-Leninists in many
countries."[16]

Some scholars have identified Reagan as Wilsonian in his worldview.[17] But Reagan was not: To be pro-freedom and anticommunist
was not the same as being an idealist. Rather, he looked at regime types
and defended what he viewed as the best form in both theory and practice. Democracy and freedom, according to Reagan, were intercon-
nected. The president identified a "campaign for democracy" that had
been gaining strength around the world throughout the twentieth century and saw it complemented by a "global campaign for freedom"; he
called for a "crusade for freedom that will engage the faith and forti-
tude of the next generation," which in turn would assist the campaign

for democracy. Such campaigns, however, were rooted in individual governments—which were formed by different countries with diverse populations around the world making their own free and democratic choices—not in international organizations or with a goal of world government. Rejecting the notions that democracy and freedom were either only theoretical constructs or aspects of cultural imperialism, he maintained that fostering the infrastructure of liberal democracy was necessary and proper for people to live fully and freely as they should.[18]

With hindsight, we can see that the whole of Reagan's foreign policy is prefigured in the Parliament address. The president set forth his views that Western military strength was a prerequisite for peace and that such strength was maintained in the hope that it would never be used; that a campaign for freedom and democracy would be pursued worldwide; that a free, representative form of government is best, and democracy requires cultivation; that the greatest threats to human freedom in the twentieth century came, at the same time, from global war and the "enormous power of the modern state"; and that the "decay of the Soviet experiment" should come as no surprise to anyone and should be encouraged. In the context of saying that Western strength and resolve were required as the basis for any way to reach a post–Cold War world, he believed that his worldview and policies—past, present, and proposed—were grounded in an accurate understanding of the long term. As Reagan put it: "the march of freedom and democracy which will leave Marxism-Leninism on the ash-heap of history as it has left other tyrannies which stifle the freedom and muzzle the self-expression of the people." Reagan had confidence that "[a]ny system is inherently unstable that has no peaceful means to legitimize its leaders," and that ultimately people would resist—by force, if necessary—the very repressiveness of the state.[19] Believing that such resistance had been occurring for years and would continue in Communist countries on many levels, he urged the United States and the free world to do their part to help peoples win their freedom.

Where the union of rhetoric and politics illuminates Reagan's thought, another speech deserves mention. In March 1983, many castigated the president for calling the Soviet Union an "evil empire." It should be noted that this analysis of the USSR was a small but significant part of a far-ranging presidential address given to the annual convention of the National Association of Evangelicals. And what Reagan told his audience about the Kremlin that day must be understood: He took the Soviets seriously when they said that they acted according to Marxist-Leninist doctrine and thus argued that the Kremlin subordinated morality to the interests of class war and world revolution. While stressing that the United States would seek both fair negotiations with the Soviets and "to persuade them of our peaceful intent," he maintained that the Kremlin "must be made to understand we will never compromise our principles and standards. We will never give away our freedom. We will never stop searching for a genuine peace." In this context—and in the critical year (1983) of planned deployment of the Euromissiles—he clarified his problem with the nuclear freeze movement. Reagan defended his two tracks of "peace through strength" and negotiations from that position of strength: He maintained that a freeze under current conditions would be a fraud since it would reward the Soviet Union for its offensive military buildup, would prevent the United States from modernizing its aging forces, and would be "virtually impossible" to verify; he added that a freeze would end any incentive for the Soviets to negotiate seriously on America's proposals in Geneva for majors arms reductions. Stating plainly his understanding of ideology and regime distinctions, he said, "I would agree to a freeze if only we could freeze the Soviets' global desires."[20]

Reagan applied that understanding to the whole East-West conflict. "The real crisis we face today is a spiritual one," he said of the Cold War, and "at root, it is a test of moral will and faith." In the way that presidents and preachers had done in the 1940s and 1950s, he urged everyone to pray for "the salvation of all of those who live in that totalitarian darkness—pray they will discover the joy of knowing God. But until they do, let us be aware that while they preach the supremacy of the state, declare its omnipotence over individual man, and predict its eventual domination of all peoples on the Earth, they are the focus of evil in the modern world." It was common in the 1980s to draw a moral equivalence between the two sides in the Cold War. Reagan refused to do so and exhorted his audience to beware this temptation or that of removing themselves "from the struggle between right and wrong and good and evil." In the end, he believed that the Cold War struggle between good and evil was one that the free world would win. But he did not think that America and its friends would ultimately win because of military might; rather, he found the source of the Western world's strength in the quest for human freedom to be spiritual, not material, in nature. And so he extended what he had suggested in his address to the British Parliament, in words that many dismissed as a rhetorical flourish for his Christian audience: "I believe we shall rise to the challenge. I believe that communism is another sad, bizarre chapter in human history whose last pages even now are being written." Echoing Truman's religious campaign of truth in the early 1950s, Reagan identified a spiritual emptiness in communism and held that people of all faiths could achieve together what no one church could do by itself.[21]

Freedom had, in Reagan's mind, both moral content and responsibilities in it. His serious treatment of freedom in the speeches before Parliament and the National Association of Evangelicals revealed the basis of his understanding of ethics and politics. Free, constitutional governments were not always perfect, but Reagan knew that they were legitimate and oriented toward a full understanding of liberty. By contrast, he viewed the Soviet Union as an illegitimate regime—indeed, as the worst yet seen. Reagan raised the question about the illegitimacy of the Soviet regime at a time when elite opinion called for accommodation and enhancing Moscow's sense of security. Such elites viewed U.S.-Soviet relations within the context of the arms race; Reagan reversed that thinking so that the arms conflict was derivative of the ideological conflict. Because the USSR was not only illegitimate but also offensive by nature, he thought, the next logical step was to "delegitimize" the Soviet regime on all fronts. He would support his rhetorical and political offensive with military muscle and revolutionary strategic thinking. If the West could win the ideological battle, reasoned Reagan, then the nuclear dilemma could be mitigated or even resolved through a renewed commitment and some original thinking outside the box of conventional arms control.

PEACE THROUGH STRENGTH

By asking what Reagan meant by "peace through strength," we also ask how he defined peace. When championing freedom and democracy, he often said that the United States desired peace. Reagan was careful, however, to frame peace as an environment of free nations and liberal democracies. It would have been wordier, but "peace through strength" might have been rendered more accurately as peace through strength and freedom. Not only did Reagan reject the realist view that peace was merely an absence of war, but he also shunned the idealist belief that peace was a policy to be achieved through international organization and agreements. "We desire peace," he said in late 1982. "But peace is a goal, not a policy. Lasting peace is what we hope for at the end of our journey; it doesn't describe the steps we must take nor the paths we should follow to reach that goal." As a result, he announced that he would "search for peace along two parallel paths": deterrence and arms reductions.[22] In practical terms, deterrence ended up being synonymous with the overall defense buildup, and included enhancing conventional forces, strategic modernization, improvements in readiness and mobility, and eventually the Strategic Defense Initiative (SDI), which was announced in 1983; arms reductions began in 1982 with the Strategic Arms Reductions Talks (START) and culminated with the elimination of two entire classes of nuclear weapons in the Intermediate Nuclear Forces (INF) Treaty of 1987.

Reagan did not believe that America should accommodate the Kremlin, and he resurrected Truman's policy that the United States should negotiate with the Soviets only from a position of strength. Unlike the Truman era, the United States did not possess a position of sufficient strength relative to its opponents when Reagan became president. Reagan set out to reestablish a position of strength before he would consider negotiating with the Soviets. In his view, the military buildup was necessary and targeted: His defense outlays never moved much above one-fourth of federal spending and, as such, were below the levels during the Vietnam War and a couple of percentage points above the level under Carter; but they represented a reallocation of resources toward defense overall, which included making key weapons systems operational and upgrading the defense of Western Europe.[23] The impact of the spending increase was great. Although the defense budget had begun to grow under Carter, Reagan added $6.8 billion more for defense in Fiscal Year (FY) 1981—which was a quarter higher than when he entered office—and $25.8 billion in FY 1982.

With the assistance of Secretary of Defense Caspar Weinberger, he consistently overruled the budget director, David Stockman, and overcame the opposition of many in the Washington and NATO bureaucracies. The United States had often allotted 10 percent or more of its GNP to defense in the 1950s and early 1960s, whereas Reagan spent 6.3 percent in the first budget for which he was completely responsible (FY 1982) and a high of 6.5 percent in FY 1986. Because the American economy had grown enormously since the early 1960s, each percentage point represented more money in absolute terms, even taking into account that many new weapons systems cost more than those of earlier generations.[24]

The blow dealt to the USSR by the president's announcement of SDI was severe. But Reagan hoped for more than to convince the Soviets of U.S. superiority in technology and economics.[25] Like Carter, he had an aversion to the threat of nuclear destruction and often said that a nuclear war must never be fought because it could never be won. Unlike Carter, he did not let this aversion determine his Cold War foreign policy. His commitment to deploy Pershing II and cruise missiles in Western Europe beginning in the fall of 1983 was firm. Building on that base, SDI and START provided the twin supports to Reagan's efforts to rise above and address the nuclear dilemma. While hoping that the Soviet Union would accept the "zero option," which he had announced in November 1981 and which proposed to eliminate all intermediate-range nuclear force weapons in Europe on both sides, Reagan looked for an alternative. He placed his alternative before the American people in March 1983: "What if free people could live secure in the knowledge that their security did not rest upon the threat of instant U.S. retaliation to deter a Soviet attack, that we could intercept and destroy strategic ballistic missiles before they reached our own soil or that of our allies?" The Strategic Defense Initiative was ridiculed as "Star Wars" by many experts, pundits, and even comedians, but Reagan thought that advanced technology and ability were on America's side and allowed for failures and setbacks over the course of "probably decades." In the long run, he viewed SDI as a program "to achieve our ultimate goal of eliminating the threat posed by strategic nuclear weapons" and part of the "necessary task of preserving peace and freedom."[26]

It turns out that Ronald Reagan was both anticommunist and anti-nuclear. Both totalitarianism and the threat of nuclear destruction endangered freedom, liberal democracy, and their fruits. Some observers have weighted the anti-nuclear over the anticommunist in order to explain why Reagan was willing in his second term to negotiate with the Soviets. Yet as early as summer 1983, the president had written a private letter to Soviet General Secretary Yuri Andropov proposing joint steps toward eliminating all nuclear weapons. Reagan wanted a nuclear-free world, but he wanted more a Communist-free world. He did not let his anti-nuclear attitude define his anticommunism; rather, he exercised his anti-nuclearism in light of his anticommunism. It mattered that nuclear weapons existed, but it mattered more to Reagan that totalitarian regimes like the USSR possessed them. To Reagan, SDI meant the protection of the United States and its allies from tyrants—whether the Kremlin or a terrorist group—that had nuclear arms. His long-term goal was to reduce, even eliminate, classes of nuclear weapons through verifiable negotiations and treaties. On a different albeit complementary level, the Strategic Defense Initiative was meant to help make nuclear weapons obsolete or, at least, not worth developing and possessing, since Reagan—as dedicated as he was to pursuing START—did not expect that a string of treaties would be the ultimate vehicle by which to eliminate all classes of nuclear weapons.

How essential anti-ballistic missile defense was to Reagan is evidenced by an oft-told story. When Soviet Premier Mikhail Gorbachev said at the Reykjavik summit meeting in 1986 that he would accept reductions—and the eventual elimination—of all intercontinental and intermediate missiles if Reagan gave up SDI, the president responded, "The meeting is over," and added, "we're leaving."[27] Reagan was striving to overcome the nuclear threat and the détente-era arms control regime (whether Nixon's or Carter's version), and saw the development of missile defense as the key to transcending the intertwined nuclear and arms control problems. From this line of reasoning came his revolutionary approach to treaties with the Soviets: reductions and elimination, not limitations, of arms. Later Reagan would joke that the Soviet leaders kept dying on him—and so he was unable to meet with them. But he never embraced the belief in summitry for its own sake that was characteristic of Nixonian realism, and the military buildup of his first administration meant that in his second term he could meet with Gorbachev.[28]

In addition to years of talks between Secretary of State George Shultz and his Soviet counterparts and Reagan's overtures to Gorbachev in private correspondence and at the Geneva summit, Reagan's firmness at Reykjavik led to the INF Treaty. One prominent American ally saw Reykjavik as decisive. "President Reagan's refusal to trade away SDI for the apparent near fulfillment of his dream of a nuclear-free world was crucial to the victory over communism," wrote former British Prime Minister Margaret Thatcher. "He called the Soviets' bluff. The Russians may have scored an immediate propaganda victory when the talks broke down. But they had lost the game and I have no doubt that they knew it."[29] Negotiations on START would continue, but the INF agreement was Reagan's legacy. Although critics had dismissed the viability of the "zero option" in 1981, the Soviets in the INF treaty agreed to eliminate two classes of intermediate-range ballistic missiles as well as to accept unprecedented procedures for onsite verification.[30] When McGeorge Bundy, George F. Kennan, Robert McNamara, and Gerard Smith lamented in *Foreign Affairs* that "Star Wars" would mean the end of arms control, they were right.[31] Reagan transformed the meaning of arms control through "peace through strength."

NEOCONTAINMENT

The Brezhnev Doctrine seemed unassailable for much of the 1970s. In 1968, Soviet Premier Brezhnev had proclaimed that once a regime became Communist, it would stay Communist, because gains for the Soviet bloc were irreversible. Since then, there had been no evidence to the contrary. Although global in scope, the Brezhnev Doctrine was invoked particularly to describe Soviet expansion into the developing world. Reagan, with support from others in the administration, decided to counterattack the Brezhnev Doctrine by putting strain on some of the more recent Soviet acquisitions and on Poland.[32] In terms of people, funds, and weapons, the Reagan Doctrine—as it came to be called—pushed containment to its logical conclusion by helping those who wanted their freedom to win their freedom. The Reagan Doctrine

was part of Reagan's larger strategy to pressure the Soviets at their political, economic, military, and moral weak spots, build up Western
strength, and press for signal victories on key Cold War battlefields.

There had been one doctrine for almost every president of the Cold
War era. The Truman Doctrine had been the best known and most important and is the most relevant with respect to Reagan. In a March
1947 special message to Congress on Greece and Turkey, Truman presented several important points which became tenets of containment:
that the foreign policy and national security of the United States were
threatened by Communist totalitarianism; that the United States was
the only country—by a combination of its position and principles—
that could lead the free world; that one of the primary objectives of
U.S. foreign policy was the "creation of conditions in which we and
other nations will be able to work out a way of life free from coercion";
and that the United States strongly disapproved of totalitarian regimes
being imposed on peoples. "At the present moment in world history,"
Truman said, "nearly every nation must choose between alternative
ways of life. The choice is too often not a free one."[33]

Reagan would have felt comfortable using Truman's words. In the
Cold War circumstances he faced, he started from the same understanding of the conflict; then he determined what he wanted to do with respect
to regions and specific countries within the global conflict. The Reagan
Doctrine developed over the course of several years, although we can
see the seeds for it in public statements from Reagan's first inaugural address to his 1982 remarks before Parliament to the "evil empire" speech.
The president fully articulated what he meant by the Reagan Doctrine in
his 1985 State of the Union address. "Freedom is not the sole preroga-
tive of a chosen few, it is the universal right of all God's children," he
said. Then he went on to explain: "Our mission is to nourish and defend
freedom and democracy and to communicate these ideals everywhere
we can. We must stand by our democratic allies. And we must not break
faith with those who are risking their lives—on every continent, from
Afghanistan to Nicaragua—to defy Soviet-supported aggression and secure rights which have been ours from birth." He then pointed to the
main tool of the Reagan Doctrine: "Support for freedom fighters is self-
defense."[34] The Soviets contended that the Reagan Doctrine was offensive by nature; Reagan would respond that it was a counteroffensive.

The Reagan Doctrine grew out of several National Security Decision Directives. One of the documents pertained directly to the Soviet Union and Eastern Europe. NSDD-32, which was signed by President Reagan in May 1982, was targeted primarily at Eastern Europe and recommended funding anticommunist movements as a "forward strategy" to pressure the periphery of the "Soviet empire." According to NSDD-32, the Polish government should be destabilized by keeping the Solidarity movement alive with help from the Catholic Church and Pope John Paul II. While the Carter administration had given some covert support to Solidarity, Reagan ordered more covert help in the form of money (about $8 million a year), advanced communications equipment and training (enabling Solidarity to function and publish numerous underground newsletters under martial law), and intelligence.[35] The CIA—covertly—sponsored many demonstrations, meetings, articles, and television shows, and the Voice of America (VOA)—overtly—laid bare the Soviet role in Poland through its coverage.[36] By 1987, the Soviet-backed government of General Wojciech Jaruzelski had been forced to begin discussions with the Catholic Church that ultimately led to the election of Solidarity leader Lech Walesa as president of Poland. Although the Communist regime did not topple until 1989, Poles typically credit both Reagan and the pope as the essential outside factors contributing to their liberation from totalitarian rule.

Another Reagan administration document concerned not only the USSR but also its expanding empire in the Third World. Signed by President Reagan in January 1983 and written primarily by then National Security Council staffer Richard Pipes in 1982, NSDD-75 committed the administration to seeking out Soviet weaknesses on its periphery and "rolling back" the USSR where possible. The United States, stated NSDD-75, should "contain and over time reverse Soviet expansionism by competing effectively on a sustained basis with the Soviet Union in all international arenas, particularly in the overall military balance and in geographical regions of priority concern to the United States." Then the directive singled out Afghanistan, proposing "to keep maximum pressure on Moscow for withdrawal" and to "ensure that the Soviets' political, military, and other costs remain high." American policy, NSDD-75 went on, will seek to "weaken and, where possible, undermine the existing links between [Soviet Third World allies] and the Soviet Union. U.S. policy will include active efforts to encourage democratic movements and forces to bring about political change inside these countries."[37]

The situation in Afghanistan had clearly prompted Reagan and others to contemplate a more direct way to help those resisting Soviet occupation. Despite what many thought were impossible odds, the Afghan resistance—known as the mujahideen—were fiercely defying the Soviets. A former Soviet scholar reasoned that Reagan was reversing Che Guevera's recommendation to the USSR for bringing down the West by giving the United States "many Vietnams"; the "essence of the Reagan Doctrine" was to arrange "many Afghanistans."[38] Reagan bestowed the title of "freedom fighters" on the anticommunists in Afghanistan. In March 1985 he approved NSDD-166, which sought the defeat and withdrawal of Soviet troops from Afghanistan. Ordering increased aid to the mujahideen, Reagan—over the objections of many advisors—next supplied resistance with Stinger anti-aircraft missiles to counter Soviet air power. U.S. satellite data were also provided to the Afghan rebels in order to help them target attacks. While backing the "freedom fighters," the administration supported negotiations in Pakistan that were aimed at Soviet withdrawal.[39] At least until 1985, the Soviets thought they could prevail in Afghanistan. By 1988, they had agreed to withdraw their troops, which were then gone by February 1989. Along with U.S. secret aid beginning in 1986 to mujahideen military, as well as U.S.-sponsored political operations across the Soviet border in Central Asia, the Stinger missiles were decisive in breaking the will of the Kremlin.[40]

The Reagan Doctrine was applied with greatest success in Poland and Afghanistan and with the least success in Nicaragua. Cases like Angola and Cambodia fell in between. Perhaps the key difference for Reagan between either Poland or Afghanistan and Nicaragua was his level of domestic support.[41] Carter's Undersecretary of State Warren Christopher had called the Sandinista government moderate, and this assessment had stuck in the minds of many in Congress. In December 1981, Reagan signed NSDD-17, authorizing $19 million in covert aid to the Nicaraguan Contras, which was funded by Congress in 1982. But public support would peak for Reagan's Contra aid policies by the

end of 1983, and Congress halted aid to the Contras in 1984.[42] After
then, and through the 1990 election in Nicaragua, either overt aid—in
response to increased Cuban and Soviet backing of the Sandinistas—
or no aid at all, went to the Contras from Congress. Critics in Congress
and the media argued that Nicaragua would be the "next Vietnam" if
the Reagan Doctrine were followed, and the president, despite his
communication skills, was unable to win sufficient domestic support.
In the end, the successes outweighed the failures in the Reagan Doctrine. America's active aid helped "freedom fighters" from Afghanistan
to Angola weaken and even shake off Communist rule. Through the
doctrine named for him, Reagan recovered, fulfilled, and ultimately
transcended Truman's containment.

REAGAN'S COLD WAR LEGACY

The effects of the Vietnam era and the imperial presidency ascribed to
Richard Nixon lingered, and still Reagan improved America's position
in the world and Americans' confidence in themselves. At home, he led
and shaped public opinion to support his overall Cold War strategy.
While Nixon and Carter had alienated American allies in various ways,
Reagan built successful working relationships with British Prime Minister Thatcher, West German Chancellor Helmut Kohl, and Japanese
Prime Minister Yasuhiro Nakasone, among others. From the defense
buildup to the Reagan Doctrine, from SDI and START to INF, from the
liberation of Grenada to supplying the Afghan mujahideen with
Stinger missiles, from the establishment of the National Endowment
for Democracy to the reinvigoration of America's alliances, Reagan
first revitalized and then transcended Truman's containment.[43] Further,
he always saw the fatal weakness in the Soviet Union: that it was con-
tinually expanding its empire but suffering from core political, economic, and spiritual weaknesses. The president aimed to exploit these
weaknesses through the application of the political, economic, and
military strength of the United States. In so doing, he sought to bring
the Soviets to the negotiating table on terms favorable to America and
its allies, and to freedom and liberal democracy. Ultimately, he sought
to place communism on the "ash-heap of history." Shortly after the end

of his presidency, with the liberation of Eastern Europe and the collapse of the Soviet Union between 1989 and late 1991, it looked as if
Reagan and his Cold War policies had not failed.

NOTES

1. Ronald Reagan, *An American Life* (New York: Simon and Schuster,
1990), 133. In his earlier autobiography, Reagan described himself as once "a
near-hopeless hemophilic liberal." See Ronald Reagan and Richard C.
Hubler, *Where's the Rest of Me?* (1965; New York: Dell Publishing Co.,
1981), 160.
2. Reagan is quoted in Lee Edwards, *Ronald Reagan: A Political Biography* (Houston, Tex.: Nordland Publishing International, Inc., 1981),
55–6.
3. Ronald Reagan, "America the Beautiful" (commencement address,
William Woods College, Fulton, Missouri, June 1952), copy in the author's
possession. This address is also quoted at length in Matthew Dallek, *The
Right Moment: Ronald Reagan's First Victory and the Decisive Turning Point
in American Politics* (New York: The Free Press, 2000), 36.
4. According to Reagan, he realized by 1960 that "the real enemy wasn't
big business, it was big government." See Reagan, *An American Life*, 135.
5. Dallek, *The Right Moment*, 37–40; Steven F. Hayward, *The Age of
Reagan: The Fall of the Old Liberal Order, 1964–1980* (Roseville, Calif.:
Prima Publishing, 2001), x–xii; and Ronald Reagan, "A Time for Choosing,"
October 27, 1964, copy of speech in author's possession.
6. Reagan and Hubler, *Where's the Rest of Me?* 304–5.
7. See Kiron K. Skinner, Annelise Anderson, and Martin Anderson, eds.,
*Reagan, In His Own Hand: The Writings of Ronald Reagan That Reveal His
Revolutionary Vision for America* (New York: The Free Press, 2001).
8. Dinesh D'Souza has referred to the six years from 1974 to 1980 as
"Reagan's wilderness years," since he did not have a formal job but was still
a well-known figure. Reagan had more time to read and write on his own as
well during this time. D'Souza, *Ronald Reagan: How an Ordinary Man Became an Extraordinary Leader* (New York: The Free Press, 1997), 75.
9. Skinner, Anderson, and Anderson, *Reagan, In His Own Hand*, 10, 13,
109–13, 86, 120, 147, 174–5, 480–1.
10. Ronald Reagan, "The Need for Leadership," (speech, Conservative
Political Action Conference Banquet, Washington, D.C., March 17, 1978),
copy in author's possession.

11. Hayward, *The Age of Reagan*, 616–17; Ronald Reagan, radio broadcast, September 11, 1979, in Skinner, Anderson, and Anderson, *Reagan, In His Own Hand*, 119–20.

12. For polling data and further analysis, see Benjamin I. Page and Robert Y. Shapiro, *The Rational Public: Fifty Years of Trends in Americans' Policy Preferences* (Chicago: The University of Chicago Press, 1992), 271; Daniel Yankelovich and Larry Kaagan, "Assertive America," in *The Reagan Foreign Policy*, ed. William G. Hyland (New York: New American Library, 1987), 7 (article reprinted from the 1980 America and the World issue of *Foreign Affairs*); Hayward, *The Age of Reagan*, 691; and Jeffrey M. Jones, "In Election Year 2000, Americans Generally Happy with State of the Nation," Gallup News Service, November 7, 2000. Carter's overall disapproval rating reached 55 percent in September 1980, making him the most unpopular president running for reelection to that point in the modern era; Truman had the same disapproval rating in 1952 as Carter had in 1980, but Truman did not run for reelection.

13. For more from a Reagan insider, especially about pro-Soviet regimes established during the Carter years, see Constantine C. Menges, Discussant, Eric J. Schmertz, Natalie Datlof, and Alexej Ugrinsky, eds., *President Reagan and the World* (Westport, Conn.: Greenwood Press, 1997), 29–30.

14. Jay Winik, *On the Brink: The Dramatic, Behind-the-Scenes Saga of the Reagan Era and Men and Women Who Won the Cold War* (New York: Simon & Schuster, 1996), 99–103.

15. Ronald Reagan, "Address to Members of the British Parliament," June 8, 1982, *Public Papers of the Presidents of the United States: Ronald Reagan, 1982* (Washington, D.C.: GPO, 1983), 742–8, in which Reagan adapts Churchill: "We're approaching the end of a bloody century plagued by a terrible political invention—totalitarianism. Optimism comes less easily today, not because democracy is less vigorous, but because democracy's enemies have refined their instruments of repression. Yet optimism is in order, because day by day democracy is proving itself to be a not-at-all-fragile flower. From Stettin on the Baltic to Varna on the Black Sea, the regimes planted by totalitarianism have had more than 30 years to establish their legitimacy. But none—not one regime—has yet been able to risk free elections. Regimes planted by bayonets do not take root."

16. Reagan, "Address to Members of the British Parliament," 742–8.

17. See, for example, Michael H. Hunt, *Ideology and U.S. Foreign Policy* (New Haven, Conn.: Yale University Press, 1987), 186–7.

18. Reagan, "Address to Members of the British Parliament," 742–8.

19. Reagan, "Address to Members of the British Parliament," 742–8.

20. Ronald Reagan, "Remarks at the Annual Convention of the National Association of Evangelicals in Orlando, Florida," March 8, 1983, *Public Papers of the Presidents of the United States: Ronald Reagan, 1983* (Washington, D.C.: GPO, 1984), 359–64.

21. Reagan, "Remarks at the Annual Convention of the National Association of Evangelicals in Orlando, Florida," 359–64.

22. Ronald Reagan, "Arms Reduction and Deterrence" (address to nation, November 22, 1982), copy in author's possession.

23. Edwin Meese III, *With Reagan: The Inside Story* (Washington, D.C.: Regnery Gateway, 1992), 177, 180–1; for reprints of tables from the Office of Management and Budget showing defense spending as a share of the federal budget between 1961 and 1991, see pp. 175 and 177.

24. Norman Friedman, *The Fifty-Year War: Conflict and Strategy in the Cold War* (Annapolis, Md.: Naval Institute Press, 2000), 458; Caspar W. Weinberger, *Fighting for Peace: Seven Critical Years in the Pentagon* (New York: Warner Books, 1990), 47–50; Dov S. Zakheim, "The Military Buildup," in *President Reagan and the World,* ed. Schmertz, Datlof, and Ugrinsky, 206. Also see National Defense Budget Authority, FY 1946–FY 2002, compiled by the CSBA, August 2001, based on DOD and OMB data.

25. For more on the pressure exerted on the Soviets by U.S. advances in computer and other specialized technologies, see Friedman, *The Fifty-Year War*, 458–9.

26. Ronald Reagan, "Address to the Nation on Defense and National Security," March 23, 1983, *Public Papers of the Presidents of the United States: Ronald Reagan, 1983*, 437–43.

27. Reagan, *An American Life,* 679; for Reagan's description of the negotiations leading up to this point, see pp. 675–9.

28. For an assessment that correctly argues for Reagan's involvement in U.S.-Soviet relations but incorrectly contends that Reagan's policy goals and strategies abruptly reversed course in early 1984, see Beth A. Fischer, *The Reagan Reversal: Foreign Policy and the End of the Cold War* (Columbia: University of Missouri Press, 1997). For an account that views Reagan's second term as a period of détente, see Coral Bell, *The Reagan Paradox: U.S. Foreign Policy in the 1980s* (New Brunswick, N.J.: Rutgers University Press, 1989). And for the latest post-revisionist views of Reagan's Cold War policies, see the relevant essays in W. Elliott Brownlee and Hugh Davis Graham, eds., *The Reagan Presidency: Pragmatic Conservatism and Its Legacies* (Lawrence: University Press of Kansas, 2003).

29. Margaret Thatcher, *The Downing Street Years* (New York: HarperCollins Publishers, 1993), 471. In a footnote, Thatcher makes reference to

former senior Soviet officials confirming "precisely this point" at a February 1993 conference at Princeton University on the end of the Cold War.

30. For an insightful contemporary assessment, see Michael H. Armacost, "Military Power and Diplomacy: The Reagan Legacy" (address before the Air Force Association Convention by the Undersecretary for Political Affairs, September 19, 1988) *Department of State Bulletin* 68, no. 2140 (November 1988): 40–4.

31. McGeorge Bundy, George F. Kennan, Robert S. McNamara, and Gerard Smith, "The President's Choice: Star Wars or Arms Control," in *The Reagan Foreign Policy*, ed. Hyland, 165–79 (article reprinted from the Winter 1984–1985 issue of *Foreign Affairs*).

32. Former Director of the CIA Robert Gates argues that several papers requested by then CIA Director William Casey in 1981 and a summer 1982 report from Casey to Reagan were all instrumental in suggesting that it was an opportune time to put pressure on the Soviets, especially with respect to their external empire. See Robert M. Gates, *From the Shadows: The Ultimate Insider's Story of Five Presidents and How They Won the Cold War* (New York: Simon & Schuster), 186–90.

33. Harry Truman, "Truman's Special Message to the Congress on Greece and Turkey," March 12, 1947, *Public Papers of the Presidents of the United States: Harry S. Truman, 1947* (Washington, D.C.: GPO, 1963), 176–80.

34. Ronald Reagan, "State of the Union Address," February 6, 1985, *Public Papers of the Presidents of the United States: Ronald Reagan, 1985* (Washington, D.C.: GPO, 1986), 146. For 1986, it is worth looking at Reagan's State of the Union Address and his "Message to the Congress on Freedom, Regional Security, and Global Peace," March 14, 1986, *Public Papers of the Presidents of the United States: Ronald Reagan, 1986* (Washington, D.C.: GPO, 1988), 341–9.

35. NSDD-32 is quoted from passages in James M. Scott, "Reagan's Doctrine? The Formulation of an American Foreign Policy Strategy," *Presidential Studies Quarterly* 26, no. 4 (Fall 1996): 1047–61; for description of Reagan's policy, see Friedman, *The Fifty-Year War*, 455.

36. For these details and more discussion of the CIA role in Poland, see Gates, *From the Shadows*, 358–9.

37. NSDD-75 is quoted from passages in Scott, "Reagan's Doctrine?" 1048–9.

38. Genrikh Aleksandrovich (Henry) Trofimenko, Discussant, *President Reagan and the World,* ed. Schmertz, Datlof, and Ugrinsky, 135.

39. Friedman, *The Fifty-Year War*, 454–5.

40. For more discussion of the Reagan administration's tactics in Afghanistan, see Peter Schweizer, *Victory: The Reagan Administration's Secret Strategy That Hastened the Collapse of the Soviet Union* (New York: Atlantic Monthly Press, 1994).

41. For an assessment of the degrees of success in Afghanistan and Nicaragua, see Whittle Johnston, "Reagan and America's Democratic Mission," in *President Reagan and the World,* ed. Schmertz, Datlof, and Ugrinsky, 23–4. For a useful chronological chart of Reagan Doctrine assistance to Afghanistan, Angola, Nicaragua, Cambodia, and Mozambique, see Scott, "Reagan's Doctrine?" 1055.

42. Richard Sobel, *The Impact of Public Opinion on U.S. Foreign Policy Since Vietnam: Constraining the Colossus* (New York: Oxford University Press, 2001), 115, 103.

43. For an early, prescient look at Reagan's return to containment, see Robert E. Osgood, "The Revitalization of Containment," in *The Reagan Foreign Policy*, ed. Hyland, 19–56.

4

The Conscience of a President: Ronald Reagan and Abortion

Matthew Sitman

From the time the ink dried after Governor Ronald Reagan signed the Therapeutic Abortion Act of 1967 until he raised his right hand and took the oath of office for the U.S. presidency, slightly less than one and a half million abortions were performed in California.[1] "With a stroke of a pen on June 14, 1967," Reagan biographer Lou Cannon wrote, "Reagan signed a bill that permitted more legal abortions in California than occurred in any other state before the advent of *Roe v. Wade*."[2] Upon the Therapeutic Abortion Act becoming law, the number of legal abortions in California drastically increased under Reagan's tenure, from 518 in 1967—his first year in office—to an average of 100,000 in the years between 1968 and 1974—the remaining years of his governorship.[3]

Reagan's signing of the aforementioned bill was an inauspicious beginning to his political life, certainly not the expected prelude to a record as president that would cause conservative commentator Fred Barnes to label Reagan the "father of the pro-life movement."[4] In this major, early test, Reagan's political inexperience was glaringly obvious. He was tentative and confused, and his conservative instincts provided no clear answer to an issue that required him to weigh the moral, legal, and political repercussions of his eventual decision. His top aides in Sacramento, normally able to reach a workable consensus, were divided on the issue, further convoluting the decision-making process.[5] When Reagan approached his legal staff with complicated, hypothetical questions about abortion laws,

he claimed the only answer he received from them was that they
were glad he wasn't the one who provided the questions for the state
bar exam.[6]

Reagan later admitted that at the time abortion "was a subject I'd
never given much thought to and one upon which I didn't really have
an opinion. But now I was governor and abortion turned out to be
something I couldn't walk away from."[7] Ultimately, "faced with an
abundance of contradictory and absolutist advice," Cannon observed,
"Reagan behaved as if lost at sea."[8]

Reagan's experience dealing with the abortion issue in 1967 was a
formative one. It is impossible to understand his later staunchly pro-
life positions without grasping the lessons he learned from this early
political battle. During the debate over the Therapeutic Abortion Act,
Reagan became wholly educated on the issue. In many ways, knowing
little about abortion was not a fault of Reagan's but a sign of the times.
Lou Cannon described the political and social climate surrounding
abortion:

> Abortion in the 1960s was discussed in whispers. Until mid-decade, the
> word itself was taboo in most newspapers, including the *Los Angeles
> Times*, where abortion was called an "illegal medical procedure." The
> phrases "pro-choice" and "pro-life" did not yet exist, and battle lines on
> the issue were drawn almost entirely on religious lines. Conservatives
> who were not Roman Catholics believed, in a bromide of the day, that
> government should stay out of "the boardroom and the bedroom." Lib-
> eral Democrats who were also Catholics were overwhelmingly antiabor-
> tion.[9]

Contemplating Reagan's lack of firm understanding of the issue in this
context makes his response much less surprising. Abortion was only
starting to become a major issue, and his ideas on it, understandably,
were not yet fully developed.

To combat his naiveté, Reagan vigorously studied the issue. He
turned to William P. Clark, then serving as his cabinet secretary but
also a longtime spiritual confidante, and said, "Bill, I've got to know
more—theologically, philosophically, medically."[10] Reagan biographer Edmund Morris later wrote that "by the time the Therapeutic

Abortion Act reached him on June 13 [1967], Reagan was quoting Saint Thomas Aquinas."[11] Reagan, years later, remarked that "I did more studying and soul searching than on anything that was to face me as governor."[12] In an interview with Lou Cannon he confided, "I have never done more study on any one thing than on the abortion bill."[13]

Reagan went into semi-seclusion for a long weekend to continue studying the materials he had collected and sought the advice of those he trusted. Despite this, he would sign the bill—but primarily for tactical reasons: many in his own party supported it, he had forced some changes in the bill that eliminated its worst features, and a potential veto would be overridden in the state legislature.[14] His whirlwind education came too late; his early faltering had backed him into a corner. His conservative instincts alone were not enough to get him through this complex problem.

"Reagan was left with an undefinable sense of guilt after signing [the bill]," Morris subsequently observed.[15] It was an agonizing decision, one dictated by circumstances, not Reagan's conscience. "Those were awful weeks," Reagan would later say.[16] It was a trial by fire, an instance in which the former actor was outmaneuvered by his political foes. Lou Cannon claims Reagan "would never have signed the bill if he had been more experienced as governor, the only time as governor or president that Reagan acknowledged a mistake on major legislation."[17] Bill Clark called the incident "perhaps [Reagan's] greatest disappointment in public life."[18]

Through his frustration over the Therapeutic Abortion Act, the development of Ronald Reagan, pro-life leader, began. He had learned a great deal, and not just in the realm of political tactics. He emerged from the ordeal with a profoundly intellectual understanding of the abortion issue. Reagan sought a common ground between medicine, law, and theology, and used all three disciplines to inform his thoughts on the matter. It was in 1967 that his ideas concerning the beginning of human life were fully formed. Through vigorous study he translated conviction and instinct into a cogent understanding of abortion and its implications. Tinged with guilt but equipped for battle, he declared, "When this subject arises again, we shall be prepared."[19]

If the first legacy of 1967 was an improved intellectual grasp of abortion, the second was a changed disposition toward the issue. In short, the actual effects of Reagan signing the Therapeutic Abortion Act were not what he—or the bill's sponsor—anticipated. The impact and consequences of this legislation forced Reagan into a consideration that would stay with him through his presidency: that one mistake on abortion can lead down a slippery slope with unforeseen results.

The Therapeutic Abortion Act of 1967 contained a provision allowing abortions to be performed in California on the grounds of a woman's mental health. This was an area, obviously, more subject to a psychiatrist's interpretation than the more tangible symptoms exhibited by physical ailments and thus, in the opinion of pro-life advocates in California, was open to abuse.

Reagan articulated these fears when he said at a news conference that "the prognosis of mental health would be easier to exaggerate than the diagnosis of physical health, and this of course could allow certain leeway for a doctor who wanted to do this [perform an abortion], to make a statement that he believed that this grievous suffering or this mental health deterioration would result" if the abortion was not performed.[20] Indeed, this provision was interpreted quite broadly, and, as noted, abortions increased exponentially.[21] Reagan was not the only one who underestimated just how many abortions would be performed under the auspices of deteriorating mental health; the bill's Democratic sponsor, Tony Beilenson, told Lou Cannon he also was surprised that physicians so liberally interpreted the law.[22]

Reagan learned that the law of unintended consequences undoubtedly applied to the abortion issue. He saw first how drastically an outcome can be distanced from intention. This was especially sobering because, in this case, the issue at hand was to Reagan a sacred one: human life. From this point forward, he would be particularly perceptive to what, in his mind, was any attempt to degrade the sanctity and dignity of human life—realizing how quickly the results could morph into something unrecognizable from the original goal.

This episode in Reagan's political career, which Dinesh D'Souza claims "genuinely shocked" the governor, was a pivotal moment in the training of the future president. Reagan's record on abortion in his over twenty subsequent years of public life cannot be understood apart from those trying weeks in 1967. It would be improper to look at his signing of the Therapeutic Abortion Bill as proof of a mixed legacy on the issue. Instead, the ordeal should be seen as the impetus for much of the stridently pro-life actions of his presidency. Reagan's records on abortion as governor and as president are not contradictory; rather, they are inextricably linked. Ed Meese, one of his most trusted aides, confirmed this when he conceded that Reagan's regrets over his role in promoting abortion on demand in California probably intensified his pro-life convictions and led him in later years to support measures like the Human Life Amendment.[23]

"THERE IS NO WAY I COULD OR WOULD CHANGE MY POSITION"

Though Ronald Reagan ended 1967 with a deep understanding and hardened disposition towards the abortion issue, some would wonder in the years after his governorship if Reagan truly was committed to the pro-life cause. In 1979, as Reagan was all but a declared candidate for the following November's election, reporter Robert Mauro wrote an article titled "Pro-Life View of Presidential Candidate Possibilities" in an influential, conservative Catholic publication called *The Wanderer*. The article suggested that Reagan might have been preparing to abandon his anti-abortion position, and Reagan immediately responded. Mauro was skeptical of Reagan's commitment to the pro-life movement, but Reagan put that to rest forcefully. In a letter to Mauro, Reagan said, "my position is that interrupting a pregnancy means the taking of a human life. In our Judeo-Christian tradition, that can only be done in self-defense. Therefore, I will agree to abortion only to protect the life of the prospective mother."[24] The bulk of the letter explained his actions as governor. Reagan wrote:

> Perhaps it was my inexperience in government, but, like so many pieces of legislation, there were loopholes that I had not seen, and the thing that made the California abortion bill become somewhat permissive in nature was violation of the spirit of the legislation by the very groups who were supposed to police it.[25]

Reagan went to pains to give what he called "the correct history of what took place early in my term as governor."[26] The thoroughness

with which Reagan defended his signing of the abortion bill betrayed
a defensiveness born of guilt. In one instance he even referred to the
Therapeutic Abortion Act as "the permissive bill I supposedly
signed."[27] In sum, he strove to make clear that what resulted in California was not what he intended. Ending the letter, Reagan emphati-
cally told Mauro: "There is no way I could or would change my
position with regard to my opposition to the permissive abortion that
is taking place throughout our land."[28]

   Another letter written by Reagan around this time to an individual
named Al Matt of St. Paul, Minnesota, again assured a wary correspondent of his steadfast commitment to opposing abortion. Reagan
wrote:

> I am very much in favor of an amendment . . . to curb the abortion on
> demand that we have in so much of the country. Very simply, my feeling
> is that an abortion is the taking of a human life, and that can only be jus-
> tified or excused in our society as defense of the mother's life—if her
> life is threatened by continuing the pregnancy. There is no way I could
> or would change my position.[29]

It is noteworthy that Reagan took the time to write to ordinary citizens
to rectify any misconception that he might abandon the pro-life cause
once he was in office.

A TRUE BELIEVER

By the time Reagan was a candidate in the 1980 election, concerns
over his commitment to opposing abortion should have abated. A number of clear signals were given after 1967 that ought to have convinced
the right-to-life movement that he was one of them.

   The first and perhaps most overlooked occurred in 1970. For the
second time during Reagan's governorship, legislators tried to liberal-
ize California's abortion laws. This time Reagan successfully thwarted
their efforts. In response to this second attempt, Reagan wrote a "Dear
Citizen" letter, rhetorically asking Californians what great lives may
never exist because they were never allowed to occur. Reagan said,
"Those who summarily advocate a *blanket population control* [Rea-

gan's emphasis] should think carefully. Who might they be doing away with? Another Lincoln, or Beethoven, an Einstein or an Edison? Who shall play God?"[30]

Later that year, Reagan responded to a constituent's letter regarding abortion. He told the constituent: "I am convinced that interrupting a pregnancy is the taking of human life." He added: "It is easy to refer to the unborn as a 'fetus' but most medical doctrine recognizes the presence of a living human being whose personality traits, hair and eye color, and other characteristics have already been genetically determined."[31] At the end of the letter, Reagan mused: "If, with pregnancy, a window appeared in a woman's body so that she could look at her own child develop, I wonder at what point she would decide it was all right to kill it."[32]

In April 1975, he devoted an entire radio address to the subject. He began by reviewing his actions as governor in 1967 and followed by stating his firm belief that he could "find no evidence whatsoever that a fetus is not a living human being with human rights."[33] Perhaps most importantly, however, Reagan expressed a thoughtful caveat to his opposition to abortion, offering his clearest explanation of his belief that a woman had a right to an abortion if doing so would save her own life. Reagan said, "In our Judeo-Christian religion we recognize the right to take life in defense of our own. Therefore an abortion is justified when done in self defense."[34] Just as one can rightly respond with force if under unwanted, unwarranted duress, Reagan believed "a woman has the right to protect her own life and health against even her own unborn child."[35] This exception also included pregnancies as the result of rape, because Reagan believed a woman "should not be made to bear a child resulting from that violation of her person," again making an abortion in such a case "an act of self-defense."[36] These stances came from Reagan's understanding of America's religious tradition and related core principles of self-defense. He did not condemn all abortions but perceived certain rights that he believed were always applicable. Reagan sensed an unalterable right to defend oneself against bodily harm, whether by a criminal or (in an unfortunate case) an unborn child.

There is at least one more indication of Reagan's commitment and consistency regarding abortion in the years separating his governorship and the presidency. During the 1980 presidential race, a struggle ensued in the Reagan campaign between moderates and movement conservatives, Rockefeller Republicans and *National Review* Republicans. One of the moderates, John Sears, managed the campaign. M. Stanton Evans, a conservative, described Sears as "a devout pragmatist who has little affinity for issues in general, and even less affinity for conservatives."[37] Firing conservatives who had been with Reagan since his California days, including Lyn Nofziger, and trying to diminish the influence of men like Ed Meese and Mike Deaver, Sears invariably tried to get Reagan to moderate his political positions. He wanted Reagan to campaign from the middle, and this included changing his opposition to abortion. He told Reagan he needed to be a pro-choice candidate. On this issue, however, Reagan would not compromise. Finally, when Sears persisted, Reagan snapped: "Listen, damn it, I'm running for president, not you. And I'm not changing my position on abortion!"[38]

As Reagan neared the presidency, there could be no doubt as to his thoughts on abortion. Whether he was speaking to millions on the radio, exchanging letters with common people from the Midwest, or scolding his own campaign manager (whom he eventually fired), Reagan entered the Oval Office with strong convictions on abortion forged by political battles and intellectual deliberations. His preparation for a pro-life presidency could not have been more thorough.

A COMMON THREAD

William P. Clark says that Reagan's words and deeds regarding abortion as president can only be understood if viewed through the lens of the broader philosophical context from which he approached all his policies. Underlying Reagan's major initiatives, said Clark, was his belief in "the dignity and sanctity of all human life."[39] Protecting the unborn was an outgrowth of this sentiment.

To Reagan, the dignity of man was a common thread connecting seemingly disparate issues like opposing the Soviet Union, abortion, and even the modern welfare state. Reagan did not resist the spread of communism and the expansion of the Soviet Union for purely geopolitical reasons; rather, he saw the Cold War as "a test of faith and spirit."[40] Reagan saw the Soviet Union as not just a physical enemy but an affront to man's inherent dignity. He called communism a "disease" and was disgusted at the way "the communist sickness looks upon human life."[41] He believed communism "is neither an economic or a political system—it is a form of insanity—a temporary aberration which will one day disappear from the earth because it is contrary to human nature."[42] Communism and totalitarianism deprived man of his sacred right to liberty, a right granted, as Thomas Jefferson put it in a phrase Reagan often quoted, by "the God who gave us life."[43] Again, life was sacred and each person had intrinsic dignity—because communism ignored these twin pillars of Reagan's belief system, he doggedly combated it.

Domestically, Reagan's ethic of dignity applied to his desire to reform welfare. Reagan needed to look no further than his old political hero, Franklin Roosevelt, for a description of the limitations of welfare. In 1935 Roosevelt called government relief "a narcotic, a subtle destroyer of the human spirit."[44] In his memoirs, Reagan maintained that FDR would never have supported the welfare state that existed by the 1980s. In 1971, Reagan published a *New York Times* op-ed entitled "Welfare is a Cancer," indicating his thoughts on the effects of reliance on government assistance.[45] In 1980, he wrote a letter to the Pulitzer Prize–winning columnist for the *Washington Post*, William Raspberry, describing the ideal welfare system as one in which its success was determined by how many people were taken off the rolls. Reagan said that he wanted to give people back the pride that accompanies work, not keep them in "permanent bondage under the benevolent hand of the case worker."[46] Reagan saw welfare as a slight to a person's dignity. He cautioned that he did not resent government aid to the truly needy; rather, he said that dignity comes with independence and earning a living.

Reagan applied these values to abortion as well. In 1983, he wrote, "The real question today is not when human life begins, but, *what is the value of human life?*" [original emphasis].[47] Reagan abhorred how "some influential people want to deny that every human life has intrinsic, sacred worth."[48] At the 1982 Conservative Political Action Conference, he called abortion "a great moral evil, an assault on the sacredness of human life."[49]

Reagan loosely acknowledged this common thread in his policies in a July 1982 address to the National Right to Life Convention when he said, "this Administration does not and will not have separate agendas—one for economic matters, one for the so-called 'social' issues. Our concern is to make America healthy: economically, morally, in every way."[50] Reagan's foreign, economic, and social policies all had a moral dimension and were meant to foster an ethic appreciative of every person's innate value. It was not an accident that, in his Evil Empire speech, he preceded his condemnation of the Soviet Union with a call to "never rest" until legislation ending the "tragedy" of abortion passed Congress. Reagan invoked the Declaration of Independence: "Unless and until it can be proven that the unborn child is not a living entity, then its right to life, liberty, and the pursuit of happiness must be protected."[51] The juxtaposition of abortion and a communist dictatorship in this speech demonstrates the unity of Reagan's thought and the overarching principles that guided his policy thinking. Agree or disagree, his pro-life position was part of a consistent moral framework that sought to uphold human dignity inside or outside the womb, at home or abroad.

REAGAN, ABORTION, AND GOD

When Reagan spoke about abortion as president he frequently did so in spiritual terms, speaking of sacred rights granted by God. For him, the religious faith that permeated his life informed his opposition to abortion.[52] Reagan biographer Paul Kengor asserts abortion was an "issue he found inseparable from biblical precepts."[53] Some of Reagan's most strident comments about abortion came before religious audiences, and frequently such comments were placed closely to other items of religious and moral significance in the speech. In the Evil Empire speech—given before the National Association of Evangelicals—his denunciation of abortion came after a passage about a constitutional amendment to restore school prayer and ban discrimination against religious groups and speech in public schools.[54]

In the aforementioned July 1982 speech at the National Right to Life Convention, Reagan spoke of divine rewards for pro-life advocates when he told supporters that "it is you have attempted to protect the helpless and speak for the unborn; you have carried the burden and fought the good fight. For this, God will bless you."[55] Later in that same speech he quoted Christian apologist C. S. Lewis. Reagan rebutted those who said it was an act of kindness to abort an unwanted child by using Lewis's phrase that "love is something more stern and splendid than mere kindness."[56]

Speaking before the Annual Convention of the National Religious Broadcasters in 1984, Reagan said, "God's most blessed gift to His family is the gift of life. He sent us the Prince of Peace as a babe in a manger."[57] Admitting that what he was about to say was controversial, Reagan pointed out that some 4,000 unborn children were aborted every day—one every twenty-one seconds.[58] He continued:

> We cannot pretend that America is preserving her first and highest ideal, the belief that each life is sacred, when we've permitted the deaths of 15 million helpless innocents since the Roe versus Wade decision—15 million children who will never laugh, never sing, never know the joy of human love, will never strive to heal the sick, feed the poor, or make peace among nations. Abortion has denied them the first and most basic of human rights. We are all infinitely poorer for their loss.[59]

Reagan's faith-based rhetoric against abortion continued in his 1986 State of the Union Address—a high-profile platform. Again invoking a higher power, Reagan said America was "a nation of idealists, yet today there is a wound in our national conscience. America will never be whole as long as the right to life granted by our Creator is denied to the unborn."[60] He vowed that for the rest of his time in office, he would "do what I can to see that this wound is one day healed."[61]

These rhetorical overtures should not be dismissed. Reagan made many strong statements against abortion in very public, widely publicized situations. Those remarks often offended pro-choice liberals. Still, he was undeterred, and his sometimes controversial statements thrilled pro-lifers, who still remember them fondly. No president has spoken so consistently and boldly against abortion, and his words—as Reagan's words often did—had a lasting impact.

RONALD REAGAN, AUTHOR

Part of doing his utmost to mend this "wound" was something that Reagan staff claim no sitting president had ever done: write a book in

office. Originally, *Abortion and the Conscience of the Nation* appeared
as an essay in the Spring 1983 issue of the quarterly, *Human Life Review*. In 1984, Reagan's article was packaged with other essays, including one by British commentator Malcolm Muggeridge, bound as a
book, and published by Thomas Nelson Publishers. It would also be
reprinted in 2000, with Reagan's work this time introduced with a retrospective introduction and two forwards by pro-life leaders assessing
his impact, as well as the book's, on the right-to-life cause.

The impetus for Reagan to pen *Abortion and the Conscience of the
Nation* was simple: the tenth anniversary of the Supreme Court decision in *Roe v. Wade*. He thought such an occasion "a good time to
pause and reflect."[62] The slim volume lamented that the nationwide
policy of abortion-on-demand through all nine months of pregnancy
was not a reflection of the will of the people but an act of judicial fiat.
Reagan pointed out that beforehand not a single state had permitted the
unrestricted abortion decreed to be national policy by the Supreme
Court in 1973. [63] He noted that since the decision "more than 15 million unborn children have had their lives snuffed out by legalized abortion" and that that was "over ten times the number of Americans lost
in all our nation's wars."[64]

Reagan derided the judicial thinking behind the decision, writing,
"make no mistake, abortion-on-demand is not a right granted by the
Constitution" and that "no serious scholar, including one disposed to
agree with the Court's result, has argued that the framers of the Constitution intended to create such a right."[65] He proceeded to cite John
Hart Ely, then Dean of Stanford Law School, who said the opinion "is
not constitutional law and gives almost no sense of obligation to try to
be."[66] Ultimately, Reagan thought *Roe v. Wade* had "become a continuing prod to the conscience of the nation."[67]

Reagan's primary concern, however, was not the legal context surrounding abortion but a desire to "affirm the sanctity of life" and to
cultivate a "sanctity of life ethic."[68] He believed the "real question . . .
for all of us is whether that tiny human life has a God-given right to be
protected by the law."[69] Reagan feared the consequences of denying
this spiritual dimension of human existence. He quoted British commentator Malcolm Muggeridge, who said, "Either life is always and in
all circumstances sacred, or intrinsically of no account; it is inconceiv-

able that it should be in some cases the one, and in some the other."[70] Reagan feared the slippery slope of arbitrarily deciding who could and could not live. Life was either sacred—and accompanied with corresponding inherent worth—or it wasn't. He firmly believed, and wrote, that as a nation "we cannot diminish the value of one category of human life—the unborn—without diminishing the value of all human life."[71]

During his presidency Reagan saw as proof of this general devaluation of human life the example of "Baby Doe" in Bloomington, Indiana. The newborn had Down's Syndrome and a complication that rendered him incapable of being nourished through normal feeding. In short, he was starving—but this could have been remedied through surgery. Indiana courts, however, ruled that the appropriate medical procedure could be withheld, allowing the child to wither away and eventually die. Reagan expressed grief that the "child was denied life-saving surgery and starved to death because he had Down's Syndrome and some people didn't think his life would be worth living."[72] He wrote:

> The death of that tiny infant tore at the hearts of all Americans because the child was undeniably a live human being—one lying helpless before the eyes of the doctors and the eyes of the nation. The real issue for the courts was *not* whether Baby Doe was a human being. The real issue was whether to protect the life of a human being who had Down's Syndrome, who would probably be mentally handicapped, but who needed a routine surgical procedure to unblock his esophagus and allow him to eat. A doctor testified to the presiding judge that, even with his physical problem corrected, Baby Doe would have a "non-existent" possibility for a "minimally adequate quality of life"—in other words, that retardation was the equivalent of a crime deserving the death penalty.[73]

Reagan believed such a conclusion was the direct result of a general cheapening of human life. When one category of living persons—in his mind the unborn—was denied the right to life, it put in peril that right for all other categories. He deplored those who "want to pick and choose which individuals have value."[74] The connection between abortion and Baby Doe—and perhaps other assaults on life—was obvious to the president. To drive home this point, Reagan cited Supreme Court

Justice William Brennan: "The cultural environment for a human holo-
caust is present whenever any society can be misled into defining
individuals as less than human and therefore devoid of value and respect."[75]

Reagan's essay also likened abortion to slavery, and he wrote at
length of the philosophical connection he perceived between the two.
Like the abolitionists of the 19th century, he saw pro-life forces as having "formidable obstacles" before them and encouraged them to "not
lose heart."[76] Remember, he wrote:

> This is not the first time our country has been divided by a Supreme
> Court decision that denied the value of certain human lives. The *Dred
> Scott* decision of 1857 was not overturned in a day, or a year, or even a
> decade. At first, only a minority of Americans recognized and deplored
> the moral crisis brought about by denying the full humanity of our black
> brothers and sisters; but that minority prevailed. They did it by appeal-
> ing to the hearts and minds of their countrymen, to the truth of human
> dignity under God. From their example, we know that respect for the sa-
> cred value of human life is too deeply engrained in the hearts of our peo-
> ple to remain forever suppressed.[77]

Later in the article Reagan cited Abraham Lincoln, writing that
"nothing stamped with the divine image and likeness was sent into the
world to be trodden on."[78] Not long after the publication of his essay,
Reagan continued the slavery analogy in a speech:

> This nation fought a terrible war so that black Americans would be guar-
> anteed their God-given rights. Abraham Lincoln recognized that we
> could not survive as a free land when some could decide whether others
> should be free or slaves. Well, today another question begs to be asked:
> How can we survive as a free nation when some decide that others are
> not fit to live and should be done away with?[79]

Reagan pleaded with Americans that abortion affects not just an unborn child, but all people. He quoted the English poet John Donne:
"Any man's death diminishes me, because I am involved in mankind;
and therefore never send to know for whom the bell tolls; it tolls for
thee."[80] To convey the magnitude of the issue, Reagan turned to the
words of Mother Teresa: "the greatest misery of our time is the gener-

alized abortion of children."[81] He drew his essay to a close with another quote from Muggeridge, who said of life that "however low it flickers or fiercely burns, it is still a Divine flame which no man dare presume to put out, be his motives ever so humane and enlightened."[82] To make his case against abortion, Reagan had tapped into sources from literature, religion, legal theory, the American political tradition, and contemporary opinion. To those who oppose abortion, the publication of a book devoted to this single political issue, personally written by the sitting president, was a milestone for the pro-life movement, as well as a testament to the sincerity of Reagan's belief in "the transcendent right to life of all human beings."[83]

REAGAN'S PRO-LIFE LEGACY: AN APPRAISAL

Despite his committed words and understanding of abortion, assessments of Reagan's attitude and policies toward the issue have been decidedly mixed. Lou Cannon, generally considered the top Reagan biographer, wrote in *President Reagan: The Role of a Lifetime* that "his legacy on this issue was conflicted"; he was not "as obsessive about anti-abortion legislation as he often seemed."[84] Cannon's ultimate conclusion is that "his stand was partly a product of political calculation" and that "Reagan managed to keep the pro-life forces in his corner, but he was not an especially avid crusader for their cause."[85] Edmund Morris, Reagan's official biographer, includes only a few neutral references to abortion throughout the entirety of *Dutch: A Memoir of Ronald Reagan*. William Martin, a professor of religion and public policy at Rice University, wrote that "though [Reagan] welcomed right-to-life activists to the Oval Office, he failed to stem the tide of abortions and offered no support to the Helms-Hyde bill, which would have declared that life begins at conception."[86]

Much of these criticisms tell only part of the story. It is remarkable that Cannon does not mention Reagan writing and publishing *Abortion and the Conscience of the Nation*, not even in a footnote. Cannon completely ignored Reagan's pro-life manifesto.

It is also a misconception that Reagan was unwilling to expend political capital on the issue of abortion. The publication of his pro-life essay is just one example. William Clark remembered that Reagan "wrote [*Abortion and the Conscience of the Nation*] over the advice of his political counselors." Since it was 1983, they said "Let's not publish it now so close to the election." Reagan replied, "I might not be re-elected. We're going with it now."[87] Also, former Reagan speechwriter Peter Robinson recalled an instance when the president insisted on keeping controversial references to abortion in a speech over the objections of his moderate, pragmatic chief of staff James Baker. After Baker explained why Reagan should talk about something else, the President—shaking his head and smiling—said "Now, Jim, this is just one of those things I feel very strongly about." Despite this, Baker persisted, telling him how "all the polls show the country just isn't with you on this one" and that because the country knew where he stood on abortion already "there's just no reason to go into it all over again." Reagan, again gently rebuffing Baker, said, "Well, Jim, I just don't know about that." Following this exchange, he even pulled a letter out of his desk signed by half a dozen medical doctors claiming fetuses felt pain much earlier than thought. He handed the letter to a speechwriter and actually ordered him to use it in the speech.[88]

Another question that arises about Reagan's record on abortion concerns how much he validated his pro-life rhetoric with action. Did he match his words with deeds? Wanda Franz, President of the National Right to Life Committee, argues that "the Reagan legacy includes a wide range of pro-life action—actions that defied the pro-abortion culture and often had to be pursued over the objections of a hostile leadership in Congress."[89] Franz lists the following Reagan actions:

- "Worked to pass the 'Baby Doe' regulations to protect newborn children with disabilities when they are threatened by denial of nutrition, medically indicated treatment, or even general care." (This was in direct response to the case described previously of the newborn from Indiana who was denied basic surgery because of having Down's Syndrome.)
- "Instituted policies prohibiting funding for experimentation on children."
- "Established the 'Mexico City' policy under which private organizations, which perform or actively promote abortion as a method

of family planning in other nations, are ineligible for funds under the 'population assistance' program."

- "Supported congressional efforts to limit funding of abortions" and "worked to enforce congressional directives to prevent so-called 'family planning' programs from advocating abortion as a means of birth control as part of Title X."
- "Submitted to Congress the 'President's Pro-Life Bill of 1987,' that would have put Congress on record against *Roe v. Wade*, permanently prohibited federal funding of abortion, and denied Title X 'family planning' funds to organizations which perform or refer for abortions."
- Endorsed the Human Life Bill first introduced by Senator Jesse Helms that "expressly recognizes the unborn as human beings and accordingly protects them as persons under our Constitution."
- Endorsed the Respect Human Life Act, introduced in the 98th Congress, which stated in its first section that the policy of the United States is "to protect innocent life both before and after birth." This bill, sponsored by Congressman Henry Hyde and Senator Roger Jepsen, would have prohibited "abortions or assisting those who do so, except to save the life of the mother." It also addressed "the pressing issue of infanticide."
- Endorsed a constitutional amendment banning abortion except in the case of a mother's health.

Franz claimed that, "the pro-life movement will always be indebted to President Ronald Reagan for his word and deed."[90] Whether one favored or opposed Reagan's actions, his records seem to show a substantive as well as rhetorical pro-life presidency.

Perhaps the best take on Reagan and abortion comes from Dinesh D'Souza, a pro-life conservative who worked in the Reagan White House as Senior Domestic Policy Analyst. D'Souza pointed out that "on abortion . . . Reagan would not be flexible, because he firmly believed that millions of lives were at stake."[91] D'Souza speaks to pro-lifers who complained that Reagan didn't do enough to halt abortion. D'Souza said that "the best pro-life supporters could do" under Reagan was the Hyde Amendment, a measure that restricted public funding for abortion, and that Reagan regretted not being able to do more while in office.[92] He also argued that the political configuration of the courts and the Congress worked against Reagan and that abortion in the 1980s simply "could not be outlawed."[93] Of course, Reagan began changing those courts by appointing strict constructionists who were generally socially conservative and often opposed abortion.

The proper evaluation of Reagan's record on abortion while in the White House seems to be this: strong rhetoric against abortion and a willingness to endorse measures that would chip away at abortion-on-demand while realizing the presence of nearly insurmountable limitations on what could be accomplished because of the staunch opposition coming from other branches of government. It is also vital to remember, 15 years hence, that Reagan's first priorities were to win the Cold War and rejuvenate the American economy. Any judgment about his abortion policies while president that does not account for these concerns misses the larger context of his policy agenda. There were a limited number of battles that Reagan could fight.

In sum, the record of Reagan's presidency is one of consistent thinking and the use of major speeches to elevate the visibility of the abortion issue. Reagan gave the pro-life movement a figure to rally around, and it did just that. When, over fourteen years after Reagan left office, President George W. Bush signed legislation on November 5, 2003, banning partial-birth abortion, many conservatives saw it as a victory that was the culmination of efforts starting with Reagan. The next day, Fred Barnes bestowed on Reagan the title: "father of the pro-life movement."[94] It was an honor unimaginable in 1967.

NOTES

1. Lou Cannon, *Governor Reagan: His Rise to Power* (New York: Public Affairs, 2003), 213.

2. Cannon, *Governor Reagan*, 214.

3. Among others, data cited in Dinesh D'Souza, *Ronald Reagan: How an Ordinary Man Became an Extraordinary Leader* (New York: Free Press, 1997), 67.

4. Fred Barnes, "American Conservatism: Ronald Reagan, Father of the Pro-Life Movement," *The Wall Street Journal*, November 6, 2003, A14.

5. Cannon, *Governor Reagan*, 211.

6. Ronald Reagan, radio broadcast, "Abortion Laws," April 1975, in Kiron Skinner, Annelise Anderson, and Martin Anderson, *Reagan, In His Own Hand: The Writings of Ronald Reagan That Reveal His Revolutionary Vision for America* (New York: The Free Press, 2001), 384.

7. Reagan, "Abortion Laws," 384.

8. Cannon, *Governor Reagan*, 211.

9. Cannon, *Governor Reagan*, 209.

10. Quoted in Edmund Morris, *Dutch: A Memoir of Ronald Reagan* (New York: Random House, 1999), 352.

11. Quoted in Morris, *Dutch*, 352.

12. Reagan, "Abortion Laws," 380.

13. Cannon, *Governor Reagan*, 212.

14. See Morris, *Dutch*, 352; Cannon, *Governor Reagan*, 210–14; and William Clark, "Ronald Reagan, Lifeguard," foreword to *Abortion and the Conscience of the Nation,* by Ronald Reagan (Sacramento, Calif.: New Regency Publishing, 2000), 9–10.

15. Morris, *Dutch*, 352.

16. Cannon, *Governor Reagan*, 213.

17. Cannon, *Governor Reagan*, 213.

18. Clark, Foreword to *Abortion*, 9.

19. Clark, Foreword to *Abortion*, 10.

20. Cannon, *Governor Reagan*, 213–14.

21. Cannon, *Governor Reagan*, 213–14.

22. Cannon, *Governor Reagan*, 214.

23. D'Souza, *Ronald Reagan*, 67.

24. Ronald Reagan, Letter to Robert Mauro, October 11, 1979, in Skinner, Anderson, and Anderson, *Reagan: A Life in Letters*, (New York: Free Press, 2003) 197–8.

25. Reagan, Letter to Robert Mauro.

26. Reagan, Letter to Robert Mauro.

27. Reagan, Letter to Robert Mauro.

28. Reagan, Letter to Robert Mauro.

29. Reagan, Letter to Al Matt, October 11, 1979, in Skinner, Anderson, and Anderson, *Reagan: A Life in Letters*, 199.

30. Cannon, *Governor Reagan*, 213.

31. Reagan, Letter to Kenneth Fisher, 1970, in Skinner, Anderson, and Anderson, *Reagan: A Life in Letters,* 363.

32. Reagan, Letter to Kenneth Fisher, 1970.

33. Reagan, "Abortion Laws," 385.

34. Reagan, "Abortion Laws," 384.

35. Reagan, "Abortion Laws," 384.

36. Reagan, "Abortion Laws," 384.

37. Cannon, *Governor Reagan,* 448.

38. Paul Kengor, interview with Richard V. Allen, November 12, 2001.

39. Clark, foreword to *Abortion*, 6–7.

40. Ronald Reagan, "Address before a Joint Session of the Irish National Parliament" (address, Ireland, June 4, 1984).

41. Ronald Reagan, radio broadcast, "Communism, the Disease," May 1975, in Skinner, Anderson, and Anderson, *Reagan, In His Own Hand*, 11.

42. Reagan, "Communism, the Disease," 12.

43. Reagan, "Communism, the Disease," 14.

44. Franklin Roosevelt, quoted in Cannon, *Governor Reagan*, 349.

45. Morris, *Dutch*, 373.

46. Ronald Reagan, Letter to William Raspberry, July 1980, in Skinner, Anderson, and Anderson, *Reagan: A Life in Letters*, 588.

47. Reagan, *Abortion and the Conscience of the Nation*, 43.

48. Reagan, *Abortion and the Conscience of the Nation*, 47.

49. Ronald Reagan, "Remarks at the July 1982 National Right to Life Convention," quoted in *Ronald Reagan: In God I Trust*, ed. David R. Shepherd, (Wheaton, IL: Tyndale House, 1984) 97.

50. Reagan, "Remarks at the July 1982 National Right to Life Convention," 98.

51. Ronald Reagan, "Remarks at the Annual Convention of the National Association of Evangelicals" (speech, Orlando, Florida, March 8, 1983).

52. For a detailed study of Reagan's faith, see Paul Kengor, *God and Ronald Reagan: A Spiritual Life* (New York: HarperCollins, 2004).

53. Kengor, *God and Ronald Reagan*, 177.

54. Reagan, "Remarks at the Annual Convention of the National Association of Evangelicals."

55. Ronald Reagan, quoted in Shepherd, *Ronald Reagan: In God I Trust*, 97.

56. Reagan, quoted in Shepherd, *Ronald Reagan: In God I Trust*, 100.

57. Ronald Reagan, "Remarks at the Annual Convention of the National Religious Broadcasters" (speech, January 30, 1984).

58. Reagan, "Remarks at the Annual Convention of the National Religious Broadcasters."

59. Reagan, "Remarks at the Annual Convention of the National Religious Broadcasters."

60. Ronald Reagan, "Address before a Joint Session of Congress on the State of the Union" (address, February 4, 1986).

61. Reagan, "Address before a Joint Session of Congress on the State of the Union."

62. Reagan, *Abortion and the Conscience of the Nation*, 37.

63. Reagan, *Abortion and the Conscience of the Nation*, 37.

64. Reagan, *Abortion and the Conscience of the Nation*, 38.

65. Reagan, *Abortion and the Conscience of the Nation*, 38.

66. Malcolm Muggeridge, quoted in Reagan, *Abortion and the Conscience of the Nation*, 38.

67. Reagan, *Abortion and the Conscience of the Nation*, 39.

68. Reagan, *Abortion and the Conscience of the Nation*, 57.

69. Reagan, *Abortion and the Conscience of the Nation*, 43.

70. Muggeridge quoted in Reagan, *Abortion and the Conscience of the Nation*, 59.

71. Reagan, *Abortion and the Conscience of the Nation*, 39.

72. Reagan, "Remarks at the Annual Convention of the National Religious Broadcasters." See also Reagan, *Abortion and the Conscience of the Nation*, 39.

73. Reagan, *Abortion and the Conscience of the Nation*, 45.

74. Reagan, *Abortion and the Conscience of the Nation*, 47.

75. William Brennan, cited in Reagan, *Abortion and the Conscience of the Nation*, 53.

76. Reagan, *Abortion and the Conscience of the Nation*, 41.

77. Reagan, *Abortion and the Conscience of the Nation*, 41.

78. Abraham Lincoln, quoted in Reagan, *Abortion and the Conscience of the Nation*, 50.

79. Reagan, "Remarks at the Annual Convention of the National Religious Broadcasters."

80. John Donne, quoted in Reagan, *Abortion and the Conscience of the Nation*, 39.

81. Mother Teresa, quoted in Reagan, *Abortion and the Conscience of the Nation*, 40.

82. Muggeridge, quoted in Reagan, *Abortion and the Conscience of the Nation*, 62.

83. Reagan, *Abortion and the Conscience of the Nation*, 63.

84. Lou Cannon, *President Reagan: The Role of A Lifetime* (New York: Public Affairs, 2000), 729.

85. Cannon, *President Reagan*, 729–30

86. William Martin, "How Ronald Reagan Wowed Evangelicals," June 22, 2004, available at www.christianitytoday.com/ct/2004/125/21.0.html, last accessed June 30, 2004.

87. William Clark, "Reagan Remembered," *National Review*, June 28, 2004, 20.

88. Ronald Reagan and Jim Baker in Peter Robinson, *How Ronald Reagan Changed My Life* (New York: ReganBooks, 2003), 196–7.

89. Wanda Franz, "The Pro-Life Legacy of President Ronald Reagan," introduction to Reagan, *Abortion and the Conscience of the Nation*, 33.

90. Franz, introduction to Reagan, *Abortion and the Conscience of the Nation*, 35.

91. D'Souza, *Ronald Reagan*, 212.

92. D'Souza, *Ronald Reagan*, 212.

93. D'Souza, *Ronald Reagan*, 212.

94. Fred Barnes, "American Conservatism," A14.

5

Reagan and the Courts

Mitch Sollenberger, Jack Rossotti, and Mark J. Rozell

Ronald Reagan came into office determined to impact the federal court system by selecting judges with a judicial restraint philosophy. Reagan applied an ideological litmus test to federal judicial appointments and favored relatively young jurists to ensure his long lasting influence on the courts. Thus, a key element of the Reagan legacy is the large number of judicial nominees who have shaped constitutional interpretation long past the 1980s. Despite this success, not all of Reagan's selections were confirmed and some appointees went on to issue opinions that would later stun conservatives. Perhaps the most contentious and stinging defeat of any nominee in the modern presidency was Reagan's selection of Robert Bork for the U.S. Supreme Court. And possibly the biggest disappointment to conservatives has been Reagan's first Supreme Court nominee, Sandra Day O'Connor. These high profile selections though are just the tip of the iceberg of Reagan's judicial legacy. This essay will describe and analyze Reagan's record on federal judicial selections. It will also examine some of the more contentious battles over the president's efforts to shape the courts in the 1980s.

Reagan's Judicial Selection System

President Reagan established a judicial selection system that functioned like a fine-tuned machine. The administration abolished the nominating commissions established by President Jimmy Carter.[1] In conjunction, Attorney General William French Smith and deputy attorney general Edward C. Schmults reached an agreement on the selection process with Senate majority leader Howard H. Baker Jr. and Senator Strom Thurmond, chairman of the Senate Committee on the Judiciary. The agreement, as Sheldon Goldman noted, "was designed to give the administration more flexibility in naming district judges while retaining senatorial influence."[2] Instead of permitting pluralistic commissions to choose federal judges, Reagan placed the selection power back into the hands of home-state Senators. A memorandum by Smith described the arrangement:

> By virtue of the Senator's familiarity with the members of the Bar in their respective States, the Attorney General, in making recommendations to the President for judicial appointments, will invite Republican members to identify prospective candidates for federal district judgeships. Senators are strongly encouraged to submit the names of several candidates, preferably from three to five names, to the Attorney General for a particular vacancy. This information should be shared at the earliest practicable time with the Attorney General's designated representatives so that any questions or reservations as to merit or appropriations of the proposed candidates can be identified sufficiently early to allow meaningful consultation.
>
> With respect to States with no Senators from the majority party, the Attorney General will solicit suggestions and recommendations from the Republican members of the Congressional delegation, who will act in such instances as a group, in lieu of Senate members from their respective States. It is presumed that Congressional members in such cases would consult with the Democratic Senators from their respective States.[3]

This message was a useful compromise but at the same time a powerful call to the Senate to fall in line with the way the administration intended to select judges. The administration, however, not only wanted to refocus its relationship with Senators, it also wanted to revamp the selection process altogether.

The President centralized the selection process in the White House.[4] In so doing, he established the nine-member Federal Judicial Selection Committee.[5] According to Goldman, under this system, "[t]he highest levels of the White House staff . . . played an ongoing, active role in the selection of judges. Legislative, patronage, political, and policy considerations were systematically scrutinized for each judicial nomination to an extent never before seen."[6] Unlike previous administrations that had reacted to initiatives from the Department of Justice (DOJ), the selection committee offered its own names for possible selection to the federal courts.[7]

Thus, DOJ saw its traditional role change. Although the attorney general was a member of the White House's selection committee and had traditionally carried out most of the review functions, the President decided to create a new entity called the Office of Legal Policy to promote greater coordination of the selection process within DOJ. Although the assistant attorney general in charge of that office, Jonathan Rose,[8] reported directly to the deputy attorney general, the position had a measure of independence outside of DOJ's command structure. For example, Rose had direct access to the administration, through his membership on the White House selection committee. In addition, a special counsel for judicial selection was created within the Legal Policy Office to assist Rose in the reviewing of judicial candidates.[9]

During Reagan's second term the selection process within DOJ reverted somewhat to a more traditional system. Edwin Meese became attorney general and brought back some of the authority lost earlier on. The head of the Legal Policy Office was to report to the attorney general instead of to the deputy attorney general.[10] Moreover, the special counsel position was transferred to the attorney general's office and renamed the special assistant to the attorney general.[11] The most significant change was the increased involvement of the attorney general in the selection commission.

Even with these changes, the primary decision making responsibility rested with the White House. The President became involved when the final decision was at hand.[12] The selection committee ensured that the President's conservative vision was fulfilled. In fact, the dominance of the White House can be seen in the creation of the selection committee and the placement of presidential counsel Fred Fielding as its chair. Another change occurred during Reagan's second term when Attorney General Meese became the leading figure on the selection committee.[13] This change strengthened White House control because of Meese's close ties to the President.[14]

In the case of district court judges, when a vacancy occurred, the most senior home-state Senator[15] of the President's party would submit three to five candidates to DOJ.[16] For the appellate level nominations, where a circuit covers several states, there was greater flexibility in selecting these judges.[17] As the head of the Office of Legal Policy Jonathan Rose explained, "[o]ur pride in our circuit court appointments in large part [was] due to the fact that we [were] . . . able to get by the senatorial courtesy system."[18] The result was that instead of receiving the majority of the potential candidates from Senators, the decision-making authority was centered in the White House where presidential advisors, DOJ officials, and others helped to select lower court nominations.

Whether selecting a district or circuit court nominee, all candidates were referred to the Office of Legal Policy for an investigation of professional qualifications. This included interviewing colleagues, judges, and other professional associates in their state.[19] After these investigations, the information would be sent to the DOJ Judicial Selection Working Group, chaired by the attorney general.[20] This group evaluated the candidates' records and sent recommendations to the White House.[21]

Once at the White House, candidates would undergo another screening. The Office of Presidential Personnel would review each candidate, focusing on his or her acceptability to party officials in their home state.[22] This review helped the White House fulfill its goals of favoring conservative nominees. The administration also favored young jurists. For example, in 1984 the President selected a thirty-nine-year-old named J. Harvie Wilkinson III to the Fourth Circuit. In addition, a year later Alex Kozinski was appointed to the Ninth Circuit at the age of thirty-five, making him the youngest appellate court jurist since William Howard Taft. Others that were selected that year included James F. Holderman Jr., to the Northern District of Illinois (39), Edith H. Jones to the Fifth Circuit (36), Stanley Marcus to the Southern District of Florida (39), Ronald E. Meredith to the Western District of Kentucky (39), Thomas Scott to the Southern District of Florida (37), Deanell Tacha to the Tenth Circuit (39), Henry Wingate to the Southern District of Mississippi (39), and Mark Wolf to the District of Massachusetts (39). The goal was to promote Reagan's legacy with young conservatives who would presumably serve for many years on the courts.[23]

Once the reviews and the various selection factors were taken into consideration, the committee would endorse a candidate. The committee would then direct DOJ to send the selected candidate's name to the Federal Bureau of Investigation (FBI) to undergo a background check and to the American Bar Association's (ABA) Standing Committee on the Federal Judiciary to be evaluated for professional qualifications.[24] Before the name was sent to the ABA, the attorney general would first have the candidate fill out a questionnaire, which sought background information on his or her personal, professional, and financial history.[25] The public portion of the questionnaire, which did not include the financial information, was then sent to the chairman of the ABA committee. The chairman would initiate the review process and then return the committee's rating of the candidate to DOJ.[26]

For its part, the FBI would conduct an investigation of the candidate's character, associations and reputation. This would be done through personal interviews and various record checks.[27] Once completed, the FBI would send its report to the attorney general, White House, and the chairman of the Senate Judiciary Committee. In addition to the FBI and ABA reports, the candidate would be asked to fill out a DOJ information memorandum and also a medical qualification report.[28]

Once all of the reviews and investigations were completed, the selection committee would report its final recommendation to the President. The White House counsel, as Goldman describes, would send "a memorandum to the president with the formal nomination papers attached for his signature. The cover memo contained the recommendation that the president nominate the individual and that he telephone to ask the prospective nominee to serve as a federal judge."[29] Once the President had made the call and the candidate had accepted, the nomination would be forwarded to the Senate. Although this was the President's primary and often only involvement, the Reagan administration viewed it as one of the most vital parts of the process.[30]

The process was not routine or without strife. The internal jockeying was fierce during the selection stage. Often, a compromise on a candidate would be reached before the review process began; however, on occasion a potential nominee would be pulled well after the selection process started because he or she did not receive adequate endorsement or was actively opposed by various groups. For example, in 1981 Judith Whittaker was removed from consideration to a judgeship on the Eighth Circuit Court of Appeals because of conservative opposition. She appeared to be a well-qualified candidate and had passed all the proper channels up to the final White House clearance. In fact, Whittaker had been nominated by her home-state Senator John C. Danforth (R-MO), cleared both ABA[31] and DOJ review, and had been sent to the White House with the recommendation of the attorney general.[32] Conservative opposition against her, however, soon arose in her home state and quickly moved nationwide, largely due to concern over her views on abortion rights.[33] The White House dropped her nomination.

In 1982, Lizabeth A. Moody had been suggested as a potential candidate for one of two vacant judgeships in Ohio. Her legal credentials were impressive. Her candidacy, however, was not welcomed by conservatives who thought she favored abortion rights. The White House withdrew her from consideration.[34]

Conservative pressure was not the only cause of failed selections. In 1982 Benjamin C. Toledano was considered for a judgeship to the Fifth Circuit. Although he had been recommended by Republican Governor David C. Treen (La.), Toledano's past proved to be a liability. Toledano once had an association with the States' Rights Party, which advocated segregationist polices.[35] Thus, the NAACP opposed his candidacy. Then the ABA found problems with his legal qualifications. Still, DOJ and the White House selection committee continued to support Toledano. White House counsel Fielding, however, brought to the President's attention the concern over Toledano's nomination and stated that groups opposed "will undoubtedly claim this nomination is an example of the administration's supposed 'insensitivity' to blacks in general and civil rights in particular."[36] Reagan then chose not to nominate Toledano.

These episodes demonstrate that Reagan's selection system emphasized ideological compatibility. However, to ensure that these nominations did not invite unneeded criticism, the President was unwilling to move forward certain controversial candidates. Reagan's administration also learned that the Senate could prove to be a serious obstacle. Indeed, moving from the Senate Committee on the Judiciary through floor consideration meant passing through additional investigative and review checks, senatorial courtesy procedures and norms, and finally the consent of a majority, or even a supermajority. Even the most well prepared and organized White House selection team could not account for all these various factors. Once Reagan sent his selections to the Senate, confirmation was not certain.

Senate Treatment of Reagan's Nominations

With Reagan's election in 1981, the Republican Party also took control of the Senate for the first time in a quarter of a century. The Senate, which remained in Republican control for the next two congresses, accounted for a large part of the President's success in transforming the federal bench. As a result, for six of the eight years Reagan was in office, he could count on a friendly Senate majority leader and Judiciary Committee chairman to provide quick scheduling of hearings and confirmation votes. A Republican Senate, however, did not necessarily mean that all of Reagan's judicial nominees would be confirmed. Some were never voted out of the Judiciary Committee because of blue slip problems, senatorial opposition, or failure to receive the consent of a majority in the committee. Even on the Senate floor a few nominees did not receive floor consideration, others were threatened with the use of holds, and still others experienced close confirmation votes.

The Senate Judiciary Committee

After receipt by the Senate, one of the first obstacles in the way of confirmation is the Senate Judiciary Committee. Although this stage can be a significant barrier, during Reagan's presidency the committee reported to the Senate floor 383 lower court nominations. This was, at that time, the highest number of judicial nominations moved through committee for any President. Senator Strom Thurmond was chairman of the committee from 1981 to 1987, and he was able to move Reagan's nominations along despite occasionally strong opposition.

One of the difficulties was ensuring that senatorial courtesy was honored while at the same time quickly moving nominations along. The particular problem was the long-standing committee practice of honoring blue slips from Senators of the nominee's state. For example, in

1983, Chairman Thurmond moved forward with committee action on a judicial nomination despite the presence of a "negative blue slip."[37] The nominee was John P. Vukasin Jr., who, at the suggestion of retiring Senator Samuel Hayakawa of California, was nominated by President Reagan to be U.S. District judge for northern California.[38] Vukasin was opposed by California Senator Alan Cranston, who returned a negative blue slip to the committee.[39] Traditionally, a negative blue slip would have prevented the committee from moving ahead with Vukasin's nomination; however, Thurmond, following the blue-slip policy established by his predecessor, Senator Edward Kennedy,[40] reported him out of committee where he received confirmation by the Senate.

Although, for the most part, Thurmond was able to move the President's nominations through committee, at times senatorial opposition prevented some from reaching the Senate. Two years after Vukasin was confirmed by the Senate, Reagan selected Albert I. Moon Jr. to be a district court judge for Hawaii. In this case, both Hawaii Senators, Daniel K. Inouye and Spark Matsunaga, sent back negative blue slips to the committee.[41] On November 22, 1985, the committee held a hearing on the Moon nomination. At the hearing, Senator Inouye appeared and stated his opposition to Moon. According to the Senator, Reagan had ignored the six candidates submitted to the White House from a bi-partisan selection commission in his state. Moon countered by asserting that the commission was set up by two Democratic Senators. Moreover, the President, because of "political realities," would most likely follow the recommendations of members from his own party. Senator Joseph Biden, a member of the Judiciary Committee, replied to this comment by stating, "[i]n other words, state party hacks are better qualified to determine who should be recommended than U.S. senators?"[42] This opposition proved too much. The committee took no further action on Moon and the Senate eventually returned his nomination to the President.

Senatorial opposition through the use of a blue slip was not the only way a judicial nominee was denied confirmation. During Reagan's presidency, the committee rejected four individuals. Although this was a small number compared to the 387 district and circuit court nominations that the Judiciary Committee voted on during Reagan's tenure, these rejections represented a more broad-based opposition to many of the President's nominations. The first rejection occurred in 1986 when the President nominated Daniel A. Manion to be a judge on the Seventh Circuit. While Manion was strongly supported by the President and various Senators, his conservative views,[43] lack of professional experience, and low ABA rating were used to mount an attack on his fitness to sit on the bench. In committee, initially Manion's supporters failed to receive enough votes to report him out favorably. However, a motion to report without recommendation enabled Manion's nomination to be reported to the Senate.

Once on the Senate floor, Manion's supporters moved to hold a confirmation vote. Before this vote occurred, however, Manion's opponents lost a key advantage when they agreed to pair two of their votes with absent Republican Senators Paula Hawkins of Florida and Bob Packwood of Oregon. Democratic leaders had originally thought that Packwood opposed Manion; however, Republicans suggested that Packwood would vote in favor of Manion and suggested that they could call him to confirm. In an effort to move the vote along, the Democratic leaders agreed to pair one of their votes with Packwood. It was later learned that Packwood did not support Manion. In addition to pairing votes for Hawkins and Packwood, Republican Senator Nancy Kassebaum of Kansas, a Manion opponent, paired her vote with Senator Barry Goldwater who was absent. This left Manion's opponents without three negative votes. The result was a tie of 47 to 47; however, Senator Robert Byrd of West Virginia decided to switch his vote to make it 48 to 46. Since Senator Byrd was in the majority this gave him the opportunity to move for a reconsideration of the vote, which he did.[44] The Senate voted to reconsider a few weeks later; however, this parliamentary maneuver did not work and the vote to reconsider failed by 49 to 49. After Manion, none of Reagan's nominations that were rejected by the Judiciary Committee were ever confirmed.

One month after Manion was reported from committee, the President selected Jefferson B. Sessions to a judgeship in southern Alabama. During Sessions' hearing, opposition arose over a number of statements he reportedly made. It was alleged that Sessions had once called the National Association for the Advancement of Colored People (NAACP), the American Civil Liberties Union (ACLU), and other groups "un-American organizations with anti-traditional American values" and he was also reported to have said the Ku Klux Klan (KKK) was okay until he learned some members had smoked marijuana.[45] In addition, a former black assistant, Thomas Figures, claimed Sessions told him to be "careful what [you] say to white folks" and also reportedly called him "boy."[46] The committee voted against sending his nomination to the Senate.

Two years later, Reagan nominated Susan W. Liebeler to the Federal Circuit. Liebeler had served on the International Trade Commission (ITC) for four years and before that was a corporate law professor. Opposition arose in the Senate because of a number of decisions she made while at the ITC.[47] After receiving two hearings, the committee held two votes on whether to report Liebeler. The first, on whether to report favorably, failed 6 to 7; however, on a second vote to report without recommendation Liebeler reached the Senate floor. Opposition from GOP Senator John Heinz prevented Liebeler from receiving a confirmation vote and her nomination was eventually returned to the President.[48] Unlike Manion, Liebeler failed to receive a confirmation vote.

Bernard H. Siegan, a libertarian professor at San Diego School of Law, was the final nomination rejected by the Judiciary Committee. He was nominated in 1987 by Reagan to the Ninth Circuit Court of Appeals. Opposition arose over Siegan's nomination because of some of his constitutional views. The main charge centered around his writing on the 1954 desegregation case of *Brown v. Board of Education*. Although Siegan said he agreed with the outcome of the decision, he found its reasoning faulty. In fact, he noted, "[t]he original Constitution accepted slavery and the 14th Amendment accepted segregation in contemporary public educational facilities."[49] After two votes to report out of committee, the President withdrew Siegan's nomination.

Neither Session, Liebeler, or Siegan received Senate votes. The initial battle over Manion had cost the administration leverage when moving subsequent nominations through committee.

The Senate Floor

In addition to Judiciary Committee battles, the Reagan administration had to contend with various confirmation disputes once a nomination reached the Senate floor. Although none of Reagan's nominations were formally rejected by the Senate, some did experience delays, close roll call votes, and even Senate inaction.

One of the means a Senator can use to stop a confirmation vote is a so-called hold. Although not mentioned in the rules of the Senate, a hold is an informal device that blocks action on measures scheduled for floor consideration. On several occasions Senators, for various reasons, placed holds on Reagan's judicial nominations. For instance, James L. Buckley was nominated by President Reagan to the D.C. Circuit in 1985. Originally, the President had planned on nominating Buckley to a seat on the Second Circuit; however, opposition from Connecticut Senators Lowell P. Weicker Jr. and Christopher J. Dodd persuaded the President to appoint Buckley to the D.C. Circuit. Even with this switch in circuits, the nomination was delayed because of opposition from the DC bar and the senators. The two Senators decided to place a hold on Buckley's nomination. Dodd stated that he was merely seeking debate on the nomination.[50] The Senator's hold lasted for more than a month before debate occurred. In debate Dodd noted, "Mr. Buckley is not a legal scholar who happens to hold strong conservative views. Rather, this is a very ideologically conservative person who happens to be a lawyer."[51] Weicker also expressed doubts about Buckley's nomination. In a statement on the Senate floor, he commented, "I have serious reservations about Mr. Buckley's legal experience, which in my view, is far from adequate for a lifetime appointment to the Federal bench."[52] Shortly after the debate, the Senate voted to confirm Buckley 84 to 11.

In 1987, a Ninth Circuit Court of Appeals nomination, Stephen S. Trott, was placed on hold by Senators Howard M. Metzenbaum and Edward Kennedy.[53] Unlike the Buckley case, Trott's hold had nothing to do with his qualifications. Instead, the hold was instituted because of a dispute over Attorney General Meese's refusal to provide information to the Judiciary Committee concerning its investigation of the misuse of embassy funds by Faith Ryan Whittlesey during her tenure as U.S. ambassador to Switzerland. In the hopes of pressuring DOJ, Metzenbaum and Kennedy issued a hold. The dispute lasted for more than four months after Trott was reported out of committee. Only after DOJ turned over some of the documents to Senator Alan K. Simpson, who had intervened to settle the matter, did the Senators release their hold.[54]

Roll Call Votes

Although the Senate confirmed 375 district and circuit court nominations nominated by Reagan, three of his nominations stirred almost
straight party-line opposition on the Senate floor. J. Harvie Wilkinson,
Alex Kozinski, and Sid Fitzwater each received major opposition and
near party-line confirmation votes.

Wilkinson was first nominated by Reagan in 1983 and was resub-
mitted in 1984. Two hearings were held on Wilkinson and the Judiciary
Committee eventually reported to the Senate floor by an 11 to 5 vote.
Once on the Senate floor, Wilkinson's nomination experienced intense
opposition. One of his leading critics, Senator Kennedy, noted that "Mr.
Wilkinson, who was admitted to the bar in 1972, in fact has fewer years
as a member of the bar than any circuit court nominee from the creation
of the circuit courts of appeal in 1891 through the end of 1980."
Kennedy claimed that Wilkinson had demonstrated an incompetence of
basic legal procedures while serving as Deputy Assistant Attorney General in the Civil Rights Division.[55] Kennedy also charged that Wilkinson actively tried to influence the ABA vote on his nomination.
Kennedy stated that "Mr. Wilkinson made dozens of telephone calls in
an effort to line up supporters to contact the ABA committee members
before the crucial vote."[56] Kennedy concluded that "a Federal judge
must be willing to abide by the rules, or the rule of law will fail. Mr.
Wilkinson acted injudiciously when he violated the integrity of the
ABA committee and participated in this intensive scheme to tilt the review process in his favor. On this unsatisfactory state of the record, he
is not fit for high judicial office."[57] The Senate voted 65 to 32 for clo-
ture and then 58 to 39 to confirm Wilkinson to the Fourth Circuit.[58]

In the summer of 1985, Reagan selected Alex Kozinski to fill a vacancy on the Ninth Circuit Court of Appeals. Kozinski was the second
judicial appointment of Reagan to experience a near party-line Senate
vote. In a Judiciary Committee hearing, Senators Carl Levin and
Howard Metzenbaum brought up Kozinski's actions while serving on
the Merit System Protection Board. In testimony and affidavits from
former employees, Kozinski was charged with being a "'cruel,' 'humiliating' and 'sadistic' administrator."[59] On the Senator floor Senator
Levin charged that Kozinski "woefully lacks, on a consistent basis, the
judicial temperament, the fairness, the sensitivity and the compassion

which we should all insist of our Federal judges."[60] When a roll call was held, Democratic Senators voted heavily against him, and as such he was only confirmed by 11 votes, 54 to 43.[61]

The final judicial nomination to receive a near party-line vote during Reagan's presidency was Sidney A. Fitzwater. Nominated in 1986 to the district court in northern Texas, Fitzwater came under criticism for his role in a 1982 sign-posting incident. The incident involved him and a sheriff's deputy posting signs the night before the 1982 election in some minority precincts in Dallas, Texas. The signs read: "You can be imprisoned: 1. If you offer, accept or agree to offer or accept money or anything else of value to vote or not vote. 2. If you influence or try to influence a voter how to vote. 3. If you vote without being registered."[62] Critics of Fitzwater called these signs a misleading attempt to intimidate minority voters. On the Senate floor Kennedy stated that he opposed the nominee because "he utterly lacks respect for the fundamental right which is the cornerstone of our democracy—the right of vote."[63] In defense of Fitzwater, Senator Paul Simon noted that "it was a mistake" to post the signs; however, he concluded that there was not "a pattern of racism on the part of this judge."[64] After a successful vote to end debate, the Senate confirmed Fitzwater by a 52 to 42 vote.

Reagan's Supreme Court Appointments

In the 1980 presidential campaign Ronald Reagan said that he intended to nominate a woman to the Supreme Court. This surprised some who thought that such an appointment would more likely come from a Democratic president. However, in April 1981 when the president first learned of Justice Potter Stewart's decision to retire, he immediately asked his aides to generate a list of outstanding female jurists. On July 7, 1981, Reagan announced his choice of Sandra Day O'Connor. The Senate later confirmed her by a vote of 99 to 0.

This nomination presented somewhat of a contradiction because O'Connor, a former state legislator in Arizona, was a moderate on abortion. Even the National Organization for Women and Senator Kennedy praised her selection. Conservatives were less confident of her judicial philosophy and their concerns were realized later on in crucial abortion cases in 1989 and 1992.

Reagan would later have three more chances to appoint a justice. One was the elevation of associate justice William Rehnquist to chief justice and the other two were vacancies created by retirements. The Rehnquist nomination was very contentious and was approved by the smallest approval vote ever for chief justice. However, it was the vacancy of associate justice Lewis Powell in 1987 that forever changed the confirmation process for Supreme Court nominees.

In 1987 President Reagan nominated Judge Robert Bork, a sitting member of the United States Court of Appeals for the District of Columbia Circuit, to replace Powell. The Senate eventually would reject Bork's confirmation. Reagan's first two Court nominees—O'Connor and Antonin Scalia—had won easy acceptance in the Senate. In 1986, the Democrats regained control of the U.S. Senate. From that point on, Reagan's nominations would no longer get an easy ride.

In 1987 the Supreme Court was almost evenly divided between conservative restraintists and liberal activists. In the first category, these justices consisted of Chief Justice Rehnquist and associate justices Scalia, O'Connor and Byron White. In the second were associate justices William J. Brennan Jr., Thurgood Marshall, Harry A. Blackmun and John P. Stevens III. That left the remaining justice, Lewis F. Powell Jr., as somewhat of a swing vote. Indeed in the landmark affirmative action case of *Bakke v. the University of California*, Justice Powell's concurring opinion, that no other justice joined, emerged to a great extent as the principal holding of the case. It set the stage for the Supreme Court jurisprudence on affirmative action until the 1995 case *United States v. Lopez*.

Liberal groups had grown accustomed to favorable decisions in civil liberties cases in the 1960s, 1970s, and to a certain extent in the 1980s in areas such as the role of the federal courts and the power of the federal government versus the states. Coinciding with these was the growth of liberal advocacy groups who were using the Court as one of their ways to promote a policy agenda. It was not until the 1980s that there was a significant growth of conservative interest groups as they attempted to promote their agenda in the same way.

This combination of judicial temperaments and liberal activism made for a politically explosive situation when Justice Powell announced his intention to retire in 1987. Furthermore, Democrats had lost the last two presidential elections by large margins and had been in the minority in the Senate for the previous six years. The situation was ready-made for them to score a major political win.

Beyond this was the matter of Judge Robert Bork himself. Here was a man who was sure of himself and his positions on just about every issue he might encounter as a justice on the Supreme Court. Bork had been in academia for years and later was a member of the United States Court of Appeals. As a result he had left a long paper trail for the opposition to use. Bork had repeatedly criticized the judicial activism of the Supreme Court during the post-1954 era. His jurisprudential philosophy had been one of "original intent" in which he believed that the Supreme Court should frame its decisions on the basis of what the writers of the Constitution had said. Perhaps the most controversial of his positions was his criticism of the federal right to privacy, which included the right to have an abortion. It is safe to say that no other issue motivated liberal women's groups more than that. Under a strict constructionist theory there could no federal right to privacy or an abortion. Bork's vote on the Court could make that happen.

Bork did not help himself when he was called to testify before the Democratic-led Senate Judiciary Committee. Bork came off as somewhat arrogant and pompous. After his testimony, liberals had their victory in sight. They had forged a large coalition of advocacy groups, which was very effective in putting together something like a political campaign. They put together groups who would effectively use outside Washington grassroots lobbying and insider Washington lobbying, and combine these with very efficient use of resources that pro-Bork groups could not match. Pro-Bork groups failed to organize and use resources at their disposal. They were simply outmanned. Even though he knew he would lose, Bork asked to have a vote by the full Senate and his nomination was rejected, 58 to 42.

Although conservatives lost on Bork, they learned a big lesson and four years later in a similar and even more acrimonious Supreme Court nomination by President George H. W. Bush, the result was different. Effectively using the techniques that the liberals used four years earlier, the nomination of Clarence Thomas to the Court was accepted but by an even closer vote of 52 to 48.

Since the end of the Reagan administration federal judicial nominations have been driven by interest group activity. Yet, one more thing has changed. During the George W. Bush administration liberal forces have been successful in preventing some controversial nominations to the United States Court of Appeals, one level lower than the Supreme Court. There appears to be no end in sight for this type of extrajudicial activity and interest groups will likely continue to use the techniques first used during the nomination of Judge Robert Bork in 1987.

CONCLUSION

Ronald Reagan already is recognized as one of the most significant presidents of the twentieth century. Those who write about the Reagan legacy mostly discuss the fight over the Cold War, the economic recovery of the 1980s, the towering figure known as the "Great Communicator." Yet, Reagan's judicial legacy has also been enormous. Reagan understood the long-term impact that court decisions have on the country and he set out to influence the future direction of constitutional interpretation. His administration was the first to have an explicit ideological litmus test for appointment to a federal court. The White House established a selection procedure that ensured the enactment of the president's conservative vision on the courts. Further, the president favored relatively young jurists in order to ensure that his nominees had long tenure on the courts.

Perhaps the one indelible scar on the judicial landscape from the Reagan years was the result of the contentious Bork confirmation fight. The interest group political campaign against Bork was relentless and ugly. The Reagan White House and conservative groups simply were unprepared for the assault on Bork's record and character. The lessons from the Bork episode are most regrettable: that presidents should avoid appointing jurists with long "paper trails" (i.e., distinguished records of scholarship and important lower court opinions); that interest groups on the left and the right must gear up for intense political campaigns whenever a court vacancy occurs, thus leaving Senators to base confirmation votes more on whether the nominee is politically acceptable than judicially qualified. The Bork battle profoundly changed the confirmation process at the federal level. Its effects are still felt today.

NOTES

1. Ronald Reagan, "Termination of Certain Federal Advisory Committees," Executive Order No. 12305, *Weekly Compilation of Presidential Documents* 17 (May 5, 1981): 495.
2. Sheldon Goldman, *Picking Federal Judges: Lower Court Selection from Roosevelt through Reagan* (New Haven, Conn.: Yale University Press, 1997), 287–8.
3. "The Attorney General's Memorandum on Judicial Selection Procedures," *Judicature* 64 (April 1981): 428.
4. The Justice Department had traditionally fulfilled these duties.
5. Sheldon Goldman, "Reaganizing the Judiciary: The First Term Appointments," *Judicature* 68 (April–May 1985): 315.
6. Goldman, "Reaganizing the Judiciary," 292.
7. Goldman, "Reaganizing the Judiciary," 300.
8. Rose remained head of the Office of Legal Policy until 1984; from 1984 to 1985 Harold J. Lezar Jr. was in charge of operations; finally, from 1985 to 1989, Stephen J. Markman took control.
9. Goldman, "Reaganizing the Judiciary," 315.
10. Sheldon Goldman, "Reagan's Second Term Judicial Appointments: The Battle at Midway," *Judicature* 70 (April–May 1987): 326.
11. Goldman, "Reagan's Second Term Judicial Appointments," 326.
12. As Goldman notes, "Reagan seems to have routinely approved what a consensus of his advisers recommended. This also appears to have been the case with specific judicial appointments and was consistent with Reagan's presidential management style." See Goldman, *Picking Federal Judges*, 291.
13. Goldman, "Reagan's Second Term Judicial Appointments," 326.
14. Meese served as then Governor Reagan's executive assistant and chief of staff in California from 1969 through 1974 and as legal affairs secretary from 1967 through 1968. From 1981 to 1985, Meese served as President Reagan's presidential counsel. See Edwin Meese, *With Reagan: The Inside Story* (Washington, D.C.: Regnery Gateway Publishing, 1992).
15. For states without a Republican Senator, the administration would seek the advice of Republican leaders within the state, usually House members, governors, state officials, or other high-ranking party members.
16. For example, in 1986 Republican Senator John Warner of Virginia submitted three candidates for a judgeship in Richmond. See D'Vera Cohn, "Warner Expects Black Prosecutor to Get U.S. Judgeship in Va.," *Washington Post*, February 6, 1986, D1.

17. Ronald Brownstein, "With or without Supreme Court Changes, Reagan Will Reshape the Federal Bench," *National Journal* 16 (December 8, 1984): 2338.

18. W. Gary Fowler, "Judicial Selection under Reagan and Carter: A Comparison of their Initial Recommendations Procedures," *Judicature* 67 (December–January 1984): 274.

19. At that time, candidates had to fill out a Personal Data Questionnaire, a DOJ information memorandum, a Financial Disclosure Report, and a medical report. See Federal Bar Council, Committee on Second Circuit Courts, "Judicial Vacancies: The Processing of Judicial Candidates: Why It Takes So Long and How It Could Be Shortened," 128 F.R.D. 143 (1989): 149.

20. Fowler, "Judicial Selection under Reagan and Carter," 268

21. Brownstein, "With or without Supreme Court Changes, Reagan Will Reshape the Federal Bench," 2338.

22. See Goldman, "Reaganizing the Judiciary," 315, and Goldman, "Reagan's Second Term Judicial Appointments," 327. For more information on the duties of this position, see Bradley H. Patterson Jr. and James P. Pfiffner, "The Office of Presidential Personnel," in *The White House World*, ed. Martha Joynt Kumar and Terry Sullivan (College Station: Texas A&M University Press, 2003), 165–92.

23. Goldman, "Reagan's Second Term Judicial Appointments," 335.

24. Despite the involvement of the ABA in the selection process, the administration had a distant relationship with the organization throughout Reagan's terms. For example, traditionally the Justice Department would submit several names to the ABA to ensure that a qualified candidate was selected. During Reagan's presidency, however, the White House only permitted the submission of one name and the frequency of contact with the administration was kept to a minimum. See Sheldon Goldman, "Reagan's Judicial Legacy: Completing the Puzzle and Summing Up," *Judicature* 72 (April–May 1989): 320.

25. ABA Standing Committee on Federal Judiciary, "What It Is and How It Works," available at www.abanet.org/scipts/nomination04/appointments.jsp, accessed January 25, 2004, 5.

26. To learn more about the ABA's review process, see ABA Standing Committee, "What It Is and How It Works."

27. Federal Bar Council, "Judicial Vacancies," 149.

28. Federal Bar Council, "Judicial Vacancies," 147.

29. Goldman, *Picking Federal Judges*, 293.

30. Goldman, *Picking Federal Judges*, 294.

31. She was rated Well Qualified, the highest rating given by the ABA. See Editorial, "Political Snipers and a Good Judge," *New York Times*, January

7, 1982, A26, and Sheldon Goldman, "Reagan's Judicial Appointments at Mid-Term," *Judicature*, 66, (March 1983): 343.

32. Fred Barbash, "Protestors Deny Woman Judgeship; Unlike O'Connor, Woman Candidate for U.S. Court Is Dropped," *Washington Post*, December 21, 1981, A1.

33. Associated Press, "Women off List for Judgeship," *New York Times*, December 24, 1981, B8. Also see Goldman, "Reagan's Judicial Appointments at Mid-Term," 343.

34. Phil Gailey and Warren Weaver Jr., "Briefing," *New York Times*, August 3, 1982, A14, and "Washington Update," *National Journal* 14 (August 7, 1982): 1397.

35. Arnold R. Hirsh, "David Duke in the U.S. Senate? Unabashed Racism Could Elect Louisiana's Klu Klux Kandidate," *Washington Post,* September 23, 1990, B1.

36. Goldman, *Picking Federal Judges*, 296.

37. Blue slips are an informal practice unique to the Judiciary Committee, which has historically used blue slips on all U.S. attorney, U.S. marshal, U.S. district court, and U.S. court of appeals nominations. Traditionally, blue slips have been used by some Senators to delay, and sometimes prevent, the confirmation of persons whom they find objectionable. In practice, the chairman will send a blue-colored form to the Senators, regardless of party, of the state where the President has nominated an individual to be either a U.S. circuit or district court judge, a U.S. marshal, or a U.S. attorney. The Senators may then return their blue slips to the Judiciary Committee with comments on the particular nominee in question. In most cases, the blue slip is considered to be a pro forma gesture and will be given a positive review by the Senators; however, in a select number of cases, a negative review may occur. See Brannon P. Denning, "The Judicial Confirmation Process and the Blue Slip," *Judicature* 85 (March–April 2002), and Elliot E. Slotnick, "The Changing Role of the Senate Judiciary Committee in Judicial Selection," *Judicature* 62 (May 1979).

38. Rich Arthurs, "Judicial Nominations Doggedly Backed by Administration," *The Legal Times*, December 26, 1983, 1.

39. David F. Pike, "The Court-Packing Plans: Politicians Gain More Savvy in Selecting U.S. Judges," *The National Law Journal*, August 29, 1983, 1.

40. As chairman, Senator Kennedy informed his colleagues that when a Senator failed to return a blue slip, he would let the full committee vote on whether to proceed. See U.S. Congress, Senate Committee on the Judiciary, *Selection and Confirmation of Federal Judges: Hearings before the Senate Committee on the Judiciary*, Part I, 96th Cong., 1st Sess. (Washington, D.C.: GPO, 1979), 4.

41. Memorandum from Senator Strom Thurmond to Senator Arlen Specter, *Blue Slip Policy*, June 8, 2001, 2, and "No Action on Moon nomination," United Press International, December 12, 1985, Washington News.

42. Howard Kurtz, "Judicial Nominee Draws Fire of Home-State Senator," *Washington Post*, November 23, 1985, A7.

43. His father, Clarence Manion, was a founding member of the John Birch Society.

44. "Nomination of Daniel Manion," *Congressional Record* 132 (June 26, 1986): 15808–10.

45. Lena Williams, "U.S. Court Nominee Says He Won't Drop Out," *New York Times*, April 15, 1986, A23.

46. Glen Elsasser, "Presidential Nominee Vetoed as U.S. Judge," *Chicago Tribune*, June 6, 1986, C1.

47. Christopher Ladd, "Trade Route to Grow Rockier; With Ethics Law Looming, Officials Head for Revolving Door," *Legal Times*, November 7, 1998, 1.

48. Senator John Heinz, "Court of International Trade Rejects Liebeler Analysis," remarks in the Senate, *Congressional Record* 134 (April 12, 1988): 6478–81, and "Nomination of Susan Liebeler," remarks in the Senate, *Congressional Record* 134 (June 9, 1988): 14031–3.

49. Jenifer Warren, "Court Nomination Turned Quiet, Scholarly Life into Maelstrom," *Los Angeles Times*, August 28, 1988, 1.

50. Michael Oreskes, "2 Senators Ask a Delay on Buckley Nomination," *New York Times*, December 5, 1985, B3.

51. Senator Christopher J. Dodd, "Nomination of James L. Buckley," remarks in the Senate, *Congressional Record*, daily edition, 131 (December 17, 1985): S36832.

52. Senator Lowell P. Weicker Jr., "Nomination of James L. Buckley," remarks in the Senate, *Congressional Record*, daily edition, 131 (December 17, 1985): S36836.

53. Ruth Marcus, "No Judgeship under Trott's Tree," *Washington Post*, December 23, 1987, A13.

54. Ruth Marcus, "Impasse over Justice Documents Ends," *Washington Post*, March 25, 1988, A23.

55. Senator Edward Kennedy, "Nomination of J. Harvie Wilkinson," remarks in the Senate, *Congressional Record*, daily edition, 130 (July 31, 1984): S9501–2.

56. Senator Edward Kennedy, "Nomination of J. Harvie Wilkinson," remarks in the Senate, *Congressional Record*, daily edition, 130 (August 9, 1984): S10200.

57. Kennedy, "Nomination of J. Harvie Wilkinson, August 9, 1984," S10200.

58. Kennedy, "Nomination of J. Harvie Wilkinson, August 9, 1984," S10211.

59. Ben A. Franklin, "Angry Democrats Examine Nominee 6 Hours," *New York Times*, November 3, 1985, 36.

60. Senator Carl Levin, "Nomination of Alex Kozinski," remarks in the Senate, *Congressional Record* 131 (November 7, 1985): 31067.

61. Levin, "Nomination of Alex Kozinski," 31069.

62. Robert Pear, "Texan's Nomination as U.S. Judge Confirmed," *New York Times*, March 19, 1986, A24.

63. Senator Edward Kennedy, "Nomination of Sidney A. Fitzwater," remarks in the Senate, *Congressional Record* 132 (March 18, 1986): 5134.

64. Kennedy, "Nomination of Sidney A. Fitzwater," 5137.

6

Ronald Reagan, Iran-Contra, and Presidential Power

Ryan J. Barilleaux and Christopher Kelley

On March 4, 1987, President Ronald Reagan addressed the nation from the White House to confront an issue that had gained broad public attention, shaken confidence in the popular chief executive, and opened Mr. Reagan to severe criticism from his political opponents. In his speech, the President took responsibility for the events that had come to be called the "Iran-Contra Affair," a foreign-policy scandal that had burst upon the national scene a few months before. By his admission, the President acknowledged that some of his subordinates had engaged in actions that were probably illegal and politically damaging, but he defended himself for trying to advance noble goals in a political environment marked by disagreements between the White House and Congress over the direction and operation of American foreign policy.

REVELATION

In November 1986, the White House confirmed news reports that the Reagan Administration had secretly sold arms to Iran and used that money to support the *Contra* rebels fighting the Sandinista government of Nicaragua. These revelations sparked a scandal for the President. Americans regarded Iran with hostility ever since the imprisonment of U.S. diplomatic personnel during the hostage crisis of 1979–1981, and the arms sales were intended by the administration to

115

gain help in securing the release of Americans held captive by pro-Iranian groups in Lebanon. These transactions thus contradicted the President's stated policy of not trading arms for hostages. Clandestine financial support for the Nicaraguan *Contras* was not only controversial, but possibly illegal and potentially even unconstitutional. Questions about the affair multiplied, and included such issues as what had happened, who authorized or knew of the different actions, and whether criminal or constitutional violations had occurred.

Revelations from the Iran-Contra Affair prompted investigations within the administration. In December 1986 Lawrence Walsh, a former federal judge, was appointed as Independent Counsel to conduct a criminal investigation. In response to the growing political scandal, President Reagan appointed a Special Review Board, known to the press as the "Tower Commission" (after its chair, former Senator John Tower of Texas), to investigate the affair, and the board's report had been made public only a few days before the President's address.[1] The Tower Commission was highly critical of Mr. Reagan's control of the foreign-policy planning and decision process as well as the President's inability to recall even those details of the affair which concerned his own involvement. The White House hoped that the President's public acceptance of responsibility and his pledge to reform the workings of his administration would settle the matter, but the controversy dragged on.

In the months that followed, Congress conducted its own investigation and the Walsh inquiry continued. Over the summer of 1987, a joint congressional committee conducted televised hearings on Iran-Contra, which featured a dramatic appearance by Marine Lieutenant Colonel Oliver North testifying on the inception and conduct of the whole affair. The committee's hearings gripped national attention and stimulated extensive debate on the extent and gravity of what had occurred.

Two divergent interpretations of Iran-Contra emerged during this debate. On one side were those, including many Democrats in Congress and critics of the Reagan Administration, who saw the Iran-Contra Affair as events that rose to the level of a constitutional crisis. By their reasoning, Ronald Reagan and his subordinates had created a clandestine extra-legal foreign-policy government that was unaccountable and out of control. Collecting money from the arms sales and transferring it to the *Contras* violated an act of Congress and possibly the Constitution's provision giving the legislature control over revenues and appropriations. On the other side were those, including many Republicans and other defenders of the President, who charged that Reagan's critics were trying to criminalize policy differences and that the whole affair had been caused by executive officials driven to unorthodox measures in response to an imperial Congress bent on infringing on the President's constitutional powers and responsibilities. By their reasoning, the events of the Iran-Contra Affair were a defensible effort to prevent "foreign policy by Congress."[2]

While these competing interpretations are provocative, they tend to distort the nature and significance of the Iran-Contra Affair. They are built on a foundation of immediate events and tend to overlook the larger political context of executive-congressional relations in the post-Vietnam and post-Watergate era. Indeed, each interpretation views Iran-Contra in isolation from a larger struggle between the executive and legislative branches that began before the Reagan era and is still going on today. Understanding the Iran-Contra Affair requires putting it in context, and that means reaching back to executive-congressional struggles before the late 1980s.

THE CONSTITUTIONAL STRUGGLE OVER EXECUTIVE AUTONOMY

E. S. Corwin famously described the United States Constitution as an "invitation to struggle"[3]—a struggle over the privilege of directing American foreign policy. On one hand, the Constitution gives the President broad power to communicate with international actors, make treaties, command the armed forces, and direct foreign policy. On the other hand, Congress is given a large potential role in shaping national policy through its control over appropriations, taxes, and the institutional structures of foreign relations. The Senate possesses the power to approve treaties and nominations, and the legislature has the power to declare war. The result of this division of powers is the unending struggle that Corwin commented on, and since the Founding there have been many episodes to illustrate his point.

AN ENDURING STRUGGLE

Presidents have often sought autonomy to conduct foreign policy, while Congress has at times acquiesced in presidential autonomy and at other times worked to restrain it. But for most of American history, the struggle over foreign policy was not as bitter or divisive as it would become in the late twentieth century.

When Washington issued the Proclamation of Neutrality in 1793, it sparked a national debate over whether the President had the power to do so in the absence of Congress. In 1803 Thomas Jefferson agreed to buy the Louisiana Territory, despite his own reservations about the constitutionality of the action. Congress went along with the President because, like Jefferson, it could not resist the offer. When James K. Polk launched a war against Mexico over Texas, he received a mixed reaction from Congress. In May 1846 Congress supported Polk's initiative by voting to declare war on Mexico, yet two years later the House of Representatives censured him on the ground that the war had been "unnecessarily and unconstitutionally" begun by the President.[4] Decades later, war hawks in Congress tried to press Presidents Cleveland and McKinley into war with Spain; Cleveland made it clear he would not prosecute a war even if Congress declared it, and McKinley acquiesced in war only after the sinking of the U.S.S. *Maine*. When Theodore Roosevelt proposed sending the Great White Fleet around the world to "show the flag" and demonstrate growing American power, several senators objected to the cost and the questionable need for such an expedition. They told TR that they would not give him the money for the endeavor. Roosevelt responded that he had enough money to send the Navy halfway around the globe, and if the Senate wanted the ships back it had better make up the difference. In the end, TR won. Later, both Woodrow Wilson and Franklin Roosevelt would bring a reluctant United States into world war, the former finding that an almost reflexive isolationism replaced war fever in America as soon as the fighting was over, and the latter dying before he could see a nation that now regarded itself as a world power, with responsibilities to match. In general, these episodes point to the overall thrust of Corwin's struggle: presidents initiate and Congress tends to follow, sometimes enthusiastically and sometimes reluctantly.

ASCENDING PRESIDENTIAL POWER IN THE COLD WAR

Subsequent Presidents would accelerate presidential dominance over foreign affairs, including wars during Korea and Vietnam, and through a web of international commitments, and a range of executive agreements, covert actions, and foreign-policy doctrines. In the age of the modern presidency—from the New Deal to the collapse of domestic support for the Vietnam War—Congress generally supported these presidential actions. But legislators tended to worry about excesses of executive zeal in support of presidential diplomatic goals. For example, when in 1961 Congress agreed to John Kennedy's proposal to create the Arms Control and Disarmament Agency, the House inserted a provision specifying that the United States could not participate in any arms control or disarmament agreement without congressional approval.[5] Nevertheless, Congress was supportive of the expansive powers of the presidency exercised in the early decades of the Cold War, until the bipartisan consensus that underlined American foreign policy began to dissolve over the stalemate in Vietnam.

The turning point in presidential-congressional relations over foreign policy came during Richard Nixon's first term in the White House. Nixon came to power in the wake of the collapse of Lyndon Johnson's presidency. Johnson led a nation that largely supported his policies in Vietnam (he had the opinion polls to show his critics), until the Tet Offensive in 1968 suggested that the American-backed effort to forestall North Vietnamese attacks might be less successful than the Administration claimed.[6] Nixon was determined not to be undermined by an unsuccessful war, or by opposition to his policies from within the State Department and other branches of the foreign-policy bureaucracy, so he moved control over international affairs more and more into the White House. There, Henry Kissinger, Nixon's Assistant for National Security Affairs, directed the progress of the war (including its expansion into the ostensibly neutral country Cambodia), covert operations in Latin America and elsewhere, nuclear diplomacy with the Soviet Union, and the President's secret overtures to the People's Republic of China.[7] On one hand, many Members of Congress and much of the nation were dazzled by Nixon's success as a foreign-policy President; others were outraged by what they saw as an even more presidential unilateralism in conducting foreign policy. Congress responded with legislation.

Congress Strikes Back

Beginning even before Watergate became a household word, Congress sought to rein in presidential autonomy through a series of bills aimed at restricting the chief executive: the Case Act, which required the President to report all executive agreements to Congress; the War Powers Resolution, which was intended to limit the scope and duration of a war initiated by a president; the National Commitments Resolution, which called for all significant foreign-policy commitments to be made in consultation with Congress; and as a domestic corollary to these actions, the Budget and Impoundment Act of 1974, which effectively prevented the use of impoundment as an instrument of presidential policy.[8] Following Nixon's resignation from office, the legislature moved the nation into a period that some scholars have characterized as one of "foreign policy by Congress."[9] Not long after Gerald Ford assumed the presidency, Congress legislated an end to the Vietnam War, prohibited American intervention in the civil war in the African nation of Angola, began an investigation of American intelligence and covert operations around the world, and showed an overall resistance to presidential leadership in foreign policy.

Another action in this period would be indicative of future congressional attempts to limit presidential freedom in foreign policy: Congress adopted the Jackson-Vanik Amendment to the 1974 Trade Act, which prevented the President from granting "most-favored-nation" trading status to countries—specifically the Soviet Union—that restricted emigration by their citizens. In subsequent years, the legislature would employ amendments attached as "riders" to bills to restrict various actions, agreements, and initiatives that the chief executive could engage in when conducting foreign policy.

This congressional reaction to presidential dominance over foreign policy in turn sparked in Presidents a determination to seek even more autonomy, particularly in international affairs. During the Carter years, for example, congressional critics of arms control sought to shape the developing SALT II treaty being negotiated with the Soviet

Union. The Carter Administration replied by suggesting that the President might use an executive agreement to achieve his goal of "deep cuts" in nuclear arsenals if the Senate stood in the way of SALT II, further angering Carter's political opponents. Ultimately, when he saw that the Senate would not endorse his treaty, Carter implemented it through a new device that circumvented Congress's role in shaping arms-control policy: parallel unilateral policy declarations (PUPDs).[10] This device, a kind of "non-agreement," allowed Carter (and subsequently Ronald Reagan as well) to make arms-control policy with little or no input from Congress.

The Post-Modern Presidency

Presidents who have held office in the decades since Watergate and the end of the Vietnam War—the period of the post-modern presidency— have endeavored to enhance their ability to conduct foreign policy with minimal restrictions from Congress.[11] They have employed PUPDs to manage arms control, tested the limits in the War Powers Resolution, delayed compliance with the Case Act, and—in the case of George H. W. Bush and the Persian Gulf War of 1991—used a mandate from the United Nations Security Council to legitimize military action. Taking up the constitutional struggle, Congress has used the appropriations process, restrictive amendments on bills, investigations, and other tools to try to rein in executive autonomy. The decades since the Nixon presidency have been marked by a back-and-forth contest between the branches, with the months following September 11, 2001, as a rare exception to the overall trend. It was in this environment of executive-congressional struggle that the events of the Iran-Contra Affair occurred.

REAGAN AND THE IRAN-CONTRA AFFAIR

The Iran-Contra Affair marked a low point in the eight years of the Reagan Administration, and will always be a black mark on Ronald Reagan's presidency. As significant as this event was, it is nearly always studied as an isolated event, or it is mired in charges and counter-charges about who really was to blame for starting it all.

As the preceding discussion suggests, the affair ought to be viewed in light of the larger struggles between the president and the Congress that began with the Vietnam War and Watergate.[12]

THE AFFAIR EMERGES

On October 5, 1986, an American cargo plane flying over Nicaragua was shot down by forces of that country's Sandinista (Marxist) government. Only one person, an American named Eugene Hasenfus, managed to survive the crash. After he was taken captive, the Sandinistas discovered that Hasenfus was actually working for the United States Central Intelligence Agency (CIA) and had an address book that contained contact information for several senior American officials.

Nearly a month later, on November 25, a Lebanese magazine broke a story that detailed United States weapons sales to Iran—a claim that ran contrary to both the official statements of the Reagan administration and a federal law against dealing with countries that sponsored terrorism. The newsmagazine detailed meetings between Lt. Colonel Oliver North and Robert McFarlane, both officials on the staff of Reagan's National Security Council (NSC).

What appeared to be two disparate events, albeit embarrassing, were brought together on that same November 25, when President Reagan and Attorney General Edwin Meese went public and tied the two events together. The link between them was a scheme, outlined in a diversion memo prepared by North, in which the profits from arms sales to the Iranians could be diverted to the Nicaraguan rebel force— the *Contras*—which was fighting to overthrow the Sandinista regime.

The proximate cause of the affair was a series of events that had swirled around the 1980 presidential election. The first was a cluster of foreign policy crises that occurred at the end of the Carter administration, while the second was the shift in American foreign policy—a renewed anticommunism and assertion of American power—marked by the victory of Ronald Reagan.

The second half of Jimmy Carter's presidency witnessed a string of crises. In July 1979, the U.S.-backed Nicaraguan government fell to Sandinista rebels, sparking concerns in the United States about growing Marxist (and thus Soviet) influence in the Western Hemisphere. Soon after the Sandinistas assumed power, the Carter administration cut off aid to the new government. In November 1979, Iranian revolutionaries overthrew the Shah of Iran and seized the United States Embassy, taking fifty-two Americans hostage for 444 days. In December of that year, not long after the President had argued that the United States could trust the Soviet Union and endorse the SALT II treaty, Soviet forces invaded Afghanistan. These events helped define the differences between the Carter and Reagan presidencies.

When Ronald Reagan assumed the presidency, he made it clear that a cornerstone of his foreign policy would be to seek a rollback of communism everywhere, and that the United States would defeat international terrorism. He called for increased spending on defense, promoted the Nicaraguan *Contras*, the Afghan resistance and other groups fighting Marxist forces in the Third World, and adopted an assertive (critics said aggressive) tone in relations with Moscow and other adversaries. In his 1985 State of the Union Address, the President articulated what came to be known as the "Reagan Doctrine." Among other things, it placed emphasis on fighting Islamic Fundamentalism and Latin American revolutionaries that threatened American interests.

THE FIRST LEG: IRAN

Consistent with its policy of opposing Soviet influence anywhere in the world, the Reagan administration monitored activity in Iran and elsewhere. In 1985 members of the NSC staff prepared a National Security Decision Directive which warned of the Soviet Union's growing influence on the Middle East, particularly on Iran, and suggested a strategy for addressing what analysts considered a growing threat.[13] One way to offset the influence of the Soviets and to bargain for the release of Americans held hostage in Lebanon was to sell arms—in a limited fashion—to the Iranians, who were embroiled in a costly and bloody war with Iraq. Despite public statements by the administration that it would not negotiate with terrorists and public animosity toward aiding the regime that had humiliated the United States during the Carter years, the plan went forward. Working through Israel, the United States made contacts with Iranian officials to negotiate the sale of selected arms.

THE SECOND LEG: THE CONTRAS

Ronald Reagan had sought and received from Congress funds to aid the Nicaraguan *Contras*, because of their armed opposition to the Marxist government of that country. The *Contras* were guerrilla fighters made up mostly of former members of the previous Nicaraguan government, and were dismissed by their critics as a collection of thugs and bullies. By 1982 certain members of Congress began to look for ways to block support for the guerrillas, and that year Representative Edward Boland (D-MA) succeeded in attaching an amendment to an appropriations bill for the Department of Defense that prohibited the Department or the Central Intelligence Agency from furnishing "military equipment, military training or advice for the purpose of overthrowing the government of Nicaragua or providing a military exchange between Nicaragua and Honduras."[14] This amendment would be the first of several that Representative Boland would add to appropriations bills in order to limit the Reagan administration's ability to intervene in the affairs of Nicaragua, and it came to be known as *Boland I*. Boland I eventually proved ineffective in achieving its author's intentions, because ambiguities in the amendment allowed the administration to interpret it very narrowly and to largely ignore it.

By 1984 Congress would succeed in placing heavy restrictions upon the ability of the Reagan administration to aid the *Contras*, after it came to light that the CIA had mined the harbor in Managua, Nicaragua, an action that ran contrary to national and international law. In what would be known as *Boland III*, Congress stipulated that during FY 1985 (which ran from October 1984 to October 1985), no funds available to the Central Intelligence Agency, the Department of Defense, or any other agency or entity of the United States involved in intelligence activities may be obligated or expended for the purpose of supporting, directly or indirectly, military or paramilitary operations in Nicaragua by any nation, group, organization, movement, or individual.[15] Boland III would be the crux of the political and legal problems at the center of the Iran-Contra controversy.

Boland III represents the power that Congress has when it chooses to assert itself as a co-equal branch of government. It forbade the president from aiding the *Contras* directly or from soliciting funding from third parties, such as private citizens or foreign governments, on behalf of the United States.

Rather than challenge Congress's challenge to the foreign policy prerogatives of the executive, President Reagan and his advisors began to establish a "shadow" organization known as the *Enterprise* to direct aid and other forms of help to the *Contra* rebels.[16] The *Enterprise* undertook three types of activities: it solicited donations from foreign countries; it solicited contributions from wealthy Americans sympathetic to the Reagan administration's foreign policy goals in Latin America; and, most important to the controversy at the center of Iran-Contra, it orchestrated the selling of arms to Iran and then diverted the profits from those sales to the *Contras* (for an eventual sum of $47 million).[17] Under the direction of Admiral John Poindexter, the President's Assistant for National Security Affairs, and Lt. Colonel North, the *Enterprise* pursued these activities until it was exposed in 1986.

FALLOUT

The Tower Commission report and the President's March 1987 address did much to separate the President from political damage, but the subsequent congressional investigation and Independent Counsel inquiry kept Iran-Contra alive for a considerable time. The joint congressional committee conducted high-profile hearings into the affair,[18] and Colonel North's testimony proclaiming that it was all for a noble cause made him a celebrity and rising star in conservative political circles (but not one universally praised by conservatives). The committee came to be sharply divided mostly along partisan lines, and in the end two reports were issued.[19] This division tended to blunt the criticisms of the President and autonomous executive power that many of Reagan's critics had hoped to achieve. The Walsh inquiry continued through 1992, and fourteen individuals from the State and

Defense departments, the CIA and the National Security Council were charged with criminal offenses. President George H. W. Bush used presidential pardon power to pardon most of those who were charged, while appeals or limits on evidence due to security classifications spared three others.[20]

The issue of whether the United States should support the *Contras* was eventually resolved by a deal between President George H. W. Bush and Congress over an aid package, and then with the election defeat of Sandinista President Daniel Ortega in 1990. The new government that replaced the Sandinista regime was anticommunist, friendlier to the United States, and less controversial.

Nevertheless, Congress sought to prevent another Iran-Contra Affair by attempting to insert controlling language into a foreign operations appropriations bill[21] that prohibited the United States from attempting to influence any government or private party from carrying out foreign policy actions that are prohibited by United States law. Rather than sign the bill without objections, President George H. W. Bush took care to note that this attempt was unconstitutional and defined the influence as "quid pro quo" transactions "in which U.S. funds are provided to a foreign nation on the express condition that the foreign nation provide specific assistance to a third country, which assistance U.S. officials are expressly prohibited from providing by U.S. law."[22] He did this despite the very specific statements made by the sponsor of the amendment, Representative David Obey (D-WI),[23] and the restriction has had little effect on presidential autonomy.

WHAT WAS THE SIGNIFICANCE OF IRAN-CONTRA?

The Iran-Contra Affair was a black mark on the Reagan presidency but not a fatal blow. After President Reagan made his televised speech in March 1987, Americans seemed largely willing to believe him and let the event pass. Iran-Contra did, however, follow Vice President Bush into his administration and with it went many of the bitter conflicts between the President and Congress over the prerogatives of each branch.

After Ronald Reagan left office, his successors would continue to seek autonomy in the conduct of foreign policy. In 1990 and 1991, George H. W. Bush dispatched a large contingent of American forces to Saudi Arabia in preparation for a war against Iraq. When the United Nations Security Council authorized military force to push Iraqi forces out of Kuwait, Bush told Congress he had all the authority he needed to launch the war. His successor, Bill Clinton, would dispatch American forces to Haiti, Rwanda, and Kosovo, as well as launch unilateral cruise missile strikes against Afghanistan and Iraq. Following the attacks of September 11, 2001, George W. Bush launched a war against terrorism that resulted in the overthrow of the Taliban regime in Afghanistan and imprisonment of even American and British citizens as enemy combatants. His overthrow of the Saddam Hussein regime in Iraq in 2003 had been authorized by a prior vote of Congress, but by the time it occurred was controversial and was more a reflection of executive autonomy than executive-congressional cooperation in foreign affairs.

In the end, Iran-Contra was a significant but not isolated instance in a series of struggles between the presidency and Congress—struggles that began in the fights over the Vietnam War and Watergate, but which have their ultimate roots in the constitutional system of separated powers and institutions. The struggles of the post-modern presidency, of which the Iran-Contra Affair was a part, were fueled by two competing forces: a determination by many in Congress to gain greater influence over executive decisions in foreign policy, and the contrary force of an executive seeking maximum autonomy and resistance to congressional influence.

In the landmark case, *Youngstown Sheet & Tube v. Sawyer*,[24] Justice Jackson wrote that a President's power is at its lowest when the President works contrary to the expressed wishes of Congress. In the era of the post-modern presidency, Congress has often tried to restrain the President through expressions of its wishes in amendments and other legislative action, while Presidents have tried to act autonomously when their foreign-policy goals were at odds with the wishes of Congress. To that extent, the Iran-Contra Affair was neither a constitutional crisis nor an overrated flap about divergent policy goals; it was an illustration of executive-congressional struggle.

NOTES

1. For details, see John Tower, Edmund Muskie, and Brent Scowcroft, *The Tower Commission Report* (New York: Random House, 1987).

2. The term "foreign policy by Congress" is borrowed from Thomas Franck and Edward Weisband, *Foreign Policy by Congress* (New York: Oxford University Press, 1979).

3. E. S. Corwin, *The President: Office and Powers, 1787–1984*, 5th rev. ed. (New York: New York University Press, 1957), 71.

4. Quoted in Louis Fisher, *Presidential War Power* (Lawrence: University Press of Kansas, 1995), 34.

5. For a fuller discussion, see Ryan J. Barilleaux, "Executive Non-Agreements, Arms Control, and the Invitation to Struggle in Foreign Affairs," *World Affairs* 148 (Fall 1986): 217–27.

6. For elaboration, see Barbara Kellerman and Ryan J. Barilleaux, *The President as World Leader* (New York: St. Martin's Press, 1991), ch. 6, "Lyndon Johnson's Involvement in Vietnam."

7. See Kellerman and Barilleaux, *The President as World Leader*, ch. 7, "Richard Nixon's Overtures to the Communist Superpowers."

8. See Ryan J. Barilleaux, *The Post-Modern Presidency* (New York: Praeger, 1988), 8–9.

9. Franck and Weisband, *Foreign Policy by Congress.* See also U.S. Congress, *Legislation on Foreign Relations through 1983*, vol. 1 (Washington, D.C.: GPO, 1984).

10. See Ryan J. Barilleaux, "Parallel Unilateral Policy Declarations: A New Device for Presidential Autonomy in Foreign Affairs," *Presidential Studies Quarterly* 17 (Fall 1987): 107–17.

11. See Barilleaux, *The Post-Modern Presidency*, especially chs. 1 and 2.

12. The struggle is captured best by supporters of the "imperial presidency" thesis versus those who supported the "imperiled presidency" thesis.

13. Malcolm Byrne and Peter Kornbluh, "The Iran-Contra Scandal in Perspective," in *The Digital National Security Archive*, available at http://nsarchive.chadwyck.com/icessayx.htm, last accessed January 11, 2005.

14. Lance T. LeLoup, *The President and Congress: Collaboration and Combat in National Policymaking* (New York: Longman, 2003), 124.

15. Louis Fisher, *Constitutional Conflicts between Congress and the President*, 3rd ed. (Lawrence: University of Kansas Press, 1991), 211.

16. Byrne and Kornbluh, "The Iran-Contra Scandal in Perspective."

17. Lawrence Walsh, *Final Report of the Independent Counsel for Iran–Contra Matters*, Executive Summary, U.S. Court of Appeals for the Dis-

trict of Columbia Circuit, August 4, 1993, available at http://www.fas.org/irp/offdocs/walsh/execsum.htm, last accessed January 11, 2005.

18. For the record of the investigation, see U.S. Congress, House, Joint Hearings before the Select Committee to Investigate Covert Arms Transactions with Iran and the Senate Select Committee on Secret Military Assistance to Iran and the Nicaraguan Opposition, 100th Cong., 1st Sess. (Washington, D.C.: GPO, 1988).

19. U.S. Congress, House, Select Committee to Investigate Covert Arms Transactions with Iran, *Report of the Congressional Committees Investigating the Iran-Contra Affair: With the Minority Views*, ed. Joel Brinkley and Stephen Engelberg, abridged ed. (New York: Times Books, 1988).

20. See the Executive Summary of the Independent Counsel's Report on Iran-Contra, available at www.webcom/pinknoiz/covert/icsummary.html.

21. "Foreign Operations, Export Financing, and Related Programs Appropriations Act," Public Law 101–67, 1990.

22. George H. W. Bush, "Statement on Signing the Foreign Operations, Export Financing, and Related Programs Appropriations Act, 1990," *Weekly Compilation of Presidential Documents*, November 21, 1989, 1811.

23. See Charles Tiefer, *The Semi-Sovereign Presidency: The Bush Administration's Strategy for Governing without Congress* (Boulder, Colo.: Westview Press, 1994).

24. *Youngstown Sheet & Tube v. Sawyer* 343 US 579 [1952.]

7

Ronald Reagan and the Rebuilding of the Symbolic Presidency

Gary L. Gregg II

What does it mean to say that Ronald Reagan rebuilt the symbolic presidency? Critics might contend that Reagan's presidency was all smoke and mirrors; that the political wool had been pulled over the eyes of the public by waving flags and a grandfatherly smile that masked a more sinister agenda. Or, they might argue that President Reagan's aides did a masterful job of covering for an "amiable dunce," to use a phrase often heard in the 1980s; they crafted the image of a man who seemed to be in charge when the reality was much different.

In this essay, I use a less cynical view of symbolic leadership. I maintain that symbolism and leadership inevitably go together—a claim almost unheard of among political scientists today. A man with a vision must be able to articulate and embody that vision if he is to become a leader of others. Ronald Reagan had a vision for the office of the presidency, and he had a vision of what he wanted to do with that office. That he was also able to successfully articulate that agenda through rhetoric and other symbols made for a successful and historically important presidency.

BEING PRESIDENTIAL AND THE SYMBOLIC PRESIDENCY

"Being presidential" is one of those phrases often invoked but seldom with any kind of common understanding or definition. No doubt, many of us would argue over what it means to be "presidential," and at least to a certain degree the argument would inevitably involve a discussion of personal preferences. What certainly is clear is that "being presidential" is about more than policy substance and decision-making. It is about style and symbolism; image and imagination. To those concerned with such elements of leadership, *how* a leader does what he does is just as important as what is done. The American presidency is about more than just executive orders, staffing decisions, negotiations with Congress, and policy positions. Since George Washington established the precedents that would inspire and constrain his successors, presidential leadership, at least in part, has been about offering symbolic leadership for the nation.[1]

In the United States, we have maintained the ancient fusion of Kingship—a symbolic leader and decision maker contained in the same person. This helps explain the unique nature of our relationship to our presidents. We love them and we hate them; we respect some and despise others. This is because we recognize them as more than political decision makers. They are our symbolic representatives; they are part of what we are and we are part of them. As James David Barber has said, this leads to the presidency being "the focus for the most intense and persistent emotions in the American polity."[2]

Nearly everything a president does in some way holds symbolic import. Though his actions do not always mean the same thing to different interpreters, there is little doubt that what a president does and how he does it holds important meaning beyond the immediate material and political consequences. Advance teams, communications specialists, and speechwriters in the White House script his appearances. Presidents enact those scripts, and, mostly through the intermediary of the media, the American people and the world observe, and, sometimes consciously, take in the images and the actions of the man. In an age where the visual image and symbolism have become so pervasively important, the public presidency has also become central to governing from the White House. And, the public presidency itself is about more than rational arguments made for specific public policy positions; it's also about the photo, the style, the connection made with the public. To one degree or another, the image is also the message. Perhaps because of his experience in Hollywood and on the radio, Reagan seemed to understand all this very well.

In so many ways, George Washington established the basic precedents and expectations that have become known by the phrase "being presidential." After being inundated with visitors and well-wishers early in his administration, for instance, he developed the practice of setting aside Tuesday afternoons during which the public could be received by its president. These would not be informal gatherings of equals and pals, but neither would they be audiences with royalty based on a European model. They would, however, satisfy the need of the public to see and commune with its president while permitting its president the dignity of separation demanded by the office. In his own words, Washington was trying to create a "just medium between much state and too great familiarity."[3]

Washington had his finger on one of the great symbolic challenges of the presidency: to appear dignified and yet humble; powerful and yet republican. Not all presidents have risen to Washington's challenge. Nearly every gradation between the informality of an Andrew Jackson and the formalism and distance of a Woodrow Wilson can be seen in one presidency or another. The symbolic presidency of Ronald Reagan can best be understood in contrast to the presidencies of the 1970s that came immediately before his move to the White House in 1981.

The Symbolic Presidency of the 1970s

During the late 1960s and into the 1970s, the symbolic power of the American presidency was dealt a series of blows. Lyndon Johnson's Texas informality, the Vietnam War, Nixon's Watergate cover-up and resignation all served to undermine the trust of the American people in the institution of the presidency. The general celebration of presidential power that infused elite opinion during the decades since the presidency of Franklin Roosevelt came to an end in the early 1970s following Vietnam and Watergate. That celebration of the presidency was replaced with a concern that the office had grown too powerful and hubristic. It had become, according to Arthur Schlesinger's influential book, "the imperial presidency."[4]

The symbolic reaction of Gerald Ford and Jimmy Carter was clear and understandable but ultimately did not serve themselves or the office.

They both sought to create an image of a more humble, informal, and less "imperial" presidency. On certain occasions, Ford ordered the University of Michigan fight song to replace "Hail to the Chief," renamed the living quarters of the White House "the residence" rather than "the mansion," and invited photographers to see him toast his own English muffins for breakfast. With a series of unfortunate accidents, President Ford also became the subject of ridicule and jokes by television comedians. This all contributed to the image of a presidency not very imperial or grand at all.

President Carter seemed to be the perfect embodiment of this more informal presidency. A little-known one-term Governor of Georgia, he preferred the informal "Jimmy" and began his presidency by being sworn in with that nickname. Just after his inauguration, he left the limousine and walked to the White House. For a time he banned "Hail to the Chief" altogether; sometimes carried his own luggage; conducted a televised "fireside chat" in a cardigan sweater; and sold the presidential yacht Sequoia.

Carter would eventually realize that he had taken this humbling of the presidency too far. In his memoirs he would write that in "reducing the imperial presidency, I overreacted at first. We began to receive many complaints that I had gone too far in cutting back the pomp and ceremony."[5] Carter also finished his presidency in a way that created the image of a man captured and imprisoned by forces on the other side of the world rather than as a man in charge of a superpower. The last days and hours of his presidency were spent pulling out all the stops to gain the release of fifty-two Americans who had been held hostage for more than a year in Iran.

On the day after Reagan's inauguration in 1981, Hedrick Smith captured the challenge Reagan would face assuming the presidency:

[T]he well-springs of national confidence had nearly run dry and the yearning for America to regain control of its destiny [was] palpable across the land.

A decade ago, the seemingly endless agony of the Vietnam War sapped the nation's strength and morale and left the stinging sensation that something had gone profoundly wrong. The seizure of the American hostages in Iran sharpened the pain of national humiliation. For 14 long months those hostages, pawns in internal Iranian feuding, were a metaphor for America's sense of impotence.[6]

Having humiliated Carter, the Iranians released the hostages 20 minutes after Ronald Reagan was inaugurated as the 40th president of the United States. Hollywood's best scriptwriters could not have developed more symbolically powerful circumstances to capture what the new President sought to bring to the nation.

Optimistic Formalism: An Overview

In 1981, Ronald Reagan inherited a presidency that in the previous decade had gone from "imperial" to "imperiled." It had lost the trust and respect of much of the public. Americans were gripped in an economic downturn, an energy crisis, and a general feeling diagnosed by Jimmy Carter as "malaise." Overseas, the nation's attention had been held hostage by Americans blindfolded and paraded before the cameras in Iran, and communism seemed on the march in Southeast Asia, Africa and Afghanistan.

Ronald Reagan seemed to understand that Americans were ailing from more than just policies with which he disagreed. He found an America whose best instincts were not being called out and whose confidence had been shaken. Perhaps because of his time as an actor, Reagan's instincts for public leadership were finely tuned. Beyond policy changes, Reagan understood the importance of enacting the symbolic presidency, reminding the American people of a grander vision of America, and hitting the balance George Washington laid out between "much state and too great familiarity."

Reagan's Inauguration and first actions seemed designed to return the office to its former formalism and elevated dignity. Fireworks over the Lincoln Memorial would begin what nine grand inaugural balls would finish: the most lavish series of inaugural events in the history of the presidency. Members of Congress would be asked to wear morning coats to the inauguration and the ceremony itself for the first time would be held on the West side of the capitol with a rising sun behind the new President. Reagan faced the monuments to Lincoln, Jefferson, and Washington with Kennedy's burial place beyond the Potomac. The setting was made for TV and was more majestic than sites previously used. Frank Sinatra produced part of the televised events and Washington seemed overrun by celebrities from Hollywood taking part in the festivities.

Nancy Reagan, the new first lady, would get attention for contributing to a new air of elegance in Washington. Her James Galanos gown, which was reported to have cost more than $25,000, would be a stark contrast to Mrs. Carter who, four years earlier, refused to buy a new gown for her husband's inauguration, preferring a six-year-old blue chiffon one purchased for her husband's inauguration as Governor of Georgia. Mrs. Reagan had the private residence of the White House redecorated by a Beverly Hills designer, and purchased new china for the executive mansion. Many would be critical of the new look and the ostentatious displays of wealth that came to Washington with the new president, but it was clear from the start that this would be a presidency unlike any since John F. Kennedy and his wife, Jacqueline, had arrived at the White House twenty years before. Some commentators marveled that a bit of the old Kennedy magic seemed to have returned to public life in the unsuspected character of a sixty-nine-year-old man.

Reagan's inaugural address—written entirely by himself—would be heralded both as a model in presidential rhetoric and for its masterful delivery. He began by reminding America of its special place in the world and of the rarity of the peaceful transference of power Americans take for granted. He thanked President Carter for his "gracious cooperation" in the peaceful and orderly transfer of power "which is the bulwark of our republic."[7] After a litany of economic problems, Reagan turned to his famous optimism: "They [economic ills] will not go away in days, weeks, or months, but they will go away. They will go away because we as Americans have the capacity now, as we've had in the past, to do whatever needs to be done to preserve this last and greatest bastion of freedom."[8] He would call for "an era of national renewal" that would renew "our faith and our hope" while declaring we "have every right to dream heroic dreams."[9]

But Reagan's inaugural was about more than just renewing public confidence. It was also partly an exercise in civic education. He gave his traditional and forceful arguments for limiting the power of government, but did so by talking of the origins of government in "we the people." He reminded his listeners of "the giants on whose shoulders we stand" and connected his vision of a better America with a longer tradition of civic values and the power inherent in the American people themselves.

Elevated and elevating rhetoric would be a hallmark of the Reagan presidency after that unseasonably warm inaugural day in January 1981. The American people would come to know and seem to appreciate the dignity with which Reagan enacted the office. Reagan seemed always to have in mind the fact that he would someday leave the office and wanted to leave it more stately and dignified than he had found it. That is why (out of the view of media and cameras) he never removed his suit jacket in the Oval Office. Longtime Reagan aide Michael Deaver tells the story of one particularly hot and humid summer day in 1981 when he entered the Oval Office with Reagan following a ceremony in the Rose Garden. Deaver immediately took off his coat, but despite the sweltering heat they had just suffered through, Reagan refused to remove his own. "I could never take my coat off in this office," the president told Deaver.[10] Reagan showed a real understanding of the symbolic importance of seemingly small actions.

A particularly important hallmark of Reagan's symbolic presidency was his snapping salute to men in uniform. With his crisp salute, the man who had pledged to rebuild the American military and face down imperial communism came to embody the role of commander in chief. Yet, that salute was not planned or calculated. As Michael Deaver tells the story, it first appeared at the Inaugural parade after a General told Reagan such a salute was not appropriate if his head was not covered. Not deterred by the General's discouraging reply, Reagan saluted the passing soldiers and never stopped using the gesture for the remainder of his presidency.[11] Later, President Clinton was said to have studied tapes of Reagan's salute after he took office.

The formalism apparent in the inauguration was seen throughout Reagan's presidency. Formal East Room press conferences complete with dramatic entrances down the red-carpeted hallway complemented his many other ceremonial events and photo opportunities. The optimism demonstrated during the campaign and in his inaugural speech was eventually transferred into the "Morning in America" campaign theme that was so successful to his landslide reelection in 1984.

While he lived in the White House, Reagan was unquestionably moved by an understanding of his duty to the office and to the American people. In his autobiography he talked of the White House having a "mystical, almost religious aura for me since I was a child."[12] Reagan demonstrated a reverence for the office as an office and as a home. There would be no cardigan sweaters or photo ops of him making his own breakfast or carrying his bags. This president was not ashamed to hear "Hail to the Chief" when he stepped into a room. The difference between Reagan's presidency and that of the 1970s was vast.

But, the Reagan presidency was not all about blue suits and wingtips. There was more to the symbolism of the Reagan term than just motorcades and crisp salutes. While he was in Washington in his suit jacket, Reagan pined for life on his ranch in California. Rancho del Cielo was a place Reagan could retreat to from the pressures of Washington and where he would resume his western informalism. But it was also a powerful stage on which the elderly president could demonstrate his vigor and a ruggedness reminiscent of Teddy Roosevelt. He would appear in jeans on horseback, building a fence line, clearing brush, and chopping wood when at his Ranch in California. In 1981, the White House even staged the signing of his economic recovery bill on the ranch lawn; Reagan sat in an open-collared shirt and a blue jean-jacket at the very foggy ranch. In all, he spent nearly one in every eight days of his presidency at the ranch.[13] Not unlike the first President, Reagan seemed to be aiming for a balance between formality on the one hand and an informal ruggedness on the other; not too much state, not too much familiarity.

VISUALS AND THE REAGAN PRESIDENCY

Human beings need symbols to help them understand, compartmentalize and come to grips with information. In the political realm, people communicate through symbolic language. Rhetoric—the words spoken by political leaders and candidates—is an area of chief concern to presidential scholars. But, presidents and other political leaders also communicate through visual images: picture symbols that are intended (and sometimes *not* intended) to have meaning beyond themselves. Often these visual symbols serve to reinforce a pre-existing impression. At other times, such visuals can create new impressions in people's minds about politics, policy, and personalities in office.

Historian John Lukacs has watched the growth of the use of pictures and images and the corresponding decline of reading, and has suggested that a new age in literacy is upon us. "The reproduction of more and more pictures in newspapers, magazines, and books," he argues, "the advent of moving pictures and, finally, of television led to a condition in which . . . the routine imagination of large masses of people became pictorial rather than verbal."[14] The symbolic aspects of the Reagan presidency seem to confirm Lukacs's observations.

Ronald Reagan has been called "the Great Communicator." His policy speeches and addresses to the nation have been the subject of much scholarly dissection and journalistic commentary. Indeed, during the 1980s scholarly commentary on the presidency began referring to the modern office as "the rhetorical presidency."[15] But presidential leadership in the modern era is about more than rhetoric narrowly conceived as words; it is also about the creation and use of visual symbols. No presidency relied more upon visual images and symbolic moments than Reagan's. They helped to tell the story of his administration and the nation.

In *The Great American Video Game*, Martin Schram, a veteran print journalist covering Washington politics, recounted a piece CBS News ran one evening during the 1984 reelection race. The story attempted to unmask what CBS News saw as the image deception of the Reagan White House. Leslie Stahl, the reporter for the piece (which was three times longer than the average story on a network news program), criticized Reagan for ducking responsibility on bad news, only showing up when good news was reported, attempting to mask the truth of policies in fancy backdrops, and "running a campaign in which he highlights the images and hides from the issues." That night she braced herself for a nasty call from the White House. Instead, to her great surprise, she received a thank you call from a member of the administration who told her: "They [the American people] don't hear what you are saying if the pictures are saying something different." The negative report had been accompanied by more than four minutes of stunning pictures of the president. As Schram recounts the video images accompanying Stahl's story:

> The president basking in a sea of flag-waving supporters, beaming beneath red-white-and-blue balloons floating skyward, sharing concerns with farmers in a field out of Grant Woods, picnicking with Mid-Americans, pumping iron, wearing a bathing suit and tossing a football . . . more flags. . .

wearing faded dungarees at the ranch, then a suit with Margaret Thatcher, getting a kiss and a cake from Nancy, getting the Olympic torch from a runner, greeting wheelchair athletes at the handicapped Olympics, greeting senior citizens at their housing project, honoring veterans who landed on Normandy, honoring youths just back from Grenada, countering a heckler, joshing with the press corps, impressing suburban schoolchildren, wooing black inner-city kids, hugging Mary Lou Retton . . . more flags. . . red-white-and-blue balloons ascending.[16]

Reagan and his team of media advisors, including Michael Deaver, who was given primary responsibility for creating the images that would form an impression on the American people, had a keen understanding of what the American people wanted to see in their president and how a president should be portrayed. Most observers consider such image-creation as dishonest and manipulative and a creature of modern Machiavellians.[17] But a longer view would see that symbolic leadership has been an essential aspect of the presidency since George Washington first sat for a portrait to be mass-produced for the public. Its power may be enhanced in the television age, but symbolic leadership and political visuals are not inventions of the modern era.

Symbolic Moments That Made a Presidency

Considering a presidency through the lens of symbolic leadership reveals a fundamental fact: Rather than being the accumulation of everyday activities, judgments, and actions, symbolic leadership is more often provided by a series of highs and lows when the actions, images, and words of the president strike the public's imagination. As such, the presidency of Ronald Reagan was punctuated by great symbolic moments that held import well beyond their immediate circumstances and together created an enduring image of the man and his time in office.

Reagan's inaugural address and related festivities cast a very different presidential image than the presidencies of the 1970s. In numerous symbolic moments across the eight years of his presidency, he argued for his conservative vision of smaller government, less taxes, and a strong defense. His touching address to the nation when the space shuttle Challenger exploded in 1986 will long be remembered, particularly his delivery of the last line: "We will never forget them, nor the last time we saw them, this morning, as they prepared for their journey and waved good-bye and 'slipped the surly bonds of earth' to 'touch the face of God.'"[18] Reagan left the American memory and presidential history with important symbolic milestones that mark our understanding of the 1980s and modern America. Here are just three such moments:

The Heroic Victim as President. On March 30, 1981, the image of Ronald Reagan was changed forever. Reagan had just delivered a speech at a Washington, DC hotel when, as the president waved and walked toward his waiting limo, John Hinckley, the president's would-be assassin, opened fire. One bullet entered the president's chest in an instant caught forever by television cameras. The image of the president waving and then bending and being thrown into his limousine would be played on television sets over and over again for years. It was only many years later that we would learn of how close the President had come to dying that day. What the American people did see, however, was a heroic president strong enough to walk into the hospital on his own legs and make jokes with doctors and with Nancy. Reagan famously told Nancy after the shooting, "Honey, I forgot to duck," and joked with the doctors, "Please tell me you're all Republicans." Such images of the strong and unbowed president filled the airwaves for weeks.

Twelve days after being shot, wearing a bright red sweater, the seventy-year-old President walked out of the hospital under his own power. Four weeks later, he received a hero's welcome from a joint session of Congress and a national audience whom he addressed to sell his economic recovery program. Reagan's poll numbers soared, his record-setting tax cuts were passed, and his heroic image during the crisis was solidified in the imagination of the American people. This was a nation so recently on its knees from Vietnam, Watergate, and hostages held in Iran.

The Optimistic Warrior President. Ronald Reagan was a Cold Warrior's Cold Warrior. Since the 1950s when he led the fight against communist infiltration of Hollywood, Reagan had been an avowed anti-communist. Becoming president, he launched a huge military build-up and vowed to draw a hard line against imperial communism. Indeed, Reagan's support of anti-communist rebels, particularly in Angola, Afghanistan, and Nicaragua, can be understood as a move to take the Cold War beyond containment and to roll back recent communist gains. Similarly, he supported the Solidarity trade movement in Poland, which was fighting for a free and open society in that communist country.

He was an optimistic cold warrior, always believing the side of freedom would triumph over the side of tyranny. Communism would end up "on the ash heap of history." The last few years of the Cold War can be understood as a series of important symbolic moments. Reagan's Strategic Defense Initiative has been credited with helping to break the back of Soviet resolve.[19] Similarly, his defying the nuclear freeze movement in Europe by deploying new medium-range missiles in Germany was a singular symbolic triumph that strengthened his negotiating hand with the Soviets—evident when he finally met with Mikhail Gorbachev in a series of summits. He deemed the Soviet Empire "the focus of evil in the modern world"[20] and would go to the Berlin Wall, one of the greatest symbols of that evil, and admonish the leader of the Soviet Union to "tear down this wall." As commander in chief, Reagan was the optimistic warrior who never doubted the ultimate outcome of the war.

The Disengaged President. Negative images of Reagan also developed during his presidency. Perhaps the most persistent negative image was of a disengaged and perhaps not even very smart president. Stories of Reagan falling asleep in cabinet meetings and pictures of him appearing to doze off while meeting the Pope intensified the speculation. During one press talk at the ranch, Nancy appeared to be feeding him answers. Worse, a story circulated that he did not even recognize Samuel Pierce, his own Secretary of Housing and Urban Development. Such a negative image came to a head came during the Iran-Contra Scandal. The President was portrayed as not even knowing what was going on in his own White House as members of his administration traded arms for hostages and then funneled the proceeds to Nicaraguan rebels fighting the Sandinista government. The image of a disengaged president continues to haunt his legacy.

CONCLUSION

Michael Riccards has written that Reagan's presidency succeeded "by substituting images for ideas."[21] Nothing could be further from the truth. Ronald Reagan was the most ideologically dedicated president of the second half of the twentieth century. He came to Washington holding and espousing a core set of ideas and ideals that had remained firm in his own mind for a quarter of a century.[22] It is true that Reagan and his team were masterful in creating powerful symbolic moments through which the American people came to understand the man and his presidency. But there can be little doubt that those symbolic events, from his flag-waving patriotism of 1984, to his challenge to the premier of the Soviet Union to tear down the Berlin Wall, were in the service of bigger ideas about economics, human dignity, and America's place in world history. Presidential leadership requires vision, but it also requires an ability to communicate that vision to the public. Reagan had both.

During his presidency, much of the American public admired Ronald Reagan. He won two sweeping electoral victories and ended his presidency highly regarded in public opinion polls. Others, of course, reviled Reagan and distrusted him. This dichotomy of opinion went beyond policy differences. Reagan embodied a vision of leadership and America in stark contrast to that found in the media and the academy of his time. Because his public actions were infused with meaning, he dichotomized public opinion. Such will always be the legacy of a president willing to exercise strong symbolic leadership in a pluralistic nation.

Michael Deaver, Reagan's long-time confidant and public relations master, would look back at Reagan's presidency and say, "He made it okay to look at the White House or Old Glory and get goose bumps again."[23] Ronald Reagan's legacy is often discussed in terms of economics and foreign policy. We should not forget, however, that Reagan also contributed mightily to the resurrection of the symbolic presidency following the terrible damage done to the office during the 1970s.

NOTES

1. Gary L. Gregg II, "The Symbolic Dimensions of the First Presidency," in *Patriot Sage: George Washington and the American Political Tradition*, ed.

Gary L. Gregg and Matthew Spalding (Wilmington, Del.: ISI Books, 1999), 165–98.

2. James David Barber. *Presidential Character: Predicting Performance in the White House* (Englewood Cliffs, N.J.: Prentice Hall, 1972), 4.

3. George Washington, Letter to David Stuart, June 15, 1790, in *George Washington: A Collection*, ed. William B. Allen (Indianapolis, Ind.: Liberty Fund, 1988), 545.

4. Arthur M. Schlesinger, *The Imperial Presidency* (New York: Popular Library, 1974).

5. James E. Carter, *Keeping the Faith: Memoirs of a President* (New York: Bantam Books, 1982), 34.

6. Hedrick Smith, "Reformer Who Would Reverse the New Deal's Legacy," *New York Times*, B2, January 21, 1981.

7. Ronald Reagan, *Speaking My Mind: Selected Speeches* (New York: Simon and Schuster, 1989), 60.

8. Reagan, *Speaking My Mind*, 61.

9. Reagan, *Speaking My Mind*, 63.

10. Michael K. Deaver, *A Different Drummer: My Thirty Years with Ronald Reagan* (New York: Harper Collins, 2001), 91.

11. Deaver, *A Different Drummer*, 87.

12. Reagan, *An American Life*, (New York: Simon and Schuster, 1990), 228.

13. James M. McPherson and David Rubel, eds., *To the Best of My Ability: The American Presidents* (New York: Dorling Kindersley, 2001), 294.

14. John Lukacs, *At the End of an Age* (New Haven, Conn.: Yale University Press, 2002), 26

15. In particular, see Jeffrey K. Tulis, *The Rhetorical Presidency* (Princeton, N.J.: Princeton University Press, 1987).

16. Martin Schram, *The Great American Video Game: Presidential Politics in the Television Age* (New York: Morrow, 1987).

17. See Richard W. Waterman, Robert Wright, and Gilbert St. Clair, *The Image-Is-Everything Presidency: Dilemmas in American Leadership* (Boulder, Colo.: Westview Press, 1999).

18. Speech delivered by President Reagan to the nation on the space shuttle *Challenger* disaster on January 28, 1986, in Reagan, *Speaking My Mind*, 292. For a more detailed analysis of the importance of President Reagan's rhetoric related to the explosion of the *Challenger*, see Randall A. Adkins and Gary L. Gregg II, "The Challenger Seven: Ronald Reagan and the Leadership of Healing," in *Reassessing the Reagan Presidency*, ed. Richard S. Conley (Lanham, Md.: University Press of America, 2003), 51–67.

19. See, for instance, Peter Schweizer, *Reagan's War: The Epic Story of His Forty-Year Struggle and Final Triumph over Communism* (New York: Doubleday, 2002).

20. Speech delivered by President Reagan to the National Convention of Evangelicals, Orlando, Florida, on March 8, 1983, in Reagan, *Speaking My Mind,* 178.

21. Michael Riccards, *The Ferocious Engine of Democracy: A History of the American Presidency,* vol. 2 (New York: Madison Books, 1995), 344.

22. See Ronald Reagan, *Reagan: A Life in Letters,* ed. Kiron K. Skinner, Annelise Anderson, Martin Anderson (New York: Free Press, 2003).

23. Deaver, *A Different Drummer,* 124.

8

The Other Reagan Revolution:
Managing the Departments

Shirley Anne Warshaw

The election of 1980 is often viewed as a transformative election, due in part to the massive changes in the operation of the federal government that President Reagan ushered in. No president since Franklin Delano Roosevelt had sought to so dramatically reframe how the federal government operates.

When Ronald Wilson Reagan captured the presidency in 1980, he immediately moved to reframe the management of the federal government. He pledged a "detailed review of every department, bureau, and agency that lives by federal appropriations."[1] At the heart of this review was the decision by the newly elected president to reduce the number of federal employees and to shift to state governments much of the operational decision making for federal grant and aid programs. Although these issues were discussed during the campaign to some degree, they were never at the forefront of the Reagan campaign's public rhetoric. Not until the administration took office did these issues become the central theme of presidential management of the executive branch. During the campaign, two major issues overshadowed Reagan's proposals for reframing how the federal government operates: the American hostages held in the embassy in Tehran and the need to rebuild the nation's military structure, including creation of a satellite missile defense system.

MANAGING THE PRESIDENCY: THE NIXON STRUCTURE

President Reagan's decision to downsize the federal government was not a typically Republican proposal, but rather was a significant shift from his Republican predecessors, Richard Nixon and Gerald Ford. Neither Nixon nor Ford had attempted to reduce the number of federal employees or programs. Rather, both Nixon and Ford had attempted to reprioritize where federal dollars were being directed. The Community Development Block Grant Program of 1974 was an effort strongly supported by both Nixon and then Ford to provide block grant funding to communities. Funding that emerged during the Johnson administration had largely been targeted to low-income communities through complicated calculations based on such factors as poverty indices, housing blight, quality of infrastructure, and unemployment levels.

Nixon attempted to redirect this targeted funding, which primarily had gone to urban areas, which had a Democratic political base, to more rural and suburban communities with a primarily Republican political base. The shift of federal community development grants was a political move to boost support for the Republican Party and for the Nixon and then the Ford administrations. The redirection of federal funding did not entail reducing the number of employees in the federal government or the size of executive departments. Reagan's efforts to reduce the size of the federal government and to move the administration of federal programs to the state level was framed by the Reagan staff and had few roots in recent Republican administrations. Both Nixon and Ford were comfortable with the expansion of the federal government in the post–New Deal federal structure.

Although Reagan built a new vision for the federal government that differed from his recent Republican predecessors, he shared their vision of managing the federal government. For Nixon, Ford, and Reagan, managing the federal government was central to successfully implementing the goals and objectives of the administration. Unless the White House could control the departments, these presidents believed, the federal government would become a series of fiefdoms. Each department would pursue its own agenda, often with little in common with other departments and perhaps without approval from the president. Thus a central theme that emerged during the Nixon administration was that control over the departments would be essential to carrying out the administration's agenda.[2]

Nixon did not begin his administration focused on controlling the departments but within a year saw a necessity. In contrast, Reagan entered office intent on developing a management structure that brought the departments within the direction and oversight of the White House staff. Nixon entered office in 1969 with the intent of allowing his cabinet officers to manage the departments with relatively little oversight from the White House. The Nixon White House was focused on foreign policy, including the Vietnam War, detente with China, and mitigating tension with the Soviet Union.

Under Nixon, departments at times pursued policies that lacked White House support and were at times critical of White House decisions. Nixon's solution was to develop a process that gave the White House control over departmental policy making and oversight of departmental activities. This process involved two avenues for departmental control.

TWO AVENUES FOR MANAGING THE EXECUTIVE BRANCH

The first avenue was to gain control of the subcabinet political appointees to ensure their loyalty to presidential goals rather than departmental goals when such goals were in conflict. This was managed by ensuring that all political appointees be approved by the White House personnel office. Cabinet officers were no longer able to automatically name their own deputies and their own staff. Clearance was required from the White House.

The second avenue was to gain control of the policy making process to ensure that departmental policies were in line with presidential goals and objectives. John Ehrlichman, Nixon's domestic policy advisor, developed the Domestic Council as a means to regularly bring cabinet secretaries and senior departmental staff to the White House. The Domestic Council was composed of cabinet officers from the departments involved in domestic policy, in a structure similar to that of the National Security Council, which included cabinet officers involved in foreign policy.[3]

Nixon's creation of a White House clearance system for departmental political appointees and the creation of the Domestic Council were the first steps for the White House to gain control over domestic policy. Policy making and oversight became centralized in the Nixon White House under Ehrlichman's Domestic Council. Nixon sought to further centralize the policy making process with the creation of a supercabinet reporting directly to the president. Under this reorganization plan, four cabinet officers would have responsibility for oversight of the entire cabinet, under the auspices of the White House and Ehrlichman. When the White House became embroiled in Watergate and Ehrlichman was forced to resign, the plans for a supercabinet dissolved.

However, the basic process of departmental management by the White House was firmly established by the time the Watergate crisis overtook the White House. Although both Gerald Ford and Jimmy Carter made modifications to the structure, control of departmental hiring remained firmly held in the White House. Similarly, the Domestic Council remained in both the Ford and Carter administrations as the primary tool for developing and managing departmental policy agendas.

When Ronald Reagan entered office in 1981, the concept of departmental management by the White House was firmly in place. Nixon's grand plan for improving presidential control over the bureaucracy had included not only greater White House oversight of the departments but also greater oversight from the Office of Management and Budget, a new unit within the Executive Office of the President. In 1970 Nixon had successfully gained congressional approval for creation of the Office of Management and Budget to replace the Bureau of the Budget. The new responsibilities of the Office of Management and Budget gave the president new authority for program oversight and regulatory review within the departments.

The legacy that Richard Nixon left to the presidency was the expanded role of the White House staff and the Executive Office of the President to ensure that departmental policies were in line with presidential goals and objectives. Ronald Reagan took this legacy and built on it, enhancing presidential management of the executive branch. Reagan carefully built a cabinet and a subcabinet selection process to ensure personal and political loyalty and built a management structure within the White House to oversee departmental programs. In addition, Reagan gave his director of the Office of Management and Budget, David Stockman, unprecedented authority to determine departmental budget priorities. No president has been more successful than Reagan in building a management structure in the White House to control the daily policy development process within the departments.

PRESIDENTIAL MANAGEMENT OF THE EXECUTIVE BRANCH: THE REAGAN LEGACY

Reagan's management of the executive branch entailed continuation of the Nixon model with modifications. Those modifications included a revised cabinet selection system, a strengthened White House personnel office for subcabinet selection, a revised domestic council structure, and greater management through the Office of Management and Budget.

Cabinet Selection

At the heart of Reagan's concept for presidential management of the executive branch was a cabinet that was committed to his policy agenda. Unlike his predecessors, Reagan made no attempt to use the cabinet to broaden the political base of the administration. His electoral margin of 9.7 percent was significantly stronger than either Richard Nixon's 0.9 percent electoral victory over Hubert Humphrey or Jimmy Carter's 2.0 percent electoral victory over Gerald Ford. Reagan believed he had a clear electoral mandate and broad electoral support to move the federal government in a bold new direction.

The cabinet selection process was overseen by long-time Reagan friend E. Pendleton James and a small group of old Reagan friends.[4] James managed the official transition process and developed a list of names for the cabinet while at the same time a group of Reagan's friends in California were also developing a list. Both James and the California group focused on developing names that were known to Reagan, were loyal to Reagan, and were committed to Reagan's priorities of reducing the size of the federal government, cutting taxes and cutting federal programs, and increasing defense spending.[5]

Unlike more recent presidents such as Bill Clinton and George W. Bush who sought to use their cabinets for political benefit by expanding racial and gender diversity, or past presidents who often used their cabinet to build bridges to factions within their own political parties, Ronald Reagan used his cabinet solely to support the Reagan revolution in the departments.[6] For Reagan, loyalty was the only test for serving in the cabinet. According to one member of the selection team, the three criteria were "One: was he a Reagan man? Two, a Republican? And three, a Conservative? Probably our most crucial concern was to ensure that conservative ideology was properly represented."[7] Once selected, the cabinet nominees met with William Timmons, a Washington lobbyist and newly named director of the White House Office of Congressional Relations, to review the legislative mandates on their departments. Timmons developed an organizational blueprint of each agency and the staffing needs for the department.

According to Martin Anderson, the domestic policy advisor on the transition team, once Timmons had completed his session with the cabinet officers, the cabinet officers began "an indoctrination course" on the goals and objectives of the new administration. Anderson noted that the "two primary things one wanted to indoctrinate the new cabinet on [were] *ideas and people.*"[8] The *ideas* that Anderson focused on were the goals and objectives of the Reagan White House. The White House sought to ensure that cabinet officers did not "go native" and embrace departmental goals and objectives. Rather, the White House sought to ensure during the transition that cabinet officers were thoroughly versed on presidential priorities. Policies developed within the departments were to be cleared by the White House to ensure consistency with presidential goals and objectives. The *people* that Anderson focused on were the subcabinet political appointees, which were to be chosen by the White House personnel office rather than by cabinet officers.

In addition to the sessions that Timmons ran for the cabinet officers during the transition process, Anderson and Richard V. Allen, Reagan's foreign policy advisor, developed briefing sessions on the campaign promises that would become the focus of the new administration's policy agenda. Anderson created a series of notebooks, which included all of the speeches and campaign promises that Reagan had made during the election on the policy issues that would involve a particular cabinet department.[9] The notebooks also included Reagan's policy positions for the past five years to give the cabinet officers a thorough background on Reagan's views. Ten notebooks were created by Anderson, providing information on a wide variety of domestic and economic policy issues that Reagan had addressed during the campaign and in the five previous years. Cabinet officers were given little leeway in their agenda setting, as the notebooks narrowed the options within the often repeated themes of the campaign.

Subcabinet Personnel Selection

This series of meetings between White House staff and cabinet officers during the transition was carefully crafted to build a sense of comradery among the newly appointed members of the president's advisory structure and to minimize the problems of "a government of strangers," as Hugh Heclo so aptly describes it.[10] They also firmly reiterated the administration's policy goals to ensure that the new cabinet officers understood the direction that Reagan sought to move the federal government. Cabinet officers were expected to take control of their departments, review departmental programs, and focus departmental activities on presidential goals and objectives.

In order to mitigate opportunities for cabinet officers to become coopted by their departments, the Reagan transition team devised a plan for strengthening the ties between cabinet officers and the White House. That plan involved placing Reagan loyalists in the subcabinet positions who would provide a buffer between the cabinet officers and the career staff. The White House personnel office would appoint all subcabinet personnel, rather than having cabinet officers choose the personnel that they wanted. In an interview given in 1981 to the *Washington Post,* James said, "Nixon, like Carter, lost the appointments process. They lost control to the departments and the agencies. We have maintained control of the Oval Office."[11]

Reagan became the first president to successfully implement a centralized personnel office that required clearance of all subcabinet staff from the White House. Although Nixon began the process, neither he nor Ford or Carter was able to fully implement it. Watergate stopped Nixon but Ford and Carter continued to allow many of their cabinet officers to have control of the subcabinet appointment process.

Cabinet officers in the Reagan cabinet were discouraged from recommending names to the White House personnel office as a means of building a subcabinet whose primary loyalty was to the president, rather than to the cabinet officer or to the department. Nominees for the subcabinet had to meet a five-point test developed by the White House personnel office. According to personnel director, E. Pendleton James,

1. They had to have a philosophy in tune with the president.
2. They had to have a competency to pursue the philosophy of the president.
3. They had to have personal professional integrity.
4. They had to be team players.
5. They had to be tough enough to take the abuse from the press, Congress, and constituent groups.[12]

The White House was also preoccupied with developing a subcabinet that had few ties to the career bureaucracy. Many in the administration believed that the career bureaucracy would oppose many of the administration's initiatives. As *Mandate for Leadership II*, the manual for the transition team in 1984 written by staff of the conservative Heritage Foundation, noted, "The political executive who is promoting significant policy change within his department should not be surprised by career bureaucratic subordinates engaging . . . in covert inter-bureaucratic struggle to block the [administration's] initiatives."[13] The description of the career staff written in 1984 had not varied since 1980, when the first Reagan transition team was developing guidelines for the subcabinet appointment process.

The appointment process for subcabinet staff did not meet with complete approval from cabinet members. Some cabinet members were quite bitter about the efforts from the White House personnel office to control the political appointments within the departments. Secretary of Education Terrel Bell bitterly described his experience with the White House in personnel matters:

the determination of Ed Meese and his White House staff to stack my department and my equally fervent resolve to prevent this, it is not difficult to fathom the reasons for the inordinate delays in consummating subcabinet positions in ED [Education] . . . How could I fight back? . . . I was on my own during the first months of 1981.[14]

Although Bell and others complained about the personnel selection process, they were essentially forced to accept it. Unless they accepted the subcabinet names sent to them for approval, the White House personnel office would not fill openings.

The personnel selection process was part of the Reagan administration's strategy to minimize the career staff's influence over departmental policy making. By maintaining control over the selection process, the White House sought to minimize opportunities for career staff to move into the political positions. Reagan, as had Nixon, viewed the career staff as too committed to departmental programs and often reluctant to change direction. If the Reagan administration was to be successful in reframing federal programs and in cutting departmental staff, the White House needed to have loyal political executives at the helm of the department rather than career staff who had been promoted to senior positions.

Cabinet Councils

Once the transition team had placed politically loyal cabinet and subcabinet staff within the departments, they created a structure that kept both within the presidential orbit. Building on the Nixon model of the Domestic Council, which brought cabinet officers and subcabinet staff to the White House on a regular basis, Reagan created multiple cabinet councils rather than a single cabinet council. Five cabinet councils were originally created with overlapping membership and two were later added. The seven cabinet councils were:

1. Cabinet Council on Economic Affairs
2. Cabinet Council on Food and Agriculture
3. Cabinet Council on Human Resources
4. Cabinet Council on Legal Policy
5. Cabinet Council on Natural Resources and the Environment

6. Cabinet Council for Management and Administration
7. Cabinet Council on Commerce and Trade

In addition, the National Security Council continued (as the only statutorily authorized cabinet council) and was considered an additional cabinet council. The new domestic policy cabinet councils were created by executive order "to create an orderly process for reviewing issues requiring a decision by the President."[15] The cabinet council system minimized debate on goals and objectives and focused on the narrower issues involving effective policy implementation.

The cabinet councils were composed of six to eight cabinet officers, a size that replicated a system that Reagan had with a similar structure during his tenure as governor of California.[16] According to Martin Anderson, the domestic policy advisor for the White House, the cabinet council system

> was really a smaller, tailor-made version of the cabinet. Each cabinet council was designed to deal with certain specific issues of national policy. When a cabinet council met it had the same force and authority in dealing with those issues as the entire cabinet had. The members of the cabinet councils were selected primarily on the basis that the departments they headed were deeply involved in the specific issues that would be discussed at the cabinet meetings.[17]

Anderson, who developed the White House cabinet council system in tandem with Edwin Meese, Reagan's deputy chief of staff, saw the cabinet council system as a vehicle for dealing with issues that were "polyjurisdictional."[18] Policy issues that involved several departments needed White House oversight but did not need full cabinet participation in resolving management questions. The cabinet council structure was established to bring a small group of cabinet officers together to discuss the development and implementation of policy issues and to identify the lead agency and its responsibilities.

While the cabinet council structure was publicly billed as a management system to ensure that program responsibility was clearly identified in the departments and to minimize overlapping jurisdictional conflict, the White House privately created the system as a means to maintain cabinet support for administration policies. All cabinet council meetings were held in the West Wing of the White House. In the first year of the Reagan administration, 112 cabinet council meetings had been held, either in the Cabinet Room or the Roosevelt Room.[19] Both rooms were close to the Oval Office, allowing Reagan, who was formally the chair of all cabinet councils, to attend as often as possible. While he did not attend the majority of meetings, the cabinet council members did not know when he would be in attendance. This guaranteed their presence. When he did attend the meetings, he bolstered their enthusiasm for their mission within the administration and for the administration's policies.

Reagan's presence in the meetings, although not regular, and the location of the meetings in the West Wing, routinely renewed the relationship between the cabinet officers and the White House. Cabinet officers were made to feel that they were part of the president's team rather than part of the department's team. A Reagan cabinet officer spoke on behalf of the president to the departments rather than on behalf of the departments to the president.

At the heart of the strategy of the cabinet council system was a concerted effort by White House staff to minimize the opportunities for cabinet officers to be co-opted by their departments. By making cabinet officers part of the decision structure for policy development in the cabinet council process, and by having the meetings in the West Wing of the White House to reinforce the importance of the cabinet council structure, cabinet members became invested in the administration's policies. Cabinet members believed that they were part of the president's advisory team and were an essential part of the administration's management team. They were not, as many cabinet officers in past administrations had been, the departments' representatives to the president.

The issue of cooption dominated the development of the cabinet council system. Meese in particular was concerned that cabinet officers would become representatives of the departments and champion departmental policies rather than presidential policies. As Meese noted in a speech to the American Society of Newspaper Editors in May 1981, it was "essential to make sure that the presidential policies would dominate the policy implementation of the executive branch. And that it would be the policies of the elected chief executive of the country rather than the policies of the bureaucracy that would establish what was going on in the government."[20]

Creation of the cabinet councils reduced the traditional antagonism between cabinet officers and the White House. Under Nixon, Ehrlichman's Domestic Council began to reduce these tensions, but Ehrlichman was never able to build the rapport between the cabinet officers and the White House staff that Anderson had under Reagan. Ehrlichman understood the importance of keeping cabinet officers within the presidential orbit since too many cabinet officers "marry the natives," he noted, but never understood the value of nurturing the cabinet officers in other ways.[21]

Nixon never encouraged Ehrlichman to use the White House as a source of nurture for the cabinet officers and, in fact, discouraged Ehrlichman from including him in cabinet council meetings. The war in Vietnam was dominating Nixon's attention and his interest in domestic policy making was waning. Nixon told Ehrlichman in a memo "not to bother him" with the details of policy issues. "I am only interested," Nixon said, "when we make a major breakthrough or have a major failure. Otherwise, don't bother me."[22]

The contrast in management styles between Nixon and Reagan with regard to their cabinet officers is striking. Unlike Nixon, Reagan sought to have regular interaction with his cabinet officers and sought to reinforce their value to him as part of the management team of the administration. Reagan built a personal rapport with his cabinet and created the impression that they were a key part of the Reagan team. While there was no doubt among the cabinet officers that the White House staff managed the policy process, cabinet officers felt as if they were first-class not second-class members of the president's management team.

There was a carefully constructed sense of team building during the cabinet council meetings. Members were encouraged to arrive early and stay after the meetings for informal discussions with other members. Coffee, tea and light food was available on a table outside of the Roosevelt Room or the Cabinet Room to encourage mingling and conversation among the members. This was an orchestrated attempt by Anderson and the White House to build rapport among the members and with the White House staff. The less that cabinet members perceived themselves as a government of strangers, the more the cabinet members would work together as part of the Reagan team.

Another benefit to the cabinet council system was described by John McClaughry, one of Anderson's senior staff in the White House. McClaughry saw the cabinet councils as "a series of arbitration and mediation panels" that provided the departments access to the White House to plead their cases when policies became territorial turf battles.[23] Because these issues emerged from the regular interaction of the White House staff with the cabinet members in the cabinet council meetings, the White House staff was able to resolve the disputes. This enhanced White House control over policy management, reduced the role of the career staff in resolving policy conflict, and forged stronger bonds between the White House and the cabinet as a management team.

THE WHITE HOUSE MANAGEMENT STRUCTURE

The decisions to forge a politically cohesive cabinet and to create a cabinet council system had been made by the transition team, led by the campaign chief of staff, Edwin Meese III. Meese was named the transition director the day after the election at a meeting at Reagan's Pacific Palisades home. The transition team was composed of Meese (director), E. Pendleton James (Personnel), William Timmons (Congressional Relations), Richard Allen (Foreign Policy), Martin Anderson (Domestic Policy), Caspar Weinberger (Budget), and James Brady (Press Secretary).[24]

Once in office, the transition team moved in to the senior White House staffing positions, with Meese joining campaign manager James Baker and Michael Deaver (a close friend of Mrs. Reagan) in a three-way chief of staff position. Known as the "troika," or the triumvirate, Baker, Meese, and Deaver divided management responsibilities. Baker handled foreign policy and congressional relations, Meese handled domestic policy and oversaw the Office of Policy Development, and Deaver oversaw the administration of the White House, including Mrs. Reagan's office.

Anderson became the director of the Office of Policy Development and managed the cabinet councils and policy development process.

The Office of Policy Development was the center of the policy development process for the administration. Anderson, who had been Reagan's domestic policy adviser on the campaign and had developed the transition team's notebooks for the cabinet, had a clear picture of the policy direction for the administration.

However, Meese and Anderson were not involved in the legislative side of the policy development process. Once the cabinet councils and the White House staff had developed a policy proposal and received Reagan's approval, the proposal was moved into the Legislative Strategy Group, under Baker's auspices. The Legislative Strategy Group, which included Baker and Timmons, was responsible for lobbying for public and congressional support for the president's domestic and economic policy proposals. In essence, the White House divided the policy process into the policy development process, under Meese and Anderson, and the political and implementation process, under Baker and Timmons.

Baker had substantial flexibility in revising policies that Anderson's cabinet councils and the Office of Policy Development had developed. For Baker, Reagan had to establish a strong legislative record early in his presidency. In order to build that legislative record, Baker needed to have an early string of legislative victories, and if victory meant revising policies to satisfy congressional requests, the requests were met. Baker's Legislative Strategy Group had the authority to accept compromise language in the policy legislation submitted on behalf of the administration when the legislation was in jeopardy of failing. Baker became masterful at the art of compromise in order to move legislation through Congress.

While Meese and Anderson oversaw policy development, and Baker oversaw legislative action on policy proposals, David Stockman, Director of the Office of Management and Budget (OMB), oversaw the budget process. Stockman proved to be the pivotal piece of the policy development process, for the policies developed through the Office of Policy Development and the cabinet councils had to be within the budget constraints established by OMB.

Stockman created the economic agenda for the administration, ensuring that all department proposals met stiff criteria. The Reagan Revolution was designed to cut the size of the federal government, primarily the categorical grant programs that had blossomed during the Johnson administration. The goal of the Reagan administration, according to Stockman, was to end the "wasteful economic subsidy" programs created by "the vast Great Society [which] spawned a system of federal categorical aid for nearly every imaginable purpose from rodent control to special education for gifted children."[25] The task of the Office of Management and Budget under Stockman was to significantly reduce the budget request sent to Congress for many of the social welfare programs and other categorical aid programs that Reagan distrusted.

Although the cabinet selection process and the creation of the cabinet councils was designed to produce policies that supported the economic agenda, Stockman often was forced into "brow beating the cabinet, one by one," as he referred to it.[26] Stockman nearly always won his battles, systematically cutting both domestic programs and foreign aid programs within the budget. Among his foreign policy successes were cuts in funding for the World Bank, the Peace Corps, and funding for military aid to foreign governments—regaled as "the biggest cutback of foreign aid" since World War II.[27]

Stockman faced the wrath of cabinet officers far more than did Anderson or Meese in the White House. While Anderson, in particular, was building strong relations with the cabinet officers to ensure that they were invested in the Reagan policy decisions, Stockman was tearing down those same strong relations as he cut programmatic funding from departmental budgets. The result was that Stockman operated outside of the organizational structure that Baker and Meese created in the White House for policy development and implementation. Yet Stockman was essential to the Reagan Revolution to ensure that the administration's policy agenda met the tests of the economic agenda.

CONCLUSION

The Reagan Revolution was, after all, an economic revolution. Reagan sought to cut the federal budget, reduce taxes, and reduce the number of federal programs. As Burt Rockman noted in his assessment of the Reagan presidency, "The particular contribution that Ronald Reagan brought to his presidency was clarity of purpose and a straightforward vision of his objectives."[28] When Reagan was elected president, the conservative revolution had begun for reframing the objectives of the federal government.

Cabinet officers were brought into the administration because of their ideological commitment to the Reagan Revolution. They understood when they accepted their appointments to the Reagan cabinet that their role was to review departmental programs and recommend those that could be reduced or ended. The apparatus set up by the transition team to choose subcabinet personnel that would be a buffer between the career staff and the cabinet officers was designed to reduce opportunities for cabinet cooption.

Once in office, the Reagan White House staff created a policy structure that would further reduce opportunities for career staff to influence the policy process, particularly that process which involved budget reductions. The Reagan cabinet council structure attempted to build a collegial relationship among the cabinet officers to create a team working in tandem with the White House on policy issues. The team approach was crafted to build a sense of ownership by the cabinet officers of policy decisions, even policy decisions that led to budget cuts within their departments.

The Office of Policy Development was focused on reviewing departmental programs and determining which programs could be phased out or reduced. Anderson's cabinet council structure facilitated small group meetings among the cabinet officers to determine the most effective avenues for programmatic cuts. Cabinet officers knew from the meetings that their departments were not alone in being targeted for budget cuts and could work together to cut programs that might overlap among one or more departments. If overlap occurred, one department could often salvage its part of the program.

When individual departments failed to support budget cuts in spite of the efforts of Anderson's working groups, Stockman stepped in and made the cuts himself. The Office of Management and Budget became the most powerful office within the Reagan administration, for it alone could make the final decisions on whether departmental programs survived intact or faced substantial budget cuts. Reagan unwaveringly supported Stockman throughout the first year of the administration.

Stockman's influence with Reagan plummeted in December 1981 with the publication of an article by William Greider in the *Atlantic Monthly*, in which Greider quoted Stockman as questioning the logic of Reagan's budget policies.[29] Stockman supported Reagan's antipathy for the burgeoning of the permanent government and the necessity for budget cuts, but he questioned Reagan's decision to simultaneously cut taxes and dramatically increase defense spending. While Reagan gently reprimanded Stockman in a private Oval Office meeting, he did not fire him.

The Reagan Revolution continued more modestly throughout the remainder of the first term but began to unravel as some of the key players began to leave. David Stockman and Martin Anderson left before the first term ended. The second term saw the departure of Deaver, and Donald Regan took over as chief of staff, with Meese moving to the Justice Department and Baker to the Treasury Department. The second term soon became consumed with the Iran-Contra affair, as Congress began an investigation into abuse of power by the president. Most of the machinery that had been so carefully established for moving the Reagan Revolution forward during the first year of the administration lost its luster by the beginning of the second term.

To a large degree, the Reagan Revolution had a short life but one which had lasting influence throughout the Reagan administration and future administrations. The tax cuts that Reagan successfully moved through Congress reduced the expenditures of the federal government, from which many federal programs never recovered. Future administrations failed to restore much of the funding lost during the first years of the Reagan administration, which Stockman had orchestrated.

The legacy of the Reagan Revolution should be viewed from two perspectives. The first perspective is that the role of the federal government was permanently changed by the budget reductions in federal programs that Reagan sought. This is, of course, the more significant legacy of the Reagan Revolution. But the second perspective should not be lost, which entails the management structure that Reagan set in place to oversee the massive changes in the federal budget and the service delivery structure. Reagan created a personnel selection system that ensured ideological consistency among his cabinet and subcabinet, rather than the traditional personnel selection system that relied on technocrats

and program executives to manage the departments. Reagan further created a White House oversight system through the Office of Policy
Development that ensured that cabinet officers were invested in the
policies, particularly the budgetary policies, of the administration.
Every successive administration has built on the management principles created by Reagan and his White House staff. The Reagan Revolution was a revolution in the role of the federal government but also
a revolution in how the president managed the federal government.

NOTES

1. William Lanouette, "Reagan in the White House, Don't Look for
Change Overnight," *National Journal* (November 8, 1980): 1873.
2. Richard M. Nixon, *RN: The Memoirs of Richard Nixon* (New York:
Grosset and Dunlap, 1978), 352.
3. For a discussion of Nixon's policy-making structure, see Shirley Anne
Warshaw, *The Domestic Presidency: Policy Making in the White House*
(Boston: Allyn and Bacon, 1997).
4. Once nominated by the Republican Party, Reagan gave E. Pendleton
James a budget of $80,000, an office, and staff to work on the transition
process and to develop names for the cabinet. At the same time that James
was developing his list of names, a group of Reagan friends in California was
also developing a list of names. For an excellent discussion of this process,
see Bradley H. Patterson Jr., *The Ring of Power: The White House Staff and
Its Expanding Role in Government* (New York: Basic Books, 1981), 241.
5. Dom Bonafede, "Reagan and His Kitchen Cabinet Are Bound by
Friendship and Ideology," *National Journal* (April 11, 1981): 608.
6. See, for example, a discussion of Clinton's diversity efforts in Gwen
Ifill, "Clinton Completes Cabinet and Points to Its Diversity," *New York
Times*, December 25, 1992, A1.
7. Lou Cannon, *Reagan* (New York: G. P. Putnam's 1982), 317.
8. Martin Anderson, *Revolution: The Reagan Legacy* (Stanford, Calif.:
Hoover Institution Press, 1990), 225.
9. Interview with Martin Anderson.
10. Hugh Heclo, *A Government of Strangers* (Washington, D.C.: Brook-
ings Institution, 1977).
11. "Personnel Office Grinds Out Names of Toilers in Reagan Vineyard,"
Washington Post, June 18, 1981, A13.
12. Interview with E. Pendleton James.

13. Stuart Butler, Michael Sanera, and W. Bruce Weinrod, *Mandate for Leadership*, vol. 2 (Washington, D.C.: Heritage Foundation, 1984), 491.

14. Terrel Bell, *The Thirteenth Man: A Reagan Cabinet Memoir* (New York: The Free Press, 1988), 43.

15. The White House, Office of the Press Secretary, February 26, 1981.

16. Chester Newland, "A Mid-term Appraisal: The Reagan Presidency," *Public Administration Review* 43 (January–February 1983): 7. See also Anderson, *Revolution,* 224–5.

17. Anderson, *Revolution,* 224–5.

18. Anderson, *Revolution,* 224

19. Anderson, *Revolution,* 224.

20. Quote from a speech made by Edwin Meese on April 23, 1981, to the American Society of Newspaper Editors, as quoted in "White House Decision Making Continuation of California System," *Congressional Quarterly Weekly Report*, May 9, 1981.

21. Nixon's interest in domestic affairs is exemplified by the citations in the index of *RN: The Memoirs of Richard Nixon.* There is no citation for domestic policy or of the Domestic Council. John Ehrlichman is given 9 lines in the citations, while Henry Kissinger is given 43 lines.

22. John Burke, *The Institutionalized Presidency* (Baltimore: Johns Hopkins University Press, 1992), 72.

23. John McClaughry, "White House Policy Making Maze; Has the Cabinet Council System Homogenized the Reagan Revolution," *Washington Times*, February 19, 1985, A5.

24. Edwin Meese III, *With Reagan: The Inside Story* (Washington, D.C.: Regnery Gateway, 1992), 56.

25. David Stockman, *The Triumph of Politics: Why the Reagan Revolution Failed* (New York: Harper & Row, 1986), 121.

26. Stockman, *The Triumph of Politics*, 123.

27. Stockman, *The Triumph of Politics*, 127.

28. Burt Rockman, "The Style and Organization of the Reagan Presidency," in *The Reagan Legacy: Promise and Performance*, ed. Charles O. Jones (Chatham, N.J.: Chatham House Publishers, 1988), 9.

29. William Greider, "The Education of David Stockman," *The Atlantic Monthly* (December 21, 1981).

9

The Great Composer: A Behind the Scenes Look at Ronald Reagan's Rhetorical Symphony

Wynton C. Hall

Shortly before the 1980 presidential election, national political reporter Chris Wallace and Ronald Reagan's chief strategist and pollster, Richard B. Wirthlin, boarded the candidate's plane en route to a campaign event. There, Wallace asked Wirthlin to explain how he believed his candidate could capture the requisite number of electoral votes necessary to win the White House. The former professor of economics, who also holds a Ph.D. from the University of California at Berkeley, began drawing a map of the United States on a scrap piece of a paper. With computer-like proficiency, Wirthlin riddled the page with numbers. Wallace decided to keep the paper for future reference.

On November 3, 1980, Ronald Reagan won in a landslide victory, and when he did, Chris Wallace remembered the handwritten map the president-elect's strategist had prepared for him. The next time Wallace saw Reagan, he showed the newly elected president Wirthlin's map before asking him to autograph the paper as a memento. Reagan took the paper, scrawled something on it, and returned it to the young reporter with a smile.

When Wallace looked down, the paper read: "Dear Chris, I don't understand this—Ronald Reagan."[1]

Enthusiasts and critics of Ronald Reagan are likely to find diametrically opposed meanings in the story above. Indeed, for the last quarter century, journalists, scholars, and political observers have attempted to pinpoint the origins of Ronald Reagan's leadership. This is particularly the case as it relates to his standing as one of America's most success-ful rhetorical presidents.

In the process, two dominant schools of thought have emerged. The first might be called "The Natural School." Adherents of this view of-ten assert that Ronald Reagan's ability to move audiences with his words was the result of an innate rhetorical ability and extensive prac-tice. To substantiate their claims, members of this camp often point to Reagan's prolific letter writing, which some estimate to number 10,000 over the span of his lifetime. Also, Reagan's self-authored ra-dio scripts and speeches, the 4,000 hours he spent speaking before 250,000 employees of General Electric, and his experience as a Holly-wood movie actor are often cited as further evidence of his devotion to his craft.[2] The confluence of these experiences, The Natural School ar-gues, produced a leader uniquely suited to meet the mediated demands of the modern presidency.

The second school of thought, however, represents a radical depar-ture from that of The Natural School. This camp advances a view that might be called "The Handler School." Supporters of this perspective argue that Reagan's rhetorical artistry was largely—if not entirely—the result of a highly coordinated communications apparatus that op-erated with little to no direct guidance from Reagan himself. Instead, The Handler School contends that a group of communication special-ists made up of speechwriters, public relations professionals, and Reagan's pollster, Richard B. Wirthlin, were largely responsible for producing Reagan's staging, script, and, by extension, his success. In this way, The Handler School often characterizes the Fourtieth presi-dent the way former Democratic presidential advisor Clark Clifford once did, as little more than an "amiable dunce."[3]

While The Natural School and The Handler School are rife with ideological underpinnings, both suffer from a glaring limitation: nei-ther offers a complete picture of the origins of Ronald Reagan's rhetor-ical genius or the behind the scenes methods used to enhance Reagan's ability to connect with audiences.

Thus, I offer a third option, one designed to explain the intricate relationship between Reagan's rhetorical sensibilities and the role his communications advisors played: The Symphonic School. Like a musical composer, Ronald Reagan's "music"—themes, positions, and vision—was entirely his own. The style and "instruments" used to amplify Reagan's music, however, were determined in concert with the members of his "symphony"—a select group of speechwriters as well as his longtime strategist, Richard Wirthlin. As will be shown, it was Reagan's organic understanding of communication combined with his advisor's synthetic instruments that produced a synergy worthy of the moniker "The Great Communicator." Indeed, in many ways, Reagan was The Great Composer.

THE GENESIS OF RONALD REAGAN'S RHETORICAL "MUSIC"

To varying degrees, all presidents come to the White House with a set of preconceived values—beliefs that guide decisions and order priorities. For some, these ideals are clearly defined; for others, less so. What's more, while some presidents' values shift over time, others remain unchanged. Yet regardless of a president's level of consistency, his moral underpinnings are necessarily reflected in the words he speaks. As the great Greek rhetorician, Isocrates, once wrote, "We regard speaking well to be the clearest sign of a good mind . . . and the image of a good and faithful soul."[4]

Thus, to understand the origins of a president's values one must explore the genesis of his rhetorical sensibility. This is particularly true for Ronald Wilson Reagan. As William K. Muir Jr. has written, "More than any other modern president, Ronald Reagan sought to exploit the moral possibilities of the rhetorical presidency. He used his 'bully pulpit' to try to convince the public that his values . . . were right. In other words, he sought to change the *mores* of Americans."[5] Indeed, Reagan's conscious infusion of values into his discourse raises two pivotal questions: what were his core values and from whence did they come?

Reagan possessed at least four core values that guided a tripartite vision for American renewal.

First, for Reagan, "individual freedom," in all its varied meanings, represented the "north star" of political judgment.[6] This deeply held belief stemmed from his Christian faith that had been fostered throughout his youth. As a boy, Reagan's personal commitment to the teachings of Christ had been forged by his mother, Nelle Reagan, and nurtured through the lessons learned at the First Christian Church in his hometown of Dixon, Illinois. Reagan was taught that reconciling one's sin nature with a desire for eternal salvation would require that a debt be paid on his behalf, a penance that could only be repaid through a personal commitment with Jesus Christ.

In this way, Reagan viewed the struggle for individual freedom as a quest to free oneself from the "slavery of the soul." That is, for Reagan, the battle between good and evil applied not merely to the external world, but to the inner contours of the human heart as well. Reagan's belief that God sent His only son to redeem the world meant that the Creator was not neutral on issues of spirituality or physical liberty—God preferred freedom to slavery.

Perhaps Reagan put it best in his first inaugural address, delivered on January 20, 1981, when he spoke the following words while standing on the West Front of the Capitol:

> I'm told that tens of thousands of prayer meetings are being held on this day, and for that I'm deeply grateful. We are a nation under God, and I believe intended for us to be free. It would be fitting and good, I think, if on each Inaugural Day in future years it should be declared a day of prayer.

Four years later, delivering his second inaugural address, Reagan once again linked the value of freedom to an inner spiritual reality. Indeed, wherever one finds Ronald Reagan speaking of freedom, spirituality is seldom far behind.

> Human freedom is on the march, and nowhere more so than in our own hemisphere. Freedom is one of the deepest and noblest aspirations of the human spirit. People, worldwide, hunger for the right of self-determination, for those inalienable rights that make for human dignity and progress.
>
> America must remain freedom's staunchest friend, for freedom is our best ally and it is the world's only hope to conquer poverty and preserve peace. Every blow we inflict against poverty will be a blow against its dark allies of oppression and war. Every victory for human freedom will be a victory for world peace.

In his religious biography of Ronald Reagan, Paul Kengor explores the implications of the president's faith as it relates to Ronald Reagan's approach to international relations with the former Soviet Union. Kengor notes that Reagan consistently connected the dearth of individual freedom experienced by citizens in the USSR to the spiritual void created by an atheistic regime.[7] In this way, Reagan saw individual freedom as both external and internal, as exogenous and endogenous. Moreover, his rhetoric revealed his belief that two polarities were, in fact, inextricably linked. Hence, Reagan felt the need to connect the two—the spiritual as well as secular struggle for freedom—when communicating his vision.

The second value that guided Ronald Reagan, and thus the way he communicated, was that of "individual responsibility." A central tenet of conservative ideology, Reagan believed human agents must be held to account for their actions. This facet of Reagan's rhetorical arsenal seldom failed to gain resonance with political audiences throughout his career. Going back to his days as Governor of California, Reagan had taken strong stands on issues of crime and punishment. What's more, he believed that the solutions to many of America's greatest problems were beyond the scope of the federal government.

It is important to note the relationship between the value of individual freedom and that of personal responsibility. For the conservative, these values possess a correlative relationship. That is, the less individual freedom one possesses in his or her own life, the less personal responsibility that individual will exhibit. Likewise, as personal responsibility for action and deed increases, so, too, does one's potential to live freely.

The third value operative in the Reagan Revolution was that of "common sense." Some scholars have tried to equate conservatism with a form of anti-intellectualism.[8] Indeed, this sentiment helped fuel the rise of the neo-conservative movement, which places emphasis on the more "cerebral" aspects of conservative ideology. Still, for Reagan, applying common sense to matters of public policy was essential, and thus he rejected the liberal impulse to approach governance as an exercise in theory or social experimentation.

For example, Ronald Reagan balked at the liberal suggestion that there are no simple answers to complex societal problems. In his famous 1964 televised address in support of Barry Goldwater's bid for the presidency, Ronald Reagan responded to Democratic and liberal critics who had suggested that conservatives were simpletons: "They [Democrats/liberals] say we offer simple answers to complex problems. Well, perhaps there is a simple answer—not an easy answer—but a simple one." Throughout his political career, Reagan favored what he perceived as practical policies grounded in rationality.

The final "note" in Reagan's symphony of values was his view of "common decency." Under this heading comes Reagan's commitment to protecting the traditions of a moral culture. As Reagan saw it, that culture was to be one marked by caring, tolerance, and religious conviction. This dimension of Reagan's value structure could be said to reflect a bourgeoisie sensibility that stood in contradistinction to the bohemian impulse that animates much of liberalism. Protecting traditional notions of culture, decorum, civility, and moral absolutism were all central to Ronald Reagan's rejection of the liberal forces fueling the counterculture of the 1960s. For some members of the leftist establishment, notions of "decency" were little more than a form of Victorian hegemony that sought to oppress so-called marginalized voices. Reagan, on the other hand, believed common decency to be the mark of a civil society.

The combination of these four values—individual freedom, individual responsibility, common sense, common decency—coalesced to create Ronald Reagan's vision for American renewal. Moreover, to varying degrees, these four values are operative in almost every major speech Ronald Reagan delivered throughout his public life.

According to Ronald Reagan's chief strategist and pollster, Richard B. Wirthlin, the president's vision was threefold:

1. Restore America's confidence in itself.
2. Encourage economic growth without inflation.
3. Lift the Damocles sword of Mutually Assured Destruction (MAD) through arms reduction and the normalization of relations with the former Soviet Union.[9]

Achieving the fulfillment of Reagan's vision required maximizing the power of the "bully pulpit." After all, as Richard E. Neustadt has written, "the power of the presidency is the power to persuade."[10] In this regard, Ronald Wilson Reagan was uniquely suited to meet the demands of the rhetorical presidency.[11]

According to Reagan administration speechwriter Curt Smith, Reagan viewed the bully pulpit as the primary function of the presidency. Smith says Reagan cared deeply about his ability to communicate because, "The spoken word wasn't a *part* of his career, it *was* his career."[12] For this reason, Ronald Reagan was receptive to a process of speech-craft whose primary purpose rested in continuously improving communications.

That is, Reagan The Composer welcomed the "instruments" (communication stratagems and methods for testing messages) his advisors had created. Indeed, the Reagan communications apparatus benefited greatly from the synergy between Reagan's clarity of vision and ability to communicate values on the one hand and the technological advancements of Richard B. Wirthlin on the other.

THE "INSTRUMENTS" OF THE REAGAN RHETORICAL SYMPHONY

The values and vision operative in Ronald Reagan's discourse were always his own. However, throughout his public career, Reagan benefited greatly from the strategic insight of the man responsible for strategizing two of the biggest landslide victories in American presidential politics, Dr. Richard B. Wirthlin. The two men met in the fall of 1968 when then Governor Reagan had secretly hired Wirthlin through an intermediary to conduct a study on his behalf without the pollster knowing the true identity of his client. Following their first encounter, Reagan and Wirthlin remained close friends for the next 36 years up and until the president's passing. Indeed, Reagan would place his electoral fate and millions of dollars into the strategist's hands over the course of his political career.

Wirthlin says that the secret to Ronald Reagan's ability to communicate involved his ability to tap into human emotion through the invocation of the four values discussed earlier. "You can persuade through reason," says Wirthlin, "but you motivate through emotion, and you do that by tapping into universally shared values. That's what Reagan did."[13]

Toward this end, Wirthlin devised two instruments—one quantitative and the other qualitative—to enhance Reagan's ability to connect with voters.

THE POLITICAL INFORMATION SYSTEM (PINS)

Wirthlin's Political Information System (PINS) was revolutionary. While PINS took over three and a half years to develop, the system was finished in time to be used for Ronald Reagan's 1980 campaign. Wirthlin describes PINS as "a total information system that involves virtually every quantitative, qualitative, institutional, historical data source," and as "a system that combined attitudinal, behavioral research with institutional information, demographic information from the census, and then political vote data."[14]

The system's diverse collection of data included everything from information about television coverage to lists of key opinion leaders in various states.[15] This wide array of data was designed around five central information components: (1) up-to-the-minute survey data on both candidates' positions on the national, state, and county levels; (2) a variable adjustment component that would correct for newly found demographic shifts; (3) a compendium of voting histories for all 50 states and 3,041 counties in the U.S.; (4) a numeric valuation for party organizational support (for both parties) in each state; (5) and a marginal variable for "insider information" to account for regional developments that might alter the calculus maintained by PINS—for the purpose of simulating the 1980 political campaign environment in order to assess and devise strategic decisions.

Taken separately, these bases of information were not new to public opinion research or campaign strategists. However, when combined with (a) the use of tracking polls that allowed for daily updating of data, (b) the ability to simulate multiple scenarios by either candidate, and (c) the rapidity afforded by having this information in a centralized computer system, PINS represented a powerful tool from which tactics and rhetorical strategy could be derived.[16]

One of PINS's greatest strengths was the system's ability to interpret how various rhetorical "moves" by either candidate might affect public approval percentages through a process of "war-gaming." This method relied on posing various "What if?" questions to the computer. For instance, it could measure how a certain Reagan message in County X would resonate with those particular voters, and, in turn, the impact on his overall ratings. Wirthlin explains:

We would, again, make assumptions about the profile of the electorate: Who was likely to turn out? What were the vote probabilities of various constituents? To what extent is an issue salient? Then we would run a series of "What if?" questions, knowing well before—and I would like to stress this—what Reagan's position would be. We wouldn't really run the simulation to determine a quote, "best position," but we ran them to determine where our vulnerabilities were as well as our strengths.[17]

The polling team stresses that PINS did not represent an electoral "auto-pilot" feature. According to Richard Beal, one of Wirthlin's assistants, "You never make a judgment on the basis of PINS alone. You use it to test the suggestions and theories of your political junkies, and you use the knowledge of the political junkies to test the empirical data in PINS."[18] Wirthlin and his staff are quick to stipulate that their work was never an attempt to tell Reagan what to say, rather, the best way to say it.[19] Put another way, Wirthlin's job was to create the instrument; coming up with the music was Reagan's job.

PULSELINES

Unlike PINS, Wirthlin's PulseLines did not utilize complex quantitative models to create findings. In fact, the process was fairly straightforward. First, a group of participants was selected. Members were selected on the basis of a wide array of factors, including religion, age, gender, income, and ethnic background. The idea was to construct an audience that most clearly resembled the target audience the researcher wanted his message to reach. Wirthlin says that the group size for Pulse-Lines generally ranged from 30 to as many as 100 members.[20]

Once the group was established, members were given a hand-held electronic box with a punch pad of numbers on its face. Each box was connected to a central unit to record participants' responses. The Pulse-Line session began with the researcher explaining that the group would view a recorded or live televised speech. When respondents heard or saw something they liked they were instructed to enter the number that reflected that strength of their reaction either positively or negatively (high numbers reflect a positive reaction, low numbers a negative one). Each respondent's ratings were then calculated and averaged in real time by the central unit. Following the session viewers' responses were printed out in an EKG-like chart, which displayed the moments in the speech when a message either did or did not resonate.[21] From this rating Wirthlin could then literally superimpose a tracing of the PulseLine onto a videotape of the speech each respondent originally viewed.[22] Doing so allowed Wirthlin to pinpoint the exact moment when Reagan's message resonated with viewers. It also allowed him to isolate which themes and/or words were responsible for the positive ratings recorded by the PulseLine. While this technology may seem advanced, PulseLines have been around for quite some time.

Marketing and commercial advertising professionals had used similar devices since the 1960s to test the effectiveness of proposed television ads.[23] However, it was not until Reagan entered the White House that PulseLines were integrated so directly into a sitting president's communication apparatus. Wirthlin believed that PulseLines were a tool he could use to help the speechwriters identify the words and phrases that might produce the impact Reagan desired. This process, therefore, was meant to yield a constant state of "rhetorical recycling."[24]

Wirthlin understood that for a message to get through the media's filter it must be sustained over time and singularly focused. Wirthlin says, "We found that if we hit a story a day, the press wouldn't pick it up. But if we could sustain a story for three days we would get about five or six times the impact."[25] Hence, he used PulseLines extensively throughout Reagan's second term to find out how voters were responding to Reagan's speeches. The goal was to isolate what are referred to as "power phrases" or "power lines" that could be inserted into future speech drafts. The hope was that by having the communications apparatus and the polling apparatus working in tandem, a positive rhetorical synergistic effect would take place that would sustain positive power phrases, and elide negative ones.

Table 9.1 illustrates how the process would work.

As is clear from table 9.1, these distinguishable phrases taken from Reagan's October 1985 UN speech reappeared in subsequent addresses after the president's November 1985 trip to Geneva. Wirthlin says that he ran PulseLines on almost every major speech Ronald Reagan delivered as president. Most importantly, Wirthlin's level of direct access to

Table 9.1 PulseLine Power Phrases

United Nations Address October 24, 1985	Speech before Joint Session of Congress November 21, 1985	Radio Address to the Nation November 23, 1985
"I come offering for my own country a new commitment, a fresh start." —and— "I look to a fresh start in the relationship of our two nations."	"I called for a fresh start, and we made that start."	"As I told Congress, we've made a fresh start in U.S.-Soviet relations."
"Until that day, the United States seeks to escape the prison of mutual terror by research and testing that could, in time, enable us to neutralize the threat of these ballistic missiles and, ultimately, render them obsolete."	"If our research succeeds, it will bring much closer the safer, more stable world we seek. Nations could defend themselves against the missile attack and mankind, at long last, escape the prison of mutual terror. And this is my dream."	
"One guiding star was supposed to light our path toward the U.N. vision of peace and progress—a start of freedom." —and— "Gaining a peaceful resolution of these conflicts will open whole new vistas of peace and progress."	"The fact is, every new day begins with possibilities; it's up to us us to fill it with the things that move us toward progress and peace."	"They [Soviets] recognize that the United States is no longer just reacting to world events; we are in the forefront of a powerful, historic tide for freedom and opportunity, for progress and peace."

Source: Public Papers of the President of the United States: Ronald Reagan.

the president as part of his inner circle meant he could ensure that "power phrases" were inserted into Ronald Reagan's future speeches.

CONCLUSION

Ronald Reagan entered the White House with a firm set of values and a clear vision of where he wanted to lead America. In this way, the views of The Natural School are correct. Reagan's unique experiences in Hollywood and as spokesman for General Electric had provided him with a rhetorical education unlike that of any other American president. What's more, during his childhood in Dixon, Illinois, Reagan had developed guiding values that ultimately formed his vision.

Still, along his political rise to power, Reagan enjoyed the help of others, namely Richard Wirthlin, who helped enhance his communications. Thus, The Handler School, too, offers insight into the production of Reagan's rhetoric.

Yet it is The Symphonic School, ultimately, that seeks to explain Reagan's rhetorical symphony as a collaborative effort between the Composer (Reagan) and the instruments he directed (Wirthlin and the speechwriters). While Reagan chose the score, he allowed others to determine the arrangement. In the end, Reagan's rhetorical legacy earned him the title of The Great Communicator. However, he could have just as easily been called The Great Composer.

NOTES

1. Transcript, FOX News, June 5, 2004.

2. The 4,000-hours and 250,000-employees figures can be found in Nancy Gibbs, "The All-American President," *Time* (June 14, 2004): 38. The 10,000-letter figure can be found in Kiron K. Skinner, Annelise Anderson, and Martin Anderson, *Reagan: A Life in Letters* (New York: Free Press, 2003), xiii. Also see Kiron K. Skinner, Annelise Anderson, and Martin Anderson, *Reagan, in His Own Hand* (New York: Free Press, 2001), and Ralph E. Weber and Ralph A. Weber, *Dear Americans: Letters from the Desk of Ronald Reagan* (New York: Doubleday, 2003).

3. Clark Clifford, *Counsel to the President: A Memoir* (New York: Random House, 1991), 644.

4. David C. Mirhady and Yun Lee Too, trans., *Isocrates I* (Austin: University of Texas Press, 2000), 171.

5. William K. Muir Jr., "Ronald Reagan's Bully Pulpit: Creating a Rhetoric of Values," in *Presidential Speechwriting: From the New Deal to the Reagan Revolution and Beyond*, ed. Kurt Ritter and Martin J. Medhurst (College Station: Texas A&M University Press, 2003), 194.

6. For more on the topic of Reagan and freedom, see Andrew E. Busch, *Ronald Reagan and the Politics of Freedom* (New York: Rowman & Littlefield Publishers, 2001).

7. Paul Kengor, *God and Reagan: A Spiritual Life* (New York: Regan-Books, 2004).

8. Richard Hofstadter, *Anti-Intellectualism in American Life* (New York: Vintage Books, 1963).

9. Interview with Dr. Richard B. Wirthlin by Wynton C. Hall, Wirthlin Worldwide, Salt Lake City, Utah, June 9, 2004.

10. Richard E. Neustadt, *Presidential Power and the Modern Presidents: The Politics of Leadership from Roosevelt to Reagan* (New York: The Free Press, 1990), 11.

11. Jefferey Tulis, *The Rhetorical Presidency* (Princeton, N.J.: Princeton University Press, 1989).

12. Curt Smith, interview with Wynton C. Hall at The George Bush Presidential Library on January 26, 2000.

13. Interview with Dr. Richard B. Wirthlin by Wynton C. Hall.

14. Interview with Dr. Richard B. Wirthlin by Wynton C. Hall.

15. David M. Moore, *The Superpollsters: How They Measure and Manipulate Public Opinion in America* (New York: Four Walls Eight Windows, 1995), 204.

16. Roland Perry, *Hidden Power* (New York: Beaufort Books, 1984), 102.

17. Interview with Dr. Richard B. Wirthlin by Wynton C. Hall.

18. David Burnham, "Reagan's Campaign Adds Strategy Role to Use of Computer," *New York Times*, April 23, 1984, A1.

19. Sidney Blumenthal, "Marketing the President," *New York Times Magazine*, September 13, 1981, 41–3. Also see Norman M. Bradburn and Seymour Sudman, *Polls and Surveys* (San Francisco: Jossey-Bass Publishers, 1988).

20. Interview with Dr. Richard B. Wirthlin by Wynton C. Hall.

21. Mark R. Levy, "Polling and the Presidential Election," *Annals of the American Academy for Political and Social Science* 472 (1984): 85–96.

22. Nelson W. Polsby and Aaron Wildavsky, *Presidential Elections: Strategies and Structures in American Politics*, 9th ed. (Chatham, NJ: Chatham House, 1996), 211.

23. Andrew Rosenthal, "Political Marketing; Campaigning to Instant Responses," *New York Times*, July 25, 1987, A9.

24. Wynton C. Hall, "The Invention of 'Quantifiably Safe Rhetoric': Richard Wirthlin and Ronald Reagan's Instrumental Use of Public Opinion Research in Presidential Discourse," *Western Journal of Communication* 66 (2002): 319–46.

25. Interview with Dr. Richard B. Wirthlin by Wynton C. Hall.

10

Religious Reagan: The Role of Faith in Reagan's Presidency and Attack on Communism

Paul Kengor

Few events in the twentieth century were as momentous as the end of the Cold War. Soviet communism took power in 1917; the Cold War began in the latter 1940s. Both were finished by 1989/91—ends that Ronald Reagan hoped for long before his presidency. Significantly, Reagan's religious views heavily affected his thinking and actions toward Soviet communism and the Cold War, far more so than has been recognized. The degree to which Reagan's religious faith was at the start, or base, of his politics, life, sense of mission, and belief system generally has been terribly neglected.[1]

The peak periods of Reagan's faith appeared to be the bookends of his life—growing up as an adolescent in Dixon, Illinois and fully matured as president and former president of the United States. His devoutness as president seemingly spiked up after the 1981 assassination attempt, from which it never came back down.

Reagan's religious convictions were formed in the 1910s and 1920s and remained consistent through the 1990s. While we rightly marvel at the consistency of Reagan's *political* beliefs, beginning in the 1950s (or earlier), his *religious* beliefs held firm even longer. Here, too, as in so much else, Reagan's mother, Nelle, described as a saint by those who knew her, was the formative figure. Aside from Nelle, there were other influential figures from his local Disciples of Christ denomination in Dixon, including his pastor, Ben Cleaver, and Sunday school teacher, Lloyd Emmert. Another crucial influence was author Harold Bell Wright via his book *That Printer of Udell's*, a Christian novel which preached the notion of "practical Christianity": the admonition that Christians must apply their faith in all they do, rather than placing their faith on a shelf.

THE ROLE OF FAITH IN REAGAN'S LIFE AND PRESIDENCY

Ronald Reagan's first major speaking engagement was as president of his 1928 high school senior class at commencement. Characteristically, he quoted the Bible, reading John 10:10: "I have come in order that they all have life in all its abundance."[2] This began a habit for Reagan: he mentioned God in all of his life's major speeches.[3]

In his first gubernatorial inaugural address, given on January 5, 1967, Reagan said, "It is inconceivable to me that anyone could accept this delegated authority without asking God's help." He followed, "I pray that we who legislate and administer will be granted wisdom and strength beyond our own limited power; that with Divine guidance we can avoid easy expedients as we work to build a state where liberty under law and justice can triumph."[4] In that first inaugural, Reagan intrepidly promised to conduct his public duties according to the teachings of Christ, believing anyone who did so held the potential to "revolutionize the world," as he quoted Benjamin Franklin as saying.[5] In an impromptu moment, Reagan paused, turned to the Senate chaplain who had opened the ceremony with an invocation, and said:

> Reverend, perhaps you weren't a part of my imagining of what this moment would be. But I am deeply grateful for your presence because you remind us and bring here the presence of someone else without whose presence I certainly wouldn't have the nerve to do what I'm going to try to do. Someone back in our history, maybe it was Benjamin Franklin, said if ever someone could take public office and bring to that public office the precepts and teachings of the Prince of Peace, he would revolutionize the world and men would be remembering him for 1,000 years. I don't think anyone could follow those precepts completely. I'm not so presumptuous as to think I can—but I will try very hard. I think it's needed in today's world.[6]

Here was a seeming sureness by Reagan that one might be able to "revolutionize the world" by incorporating Christian precepts. (His use of the term "Prince of Peace" was, of course, a reference to Jesus Christ.)

This sentiment was not unusual for Reagan. In most of his major statements where he talked about making historic global changes—here, in this speech, changes he saw as potentially sufficient to be remembered 1,000 years henceforth—God was invoked. To Reagan, God and historic global changes involved or depended upon the other; they were inextricably connected.

In his first inaugural as president, written completely by himself, Reagan made six direct references to either "God" or "prayer." In his second inaugural, also written by himself, he made twelve such references.[7] The final three paragraphs of the second inaugural are packed with religious meaning and imagery. He called upon the image of "a general" who "falls on his knees in the hard snow of Valley Forge." This was a reference to George Washington, the nation's first president, and Reagan relished the symbol: Washington on his knees at Valley Forge, said Reagan on another occasion, was "the most sublime image in American history." In another line in his second inaugural, Reagan said, "We raise our voices to the God who is the Author of this most tender music." That most tender music was "the American sound"—"hopeful, big-hearted, idealistic, daring, decent, and fair." That sound was America's "heritage."

Reagan's faith was a Christian faith, which he was bold in expressing explicitly. When asked before and during his presidency, he eagerly described himself as a "born again" Christian.[8] In the late 1970s, Adrian Rogers, leader of the Southern Baptist Convention, asked Reagan if he was "born again" and had "Jesus in his heart." He answered yes, replying that God is "real" to him, and that he had a personal experience when he "invited Christ" into his life. Rogers pressed: "Do you know the Lord Jesus or do you only know *about* Him?" Rogers said Reagan declared, "I *know* Him."[9]

Reagan said he "never had any doubt" that the words of the Bible—which he once cited as his favorite book[10]—were of divine origin. He was a consistent churchgoer his entire life, with the exception of the presidency, when he viewed his presence in a church as not merely a major disruption for worshippers—a "burden," as he usually described it—but a fiasco for all.[11] A man who did in fact frequently pray, mainly in private, he once said he couldn't remember a time in his life when he didn't "call upon God." He felt that the foundation of law must be grounded in certain Biblical absolutes, saying: "I have always believed that the body of man-made law must be founded upon the higher natural law."[12] Reagan seemed to know the Bible, and there is clear evidence in handwritten speeches, radio broadcasts, and letters that he read and could recall verses from the book.

Throughout the Presidential Handwriting File at the Reagan Library, one can find example after example of Reagan personally handwriting religious phrases and verses into speeches produced by his speechwriters. Peter Robinson, who wrote the historic June 1987 "Tear down this wall!" speech, recalls a meeting in the Oval Office in which Reagan stood up, walked to a bookshelf, grabbed a Bible, and turned to a passage he wanted inserted into a speech.[13] (Robinson remembers the phrase to be, "I will be their God, and they will be my people."[14]) One can personally view innumerable religious changes and additions to speeches by Reagan himself.[15]

As president, Reagan's various testimonies and demonstrations of faith were ubiquitous. He invoked God in inaugurals, prayer breakfasts, radio addresses, or during remarks to the U.S. Chamber of Commerce, the Boy Scouts, in Red Square, or to any university. He quoted Scripture not merely before the National Conference on Christians and Jews or to the 1988 Student Congress of Evangelism but also before the U.S. League of Savings Associations, the Air and Space Bicentennial Year Ceremony, and the American Bar Association.

His innumerable religious reflections were made in varied contexts, most to non-religious audiences and often in venues where secularists deemed such remarks inappropriate. His 1984 State of the Union contained ten references to God. His 1983 speech to the National Association of Evangelicals featured twenty-four references. If one tallied Reagan's multiple remarks on "God," "Creator," "Almighty," "The Lord," "Him," "Jesus," or other, the references would easily fall well over a thousand. These remarks were not merely the result of some speechwriter consciously plugging in religious phrases to, say, toss a bone to Christian conservatives.

In his 1990 autobiography, *An American Life*, Reagan repeatedly invoked God. No references to "religion," "God," "Christianity," or so on are indexed in the book to call attention to them. We read these references from the outset in the first few pages, as early as the prologue on page 12. He credits God with all the interventions in his early career that he felt were crucial to placing him on the path that ultimately led to the presidency. Like a broken record, over and over, on occasion after occasion, Reagan averred: "Then, one of those things happened that makes one wonder about God having a plan for all of us. . . ." There are God's "twists in the road," the choice of jobs and encounters and meetings, and, of course, "God's Plan"—both the "G" and "P" written in upper case by Reagan. God surely turned him away, he intimates, from that dream job at Montgomery Ward. Then there was that new teacher with a knack for teaching acting who just happened to arrive at Dixon High School just as Reagan got there. "Once again fate intervened," he interpreted the incidents, "as if God was carrying out His plan with my name on it." We are told to perceive God's Plan when Nancy enters his life. "If ever God gave me evidence that He had a plan for me, it was the night He brought Nancy into my life."[16]

In the book, Reagan makes constant references to prayer. This starts small, with a prayer before a football game. Then we read about him praying his first night in the White House. Then follow prayers for Anwar Sadat, for the Philippines and Marcos, before his summits at Geneva[17] and Reykjavik, in the note he left for incoming President George H. W. Bush in handing over the White House keys.[18] We read diary entries where he writes of his desire to help his agnostic father-in-law "turn to God" on his deathbed.[19]

We're surprised to read of him praying for John Hinckley, as he lay seriously wounded on a hospital bed. He asks God to forgive him for any bitterness he felt toward his would-be assassin.[20] We see him regularly thanking God in his memoir, such as for the January 1981 release of the U.S. hostages in Iran and the successful completion of the October 1983 Grenada mission. On the latter, his diary entry reads: "Success seems to shine on us and I thank the Lord for it. He has really held me in the hollow of His hand." He ends his 721-page memoir by asserting, "It truly is America the Beautiful, and God has, indeed, 'shed His grace on thee.'"[21]

These are just some of the references to God in Reagan's memoir.[22] That autobiography alone seems to make it obvious that religious faith was a part of his life. And it certainly doesn't stop there.[23] There are religious statements throughout his private correspondence as president.

Once one understands the Christian foundation of Reagan, numerous other things about him become clear. His unappreciated hatred of bigotry toward Jews,[24] Blacks,[25] Catholics,[26] and other groups was derived from his father, mother, and sense of fairness and right and wrong.[27] But his opposition to bigotry was also religion based.[28] The Biblical opposition to bigotry was, in Reagan's mind, simple: "The commandment given us is clear and simple: 'Thou shalt love thy neighbor as thyself.'" That commandment, Reagan insisted, rejected racism. This he noted in personal letters and in no less than the Evil Empire speech. Bigotry and racism were a "sin" and "moral evil," he said in the Evil Empire speech, which he had a Christian responsibility to "denounce" and oppose "with all [my] might."[29] (To the contrary, some critics accused Reagan of racism, a charge that probably bothered him more than any other.)

As president, Reagan urged that "religion and politics are necessarily related" because "politics and morality are inseparable." He added: "morality's foundation is religion."[30] These words were similar to those of America's first president. "Of all the dispositions and habits which lead to political prosperity," said George Washington in his Farewell Address, "religion and morality are indispensable supports . . . morality is a necessary spring of popular government." He added: "morality [cannot] be maintained without religion."[31] Reagan was well aware of this Washington warning, stating: "Washington . . . believed that religion, morality, and brotherhood were the essential pillars of society, and he said you couldn't have morality without the basis of religion."[32] Reagan quoted that Washington line on numerous occasions.[33]

The Bible, Reagan felt, had all the answers. "I'm accused of being simplistic at times," he said often. "But within that single Book are all the answers to all the problems that face us"—a view he offered over and over.[34] (Only four days later he repeated that view, calling "God's word and the Bible"—"the greatest message ever written."[35]) Reagan speechwriter Ben Elliott says that although that statement was an "annoyance" to some, even some on Reagan's staff, Reagan "believed that devoutly." Elliott recalled that when Reagan used that line before the National Religious Broadcasters convention, it "brought the house down." The audience responded with a standing ovation. Reagan was "thrilled" with the response, said Elliott.[36] This sentiment was expressed early and often by Reagan, from at least the 1960s through the 1980s.[37]

Reagan feared what might happen to free societies when they scrapped religious faith. Speaking to Georgetown University in October 1988, he declared: "Tocqueville said it in 1835, and it's as true today as it was then: 'Despotism may govern without faith, but liberty cannot. Religion is more needed in democratic societies than in any other.'"[38] Indeed, Reagan believed that one thing that "must never change" for America is that "men and women" must "seek Divine guidance in the policies of their government and the promulgation of their laws," as he said in August 1980.[39]

An understanding of Reagan's stance on certain policy issues—from education to capital punishment to abortion to even taxation[40]—can be gained through a close look at his religious beliefs. Chief among those positions was his anti-communism.

CONFRONTING SOVIET COMMUNISM

On March 8, 1983, Ronald Reagan shocked sensibilities worldwide when he declared the USSR the "focus of evil in the modern world." It was an "Evil Empire." Why he did he see the USSR as an evil empire? Obviously, in part, because of its repression of basic civil liberties, the crimes and killing sponsored by the Soviet state, and the expansionary philosophy that governed Marxism-Leninism. Yet, there were other key characteristics of the Soviet regime that influenced Reagan's view that the USSR was an Evil Empire. At the top of the list was the atheism of Soviet communism, which the Bolshevik regime translated into an assault on religion.

James Billington said that Vladimir Lenin and his cohorts aimed for nothing less than "the extermination of all religious belief."[41] From inside the empire, Soviet historian Eduard Radzinsky said the Bolsheviks had created an "atheistic empire."[42]

In calling the Bolshevik effort a "war," Reagan acquired an unexpected ally a decade after the Evil Empire speech—Mikhail Gorbachev.

"Just like religious orders who zealously convert 'heretics' to their own faith, our [communist] ideologues carried out a wholesale war on religion," wrote Gorbachev in his memoirs.[43] In a later book, he wrote that the Bolsheviks, even after the civil war ended, during a time of "peace," had "continued to tear down churches, arrest clergymen, and destroy them. This was no longer understandable or justifiable. Atheism took rather savage forms in our country at that time."[44]

Today, Reagan's declaring the Soviet empire "evil" has lost its shock value; it is now seen as a statement of the obvious more than a controversial remark. Yet, what remains as controversial as unclear is this extraordinary question: Did Ronald Reagan sense that God had chosen him for a special purpose in the Cold War struggle, and, if so, what, specifically, was that special purpose?

The answer requires some hair splitting. I asked the question to the four men who not only advised Reagan on Cold War strategy as much as (in some cases, more than) any advisers in the 1980s but also worked closely with him well before his presidency, and in some cases far into the earliest gubernatorial years: Secretary of Defense Caspar Weinberger, National Security Advisers Richard V. Allen and William P. Clark, and Chief of Staff and Attorney General Edwin Meese. Before considering their responses, it is important to step back to March–April 1981.

On Good Friday 1981, a few weeks after the March 30 assassination attempt by John Hinckley, which very nearly took his life, Ronald Reagan was especially reflective about the "Plan" he long felt God had for him. He sought and received face-to-face counsel from New York's Terence Cardinal Cooke. "The hand of God was upon you," Cooke told Reagan. Reagan grew very serious. "I know," he replied, before confiding to the Cardinal: "I have decided that whatever time I have left is for Him."[45] Edmund Morris explains what Reagan meant by that: "Which meant, among other things, a coming to terms with Evil. Not the accidental evil . . . of John Hinckley's assault, but that institutional murder of all liberties known as Soviet communism."[46] Aside from telling this to Cardinal Cooke, Reagan previously had written in his diary on his first evening back from the White House after his hospital release: "I know it's going to be a long recovery. Whatever happens now I owe my life to God and will try to serve him every way I can."[47]

He didn't keep this strictly private. He took this personal issue public in a speech to the annual National Prayer Breakfast on February 4, 1982. "I've always believed that we were, each of us, put here for a reason, that there is a plan, somehow a divine plan for all of us. I know now that whatever days are left to me belong to Him."[48]

Another prominent Catholic shared somewhat similar thoughts with Reagan, namely Pope John Paul II. In a February 1992 investigative report for *Time* magazine, journalist Carl Bernstein reported that both the Pope and Reagan believed they had miraculously survived their 1981 assassination attempts—which were only six weeks apart—because God had saved them for a special mission. The article implied that they felt the mission was the defeat of communism in the Soviet bloc.[49] At their first meeting together, the two men met and talked alone for fifty minutes in the Vatican Library on Monday, June 7, 1982. Pio Cardinal Laghi, the postalic delegate to Washington, was told that Reagan said to the Pope: "Look how the evil forces were put in our way and how Providence intervened." Bernstein reported that Reagan's then-National Security Advisor and close friend, William P. Clark, said that each man referred to the "miraculous" fact that they had survived. He said they also shared "a unity of a spiritual view and a unity of vision on the Soviet empire: that right or correctness would ultimately prevail in the divine plan."[50]

Confirming and adding to that, Clark recalled this in a November 1999 interview with the *Catholic World Reporter*: "The Pope and the president shared the view that each had been given a spiritual mission—a special role in the divine plan of life. . . . [A]t the Vatican in June 1982 . . . the two men discussed the unity of their spiritual views, and their concern [for] the terrible oppression of atheistic communism."[51]

This mutual special thinking among the two men led to real action. They and their teams agreed to aid the Solidarity movement in Poland, aiming to sustain and keep it alive as the potential wedge that could split the USSR's empire in Eastern Europe. It could be the splinter to crack the Iron Curtain and spark the downfall of the communist bloc and the USSR. Reagan firmly believed precisely that, going back years prior to his presidency. On that day, Reagan and the Pope translated their sense of divine mission into a practical mission to maintain Solidarity.[52] Bernstein quotes a cardinal who was one of the Pope's closest aides:

> Nobody believed the collapse of communism would happen this fast or on this timetable. But in their first meeting, the Holy Father and the President committed themselves and the institutions of the church and America to such a goal. And from that day, the focus was to bring it about in Poland.[53]

This extraordinary fact—which also reflects Reagan's actual intent to try to crush communism—has been reported, although it still escapes much public knowledge. Most of the correspondence on this White House-Vatican effort remains classified.[54]

WHAT WAS THE "SPECIAL PURPOSE?"

Reagan perceived a Divine Plan for his country in combating the USSR. It is no coincidence that a favorite Reagan quote, which appears repeatedly (often verbatim) in his speeches and personal letters long before and during his presidency is a remark by the late Pope Pius XII: "Into the hands of America, God has placed an afflicted mankind."[55] Richard Norton Smith was blunt in his interpretation of what Reagan saw in store for American global leadership: "Ronald Reagan believed there was an Evil Empire. And Ronald Reagan believed that the United States was put here by God to combat the Evil Empire and prevail."[56] That, indeed, seems safe to say. Reagan did appear to sense that role for America. But what about his sense of self? Did Ronald Reagan see *himself* as chosen by God to defeat the Soviet empire?

Looking back, after his public service ended, Reagan specifically said that he felt God had chosen his "team"—which, of course, included him—to take on and defeat the USSR in the 1980s. In addition to what the record shows or suggests, William P. Clark was with him when he said this after the presidency.[57] Importantly, Reagan felt that only in retrospect might one know such a thing. He knew that he could not be certain of God's will ahead of time, and God surely had not spelled it out for him on stone tablets.

The more difficult question is whether Reagan believed prior or during his presidency that God had chosen him to take on the Soviet empire. In a sense, this would seem to be the obvious conclusion. Richard V. Allen, Reagan's foreign-policy adviser during his campaign years in the late 1970s and his first national security adviser as president, tells of an incident in January 1977, when Reagan told him categorically that his intent was to vanquish the Soviet empire. Allen separately notes that Reagan generally saw himself as a "handmaiden" or "instrument" of God. Many others have noted this as well, from the Pope and Clark to Reagan himself, among others.[58] So, one might naturally assume that Reagan saw himself as doing God's work in attacking the "evil," atheistic USSR. He did, of course, repeatedly predict the demise of Soviet communism publicly throughout the 1980s. And he did feel that God had a special plan for America in facing down the Soviet empire. Since he believed God's hand guided events, he must have felt that the Almighty surely guided this one—meaning an effort to undermine the Soviet empire—and, one would naturally surmise, was guiding Reagan himself in that endeavor as well.

Yet, logical as that may be, both Allen and Clark insist that Reagan was too humble to talk or even *think* that way about his own personal Cold War role. While Reagan felt that America had that special role from God, Allen and Clark say he would not say such a thing, or think in such a way, about himself.

Clark said that he never heard Reagan say explicitly that he felt God had chosen him for the specific purpose of taking on the USSR and its empire, nor that God had selected him in particular to *defeat* Soviet communism. "No," said Clark. "He did not say that because that would be out of character for him. He would speak more in the passive voice. 'The wall or Iron Curtain will come down.' 'It will come apart.' 'The Divine Plan,' or 'DP' as I called it, 'will prevail.' . . . He said things like that." "But," Clark clarifies, Reagan "did feel a calling, as I did, to this effort and the idea that truth would ultimately prevail. Not that *he* would prevail, but the truth will prevail."[59] In a March 2000 speech in San Francisco, Clark said that Reagan confidently told him and staff "several times both as governor and many times later as president," that, "The wall around atheistic communism is destined to come down within the Divine Plan because it lives a lie."[60] In a quite momentous assessment, Clark says that Reagan expected communism to fall "in his lifetime."[61] Also significant, in an August 2001 interview, Clark continued:

> I remember one day I was with him when someone congratulated him for taking down the wall. He said, "No, I didn't bring the wall down. That was part of the Divine Plan, teamwork, and God's Will." His number one maxim is that we can accomplish anything if we don't concern ourselves with who gets the credit. . . . He just had total confidence in the Divine Will. He was there as an instrument of God, and one of many. He would refer to teamwork. . . .
>
> He would not consider making a statement like, "I have been chosen by God to lead a crusade against the Evil Empire." That would be totally out of character. . . . He would consider that to be false pride. . . . This is an amazingly humble person. True humility. There was no pride there at all.[62]

Allen agrees that Reagan was too humble to think that way.[63] Clark said Reagan's humility would force him to credit his "team" overall as acting by God's hand. When once congratulated for "your success in ending the Cold War," Clark saw Reagan smile and reply, "No, not my success but a team effort by Divine Providence."[64] He saw God's hand in this "team effort" to win the Cold War. In hindsight, then, Reagan would look back at what happened, at his administration's role in the downfall of the USSR, and would cite God's hand in that end, vis-à-vis his team as a whole.

While having no personal knowledge of Reagan saying that, Ed Meese concedes the possibility. He, too, never heard Reagan say he felt chosen by God to defeat the USSR.[65]

In offering his view on this, Allen is very careful with his words. He states:

> I don't believe Reagan believed that God chose him to defeat the Soviet empire. But he did believe America was a chosen place. He would look back [after his presidency and the Cold War ended] and say something like: "Our team has fulfilled God's purpose." I think he would look back and say that. "We were part of the Divine Plan." He did, in fact, have a vibrant, vigorous faith that we could and would prevail against the USSR.[66]

But Allen is adamant in asserting that Reagan did not prior to or during his presidency ever say or believe God chose him specifically to defeat the USSR.

Perhaps the open question is to what extent Reagan sensed any "realization" or any sort of "calling" *prior* to when it happened. Allen and Clark say he did not. Meese never heard him say such a thing.

However, we know he believed that he (and America) had a special purpose. He said so. He told this to Cardinal Cooke and others. He wrote about it. *Time* reported on it. His aides noted it. Morris said this "meant, among other things, a coming to terms with Evil," meaning "that institutional murder of all liberties known as Soviet communism."[67] Meese acknowledges that the special purpose Reagan had in mind was "probably something important relating to the USSR. I believe his 'special purpose' was related to setting in motion the forces that would ultimately lead to ending the Cold War."[68] In fact, the record shows he poured his efforts into directing that nation and himself toward a deliberate attempt to rollback an atheistic ideology and defeat an atheistic empire.

Caspar Weinberger is also cautious. "I heard him say to me and others two to three times that he had a very strong feeling after he was spared in the assassination attempt," Weinberger remembered, "that he felt he had been spared for a particular purpose, which made him all the more determined to carry out the things he wanted to do. . . . It was for a purpose, not just a random occurrence." When asked if this purpose was specifically to undo the Soviet empire, Weinberger demurs: "I don't think it was quite that specific. He had a lot of ideas that were difficult to enact. I think it was more of a general purpose regarding his ideas, persevering amid criticism and ridicule, and following his course." "That included," Weinberger added, "him continuing his war against communism."[69]

We need to be picky on this matter. It is quite something to allege that Reagan believed God chose him to attack and defeat the Soviet empire. That is historically quite noteworthy in that it would speak (dramatically so) to Reagan's deepest motivations. Historians would underscore the matter for generations when assessing Reagan's thinking. Historians aside, for many Americans—particularly those of the Christian faith or those who believe in God generally, which comprise upwards of tens to hundreds of millions of Americans—this question may be one of the most important, and certainly one of the most intriguing, about Reagan.

In sum, we can definitively say this: According to his aides and own words, in the end Ronald Reagan felt God had chosen his "team" to defeat the USSR. Though he himself did not directly make the first-person distinction when he was heard crediting his "team," he, of course, was at the head of his team. Thus, his team meant himself as well.

CONCLUSION

Ronald Reagan's devout Protestant faith greatly impacted his life and presidency. That fact stood largely unacknowledged throughout the 1980s and in Reagan scholarship. In large part, the sincerity of his faith came under fire as a result of legitimate questions about Reagan's lack of church attendance as president and over his wife's admitted consultations with an astrologer named Joan Quigley in the 1980s (issues I've dealt with in depth in a more comprehensive work[70]). Only now is the significance of Reagan's faith beginning to receive deserved attention.

His faith informed his view of the USSR as an atheistic, godless—indeed, evil—empire. We can not fully understand Ronald Reagan, including his Cold War actions, without first knowing the influence of religion on him. Observers can reject or embrace Reagan's thinking in that regard, or stand unaffected, but the fact is that it was there, it was real to him, and it was consequential. Further, how he applied his perspective to the USSR was the central calling of his lifetime.

Alzheimer's felled Reagan only a few short years after the USSR fell onto that ash-heap of history he predicted. He lived to see it happen, and he did in fact seek to facilitate that end for Soviet communism.[71] He pursued a forty-year-plus campaign against it. Part of this crusade, as he himself said, was motivated by his belief that as a Christian he was "enjoined by Scripture" to resist and attack evil wherever it lurks. He saw his confrontation with communism as a spiritual one. He told a Joint Session of the Irish National Parliament on June 4, 1984 that the "struggle between freedom and totalitarianism today" was ultimately not a test of arms or missiles "but a test of faith and spirit." It was, he said, a "spiritual struggle."[72]

Reagan's story, then, is not simply a story of an influential man in a powerful position at some point coming to think that God had chosen him for some unique reason. Reagan's religious faith was a critical factor in one of the most important events of the twentieth century. It had an immense impact on his thinking and action toward Soviet communism and the Cold War. As the Soviets themselves recognized in a formal statement from TASS, the official Soviet news agency, "President Reagan uses religion with particular zeal to back his anti-Soviet policy."[73]

Obviously, this is not to assert that his faith caused communism's downfall. But it was intricately tied to that end goal. For most individuals driven by religious thinking, their faith might merely affect those around them. For Reagan, however, it drove what he did in the supreme ideological contest of the 20th century. And that is a side of Ronald Reagan that history and scholars can no longer ignore.

NOTES

1. See my book: Paul Kengor, *God and Ronald Reagan* (NY: Regan-Books/HarperCollins, 2004).

2. Anne Edwards, *Early Reagan: The Rise to Power* (NY: Morrow, 1987), p. 75.

3. This includes his 1964 "Time for Choosing" speech, his 1976 and 1980 convention speeches, his 1981 inaugural address, his 1989 "Farewell Address," and his 1992 "goodbye" speech to the Republican convention. In the major speeches pivotal to Reagan's presidential path, he mentioned God in a meaningful (and often dramatic) way.

4. This address is known as "The Creative Society" speech. For a transcript, see: Ronald Reagan, *The Creative Society* (NY: Devin Adair, 1968), pp. 1-14.

5. Herbert E. Ellingwood, "Ronald Reagan: 'God, Home and Country,'" *Christian Life*, November 1980, p. 25; and William Rose, "The Reagans and Their Pastor," *Christian Life*, May 1968, p. 44.

6. Quoted in Nancy Reagan and Bill Libby, *Nancy* (NY: William Morrow, 1980), p. 168. Also see: Lou Cannon, *Ronnie and Jesse: A Political Odyssey* (Garden City, NY: Doubleday, 1969), pp. 130-1; Joseph Lewis, *What Makes Reagan Run? A Political Profile* (NY: McGraw-Hill Book Co., 1968), pp. 159-60; and Reagan, "First Inaugural Message as Governor of California," 1967, published in *Ronald Reagan Talks to America* (Old Greenwich, CT: Devin Adair, 1983) p. 20.

7. See Reagan's draft of his Second Inaugural, located in PHF, PS, RRL, Box 17, Folders 325-326.

8. William Rose, "The Reagans and Their Pastor," *Christian Life*, May 1968, p. 46; and Marjorie Hyer, "Reagan, Carter, Anderson: Three 'Born Again' Christians Who Differ on Meaning," *Washington Post*, July 25, 1980, p. A28. Other 1970s and 1980s sources are cited later.

9. Bob Slosser, *Reagan Inside Out* (Waco, TX: Word Books, 1984), pp. 48-51.

10. Jerry Griswold, "'I'm a sucker for hero worship,'" *The New York Times Book Review*, August 30, 1981, p. 11.

11. I examine this issue at length in my book *God and Ronald Reagan*.

12. "Reagan on God and Morality," *Christianity Today*, July 2, 1976, p. 39.

13. Interview with Peter Robinson, September 18, 2001.

14. The phrase occurs a number of times in the Old Testament, including in Jeremiah 31:33.

15. For examples, see Kengor, *God and Ronald Reagan*.

16. See: Ronald Reagan, *An American Life* (NY: Simon and Schuster, 1990), pp. 49, 57, 70, 123.

17. In a nationwide address, Reagan asked his fellow Americans to "pray for God's grace and His guidance for all of us at Geneva." Reagan, "Address to the Nation, November 14, 1985," *Presidential Papers*, 1985, Vol. 2, p. 1391.

18. See: Reagan, *An American Life*, pp. 56, 229, 263, 292, 365, 722.

19. Ibid, pp. 319 and 321.

20. Ibid. Also see: Morris, *Dutch* p. 429.

21. See: Reagan, *An American Life*, pp. 236, 455, 721.

22. For other examples, see, among others not cited: pp. 252, 261-3, 307, 379, and 459.

23. Among older remarks, see: Reagan, "America the Beautiful," commencement address, William Woods College, Fulton, Missouri, June 1952. Published in college's *Echoes From the Woods*, June 1952.

24. Edmund Morris called Reagan "the best friend Israel ever had" in the White House. On his confronting anti-semitism, see, among other sources: Ronald Reagan with Richard Hubler, *Where's the Rest of Me?* (NY: Duell, Sloan & Pearce, 1965), p. 9; George S. Smith, *Who Is Ronald Reagan?* (New York: Pyramid Books, 1968), p. 38; and Anne Edwards, *Early Reagan: The Rise to Power* (NY: Morrow, 1987), pp. 203-4. On his celebrating America's embrace of both Jews and Christians, see his June 1952 speech, "America the Beautiful," William Woods College.

25. One of Reagan's first exposures to injustice toward blacks was his father's revulsion at how blacks were portrayed in *The Birth of a Nation*, which his father boycotted. This made an indelible impression on Reagan. He frequently referred to the incident. Among others, see Reagan's *Where's the Rest of Me?*, p. 8. Also, key religious figures in his early life, such as Ben Cleaver, detested bigotry, not to mention his mother. It has been rarely noticed that Reagan, along with Ginger Rogers and Doris Day, made an anti-KKK film through Warner Bros. in 1951 called *Storm Warning*. In addition, he was involved in a number of Hollywood efforts against the KKK and on behalf of Black Americans. For a solid treatment, see: Stephen Vaughn, *Ronald Reagan in Hollywood: Movies and Politics* (NY: Cambridge University Press, 1994), pp. 11 and 171-87.

26. Reagan was deeply troubled by anti-Catholic bigotry he saw early in life. Part of Reagan's tolerance stems from the fact that his father was Catholic.

27. See: Reagan, *An American Life*, p. 20; and Reagan and Hubler, *Where's the Rest of Me?*, pp. 8-9.

28. Among many pre-presidential sources on Reagan's lack of prejudice, see: Frank van der Linden, *The Real Reagan* (NY: William Morrow, 1981), pp. 39-40, 46, 80-1, and 256.

29. Reagan, "Remarks at the Annual Convention of the National Association of Evangelicals in Orlando, Florida, March 8, 1983," Presidential Papers, Volume 1, 1983, p. 362. Also see: Reagan private letter to Rev. Kenneth Bowling, January 29, 1985, located in PHF, PR, RRL, Box 11, Folder 164.

30. Robert G. Hoyt, "Reagan as Defensor Fidei: Politics, Religion, Confusion," *Christianity and Crisis*, September 17, 1984, p. 316.

31. W. B. Allen, ed., *George Washington: A Collection* (Indianapolis: Liberty Fund, 1988), p. 521.

32. "Remarks at Kansas State University at the Alfred M. Landon Lecture Series on Public Issues, September 9, 1982," *Public Papers of the Presidents of the United States, Ronald Reagan, 1982*, Book II—July 3 to December 31, 1982 (Washington, DC: U.S. Government Printing Office, 1983), p. 1122.

33. Among the many examples, he quoted the line on August 3, 1982, January 26, 1984, March 6, 1984, August 23, 1984, November 3, 1984, to cite a few.

34. Reagan, "Remarks at Annual Convention of NRB, January 31, 1983," p. 152. For example to a secular audience: "President's News Conference, February 21, 1985," *Presidential Papers*, Vol. 1, 1985, p. 200.

35. Reagan, "Remarks at the Annual National Prayer Breakfast, February 3, 1983," p. 178.

36. Interview with Ben Elliott, September 20, 2001.

37. In the 1960s, he said it as governor, specifying Jesus as part of the equation: "[T]he answer to each and every problem is to be found in the simple words of Jesus of Nazareth." As president, he said it on February 4, 1982 and January 30, 1984. For full citations, see Kengor, *God and Ronald Reagan*.

38. Reagan, "Remarks at Georgetown University's Bicentennial Convocation, October 1, 1988," *Presidential Papers*, 1988-89, p. 1264.

39. Reagan, "Address to the Roundtable National Affairs Briefing," Dallas, Texas, August 22, 1980. Speech text located at Reagan Library, "Reagan 1980 Campaign Speeches, August 1980," vertical files.

40. I devote a full chapter to this in *God and Ronald Reagan*.

41. James Billington, "Christianity and History," 125th anniversary lecture series, Grove City College, Grove City, Pennsylvania, September 27, 2001.

42. Radzinsky speaking in interview for A&E Biography of Joseph Stalin, "The Red Terror."

43. Mikhail Gorbachev, *Memoirs* (NY: Doubleday, 1996), p. 328.

44. Mikhail Gorbachev, *On My Country and the World* (NY: Columbia University Press, 2000), pp. 20-1.

45. There are slight variations on the exact quote, though all are near identical in language and clear in precise meaning. This is the more common quote cited, including by Edmund Morris. The only witness was Mike Deaver, who arranged for Cooke to meet with the president. He remembered Reagan saying: "I have decided that whatever time I may have left is for Him." Michael Deaver, *A Different Drummer: My Thirty Years with Ronald Reagan* (NY: HarperCollins, 2001), pp. 145-7.

46. Edmund Morris, *Dutch: A Memoir of Ronald Reagan* (NY: Random House, 1999), pp. 434-35.

47. Reagan, *An American Life*, p. 263; and Morris, *Dutch*, p. 432.

48. Reagan remarks to the annual National Prayer Breakfast, February 4, 1982, published in Frederick J. Ryan Jr., ed., *Ronald Reagan: The Wisdom and Humor of the Great* Communicator (San Francisco: Collins Publishers, 1995), p. 108. The fact that he felt he had been spared for a special purpose has been well told by staff and his own family. Among many others, including his family, see: Michael Reagan with Joe Hyams, *On the Outside Looking In* (NY: Kensington Publishing, 1988), p. 198; Patti Davis, *Angels Don't Die: My Father's Gift of Faith* (NY: HarperCollins, 1995), p. 38; and Maureen Reagan, *First Father, First Daughter* (Boston: Little, Brown and Company, 1989), p. 279.

49. Carl Bernstein, "The Holy Alliance," *Time*, February 24, 1992, pp. 28 and 30. Reagan expressed his shock and prayers to the Pope in a May 13, 1981 cable on the assassination attempt, in ES, NSC, HSF: Records, Vatican: Pope John Paul II, RRL, Box 41, Folder "Cables 1 of 2."

50. Bernstein, "The Holy Alliance," pp. 28 and 30.

51. "The Pope and the President: A key adviser reflects on the Reagan Administration," interview with William P. Clark, *Catholic World Reporter*, November 1999.

52. This is seen in a number of sources. I detail the issue at length in my next book on Reagan.

53. Carl Bernstein, "The Holy Alliance," *Time*, February 24, 1992, p. 35.

54. Examples of the secrecy are seen in fully redacted documents at the Reagan Library, located in ES, NSC, HSF: Records, Vatican: Pope John Paul II, RRL, Box 41, Folders "Cables 1 of 2" and "Cables 2 of 2."

55. It was the last line of his July 6, 1976 nationally televised speech marking the bicentennial, followed only by his three-word sign off: "God bless America." Reagan, "Nationally Televised Address," ABC-TV, July 6, 1976. Speech filed at Reagan Library, "RWR—Speeches and Articles (1974-76)," vertical files. Also see statements on January 25, 1974, June 6, 1974, June 1975 radio broadcast, April 30, 1981, May 27, 1981, February 6, 1984, December 19, 1984 letter. See full citations in Kengor, *God and Ronald Reagan*.

56. Smith speaking during interview on "Reagan," *The American Experience*, PBS-WGBH, February 1998.

57. The exact quote is cited later in this section. See: Clark in Peter Schweizer, ed., *The Fall of the Berlin Wall* (Stanford, CA: Hoover Institution Press, 2000), p. 75.

58. Interview with Richard V. Allen, November 12, 2001.

59. Interview with Allen.

60. William P. Clark, "President Reagan and the Wall," Address to the Council of National Policy, San Francisco, California, March 2000, p. 2.

61. Interview with Clark.

62. Interview with Clark.

63. Interview with Allen.

64. Clark shared this during a February 22, 1999 presentation in Washington, DC. For a transcript, see: Clark in Schweizer, *Fall of the Berlin Wall*, p. 75.

65. Interview with Ed Meese, November 23, 2001.

66. Interview with Allen.

67. Edmund Morris, *Dutch*, pp. 434-35.

68. Interview with Ed Meese, November 23, 2001.

69. Interview with Caspar Weinberger, October 10, 2002.

70. See: Kengor, *God and Ronald Reagan*.

71. This is the focus of my next work on Reagan. I detail at length the fact that he intended this Soviet end.

72. Reagan, "Address Before a Joint Session of the Irish National Parliament," Ireland, June 4, 1984.

73. TASS statement, September 11, 1984, published as "Reagan Uses Religion to Support Anti-Soviet Policy," in *FBIS*, FBIS-13-SEP-84, September 13, 1984, pp. A4-5.

11

The Six-Year War: Intelligence Oversight in the Reagan Years

Jeff Chidester and Stephen F. Knott

No issue between the Reagan administration and Congress proved to be more contentious than the debate over covert operations, as Congress, eager to preserve a host of intelligence oversight powers gained in the mid-1970s, confronted an administration committed to returning power over clandestine operations to the executive branch. Since the nation's founding, the executive had the authority, with very little involvement from the legislature, to conduct secret operations in the interests of national security. This system prevailed until 1975 when, following the Watergate Scandal and the exposure of a series of abuses by the CIA and FBI, Congress dramatically expanded its oversight powers. Between 1975 and 1980, as the Imperial Presidency gave way to the Imperiled Presidency, Congress solidified this authority, effectively gaining equal partnership over covert operations.

When Ronald Reagan took over the White House in January 1981, he sought to restore presidential power over clandestine operations. Reagan felt it was imperative to keep this power in the hands of the executive if America was to maintain "a vigorous intelligence agency, capable of acting swiftly and in secret," a belief strongly supported by his new CIA Director, William J. Casey.[1] Casey had a disdain bordering on contempt for the new authority Congress asserted over the intelligence community. As a former member of the Office of Strategic Services (OSS), the forerunner of the CIA, he was a throwback to the days when the intelligence community consisted primarily of agents, not lawyers and bureaucrats, and clandestine operations were performed in secret, not debated on the front pages of American newspapers.

As a result, the Reagan administration and Congress engaged in a six-year battle over the right to control covert operations, during which time a Democratic Congress opposed nearly every facet of the administration's agenda. The focus of this conflict was the White House's policy in Central America, particularly aid to the Contras in Nicaragua. Frustrated by what the administration saw as Congress' attempts to micro-manage the executive branch, some members of the administration pursued illegal means to implement the President's agenda, a move which nearly led to the collapse of the Reagan presidency. In the wake of the Iran-Contra affair and well into the 1990s, Congress tightened its grip on covert policy through greater, more restrictive procedures, further debilitating an already weakened CIA and contributing to a series of disastrous intelligence failures in the coming years.

PROLOGUE: THE CIA AND CONGRESS, 1947–1975

The modern American national security state was born on July 26, 1947, with the passage of the National Security Act. This act merged the Navy and the War Department, along with the newly created Department of the Air Force, into a Department of Defense. It also established the National Security Council and created the Central Intelligence Agency, "for the purpose of coordinating the intelligence activities of the several Government departments and agencies." The act cryptically referred to the CIA's responsibility to "perform such other functions and duties" affecting national security, a provision interpreted by President Harry S Truman and his successors to permit covert operations.[2] Within months of its founding the CIA was intervening in the internal affairs of Italy and France, promoting opposition to the communist parties in those nations, and shortly thereafter the agency toppled regimes in Iran in 1953 and Guatemala in 1954. Those operations marked the beginning of the CIA's Cold War role in fighting an "invisible war" in the back alleys of the world.

In keeping with American practice dating back to the Revolutionary War, control of this clandestine arm of government was lodged with the President, with minimal congressional oversight. It was believed, by members of both parties, that the President needed this discretionary authority to effectively conduct secret operations, and it was also understood that the Soviet Union and its allies were a clear and present danger to the "Free World." However, it would be a mistake to assume, as many scholars have, that Congress was effectively "out of the loop" when it came to congressional oversight of intelligence during the early years of the Cold War. The House and Senate Armed Services and Appropriations Committees, particularly their powerful chairmen and other senior members, reviewed the CIA's budget and were kept informed of large-scale covert operations. Powerful Senators and Congressmen such as Carl Vinson, Clarence Cannon, and Richard Russell chaired the aforementioned Armed Services and Appropriations Committees, and as one CIA veteran later remarked, "they knew our appropriations line by line." Richard Russell once told the agency's congressional liaison that "there isn't a single member of this Senate that's so lowly that he can't make life unbearable for you fellows if he decides he wants to do it."[3]

Nonetheless, this system collapsed in the mid-1970s in the wake of the Vietnam War, the Watergate Scandal, and revelations of CIA and FBI abuses. Junior members of Congress, particularly the Watergate "Class of 1974," were convinced that their leadership had failed to check the power of the "Imperial Presidency," and in particular check the secret agencies at the president's disposal. These "Imperial Presidents" had hijacked the Constitution, so it was argued, and preempted the delicate system of checks and balances. Secrecy itself was seen as illegitimate, and the prevailing sentiment of the time was that democratized, open policy making would prevent future Vietnams. It was in this atmosphere that two congressional committees began to investigate the CIA in early 1975: the Senate Committee, Chaired by Frank Church of Idaho, and the House Committee, Chaired by Representative Otis Pike of New York, exposed a lengthy list of abuses by the CIA, including assassination plots against foreign leaders, domestic intelligence operations against the anti-war movement, mail openings, drug testing against unwitting citizens, and the use of clergymen and journalists for intelligence purposes. These incidents led one of Senator Church's investigators to conclude that the United

States had become the very vision of an "Orwellian Nightmare," and for Church to conclude that a new breed of President, quite unlike any seen before, believed in fighting "evil with evil."[4] The fact that these "abuses" had occurred in an era of greatly expanded civil rights and civil liberties was ignored by the critics, as was the fact that many of these "abuses" had been accepted American practice for 200 years. Also lost was the understanding that the CIA was engaged in a struggle with a Soviet regime that had no regard for ethics or due process; apparently, by the mid-1970s the nation had transcended, as Jimmy Carter put it, its "inordinate fear of communism."

The Church and Pike investigations occurred during the illusory era of détente with the Soviet Union, when the consensus about the nature of communism dissolved. The United States was seen as equally culpable for the conflict with the Soviet Union, and the CIA was the covert instrument by which America's Cold War Presidents flaunted the Constitution and aggravated tensions around the globe. In response to proposals from both the Church and Pike Committees, the Senate created the Select Committee on Intelligence in May 1976, and the House established the Permanent Select Committee on Intelligence in July 1977. With their creation, the United States granted its legislative branch the greatest amount of control of any Western democracy over intelligence matters, and thereby began the slow process of converting a once creative, talent rich, risk-taking agency into yet another cautious, risk averse, sclerotic bureaucracy.

REAGAN AND THE RESTORATION OF THE CIA

Ronald Reagan was more than an interested spectator as the CIA was probed and reformed in the mid-1970s, and that experience shaped his views toward the intelligence community and congressional oversight when he entered the White House. In 1975, President Gerald Ford asked Reagan to join the Rockefeller Commission, an eight-member body headed by Vice President Nelson Rockefeller, which was created to investigate allegations of CIA abuses. Ford hoped to preempt any congressional investigations that might do harm to the intelligence community, but his gambit did not succeed. Reagan joined the commission out of similar fears that the congressional investigations would lead to a wholesale assault on the intelligence community. In a private letter he admitted, "I accepted because I feel there are those in Washington who would like to destroy the CIA and the FBI."[5] Working on the Rockefeller Commission only served to confirm Reagan's belief in the necessity of a strong intelligence force. He admitted there had been cases of wrongdoing by the CIA, but argued that they had been blown widely out of proportion by an overwrought media and capitalized on by a Congress eager to reassert its authority in the wake of the Nixon presidency. Two months after the release of the commission's report, Reagan, then a California citizen who broadcast a daily radio commentary, told his radio audience that the investigation was "much ado about—if not nothing—at least very little," and decried the media for exaggerating the report in the name of "more exciting drama."[6]

What concerned Reagan most about the investigations of the mid-1970s was not the damage done to the CIA's image, but rather the effect that the new oversight powers given to Congress would have on America's national security. He frequently reminded his radio listeners that an effective intelligence force was just as important to national security as the military and that Congress was doing "inestimable harm" to these capabilities through restrictive oversight. Reagan said the "insane restriction" of the CIA and FBI was dangerous at this time because "we are flying blind at a time when we need both agencies capable of conducting counterespionage."[7] He asked, "Isn't it time for someone to ask if we aren't threatened more by the people the FBI and the CIA are watching than we are by the FBI and the CIA?"[8] His solution to this problem was laid out during a February 1977 speech to the Conservative Political Action Conference: "Let's stop the sniping and the propaganda and the historical revisionism and let the CIA and other intelligence agencies do their job."[9]

Reagan reiterated this theme when he ran for President in 1980, arguing in his first major foreign policy speech of the campaign that the CIA should be able to operate without congressional restrictions. The United States, Reagan contended, "must once again restore the U.S. intelligence community. Senseless restrictions requiring the CIA to report any and all covert actions to eight congressional committees must be eliminated."[10] He continued to assert that an effective intelligence force was a key component of national defense and essential in the fight against communism. In a nationally televised speech delivered in October 1980, Reagan said America "must restore the ability of the CIA."[11]

When Reagan came to the White House in January 1981, he immediately set out to reinvigorate a battered and besieged CIA. In the struggle against Soviet communism, Reagan felt the CIA was indispensable in stopping Moscow's advances, particularly in the Third World, and he intended to give covert operations a much more prominent role in his foreign policy than his predecessors. One of the most critical decisions for Reagan was selecting a CIA Director that agreed with his views on covert action, and more importantly, someone he could trust. Indeed, shortly after the election, he met with Colonel Alexandre de Marenches, head of the French intelligence force, who stressed the importance of placing a trustworthy ally at Langley. Reagan took this advice to heart and passed on several highly recommended candidates from within the intelligence community in favor of his campaign manager, William Casey.

The Senate Intelligence Committee was also looking for someone it could trust, and Chairman Barry Goldwater (R-AZ) aggressively lobbied the President to select Admiral Bobby Ray Inman. Inman headed the National Security Agency during the Carter Administration, and was praised almost universally within the intelligence community as a man of talent. Goldwater made a personal plea on Inman's behalf to Reagan, promising that his appointment would bolster congressional support for the CIA, yet Reagan held firm with his choice of Casey.[12]

During his nomination hearings, Casey placated many on the Senate panel when he pledged not to dramatically reorganize the CIA. He also promised to work closely with the intelligence committees and keep them apprised of all covert operations.[13] Nonetheless, Casey did not shy away from his plans to reinvigorate his agency after a period of low morale and "institutional self-doubt."[14] He cautioned that too much congressional oversight could be detrimental to the efficacy of the agency, saying, "This is not the time for another bureaucratic shake-up of the CIA."[15] Goldwater reminded Casey of the great respect the committee had for Inman and of the committee's desire to see him as Deputy Director of Central Intelligence, which Casey intimated was his job if he wanted. Inman balked at the offer at first, but after a personal pitch from Reagan he accepted the post of DDCI.[16] Although the committees preferred to have Inman running the CIA, his selection for the number two spot allayed their concerns for the time being. The strength of this relationship, however, would be tested during the first dispute between Congress and the new Director of Central Intelligence.

CASEY AT THE BAT

That first test came just six months into the new administration with the appointment of Max Hugel as the CIA's Deputy Director of Operations, a position many considered the second most important job at Langley. It was clear that some in Congress were still reeling from the appointment of Casey instead of Inman and were waiting for an opportunity to find fault with the new DCI, and the appointment of Hugel, against the advice of both the intelligence community and the Senate committee, gave them an ideal opportunity to question Casey's judgment. After less than two months in office, the *Washington Post* uncovered a series of audio tapes showing Hugel giving away insider stock information to his associates, forcing his resignation on July 14. Casey quickly named John Henry Stein, a career CIA officer, as the new DDO.[17]

Just days after Hugel's resignation, Casey himself was placed under congressional investigation over apparent "inconsistencies" in his financial records regarding involvement in a New Orleans farming company called Multiponics, Incorporated. The investigation, coupled with the departure of Hugel, led many congressional Democrats to call for Casey's resignation. Goldwater admonished the press for making "a mountain out of a molehill" in trumping up the allegations made against Casey, and said he saw no reason at that time for Casey to leave the CIA. He went on to praise Casey for doing a "commendable job" as Director—with the exception of the Hugel incident—and said that "everything's going good at the agency."[18]

Yet behind this public show of support, there were growing signs of discontent with Casey's stewardship of the CIA during his first six

months in office. There was an obvious decline in consultation between top CIA officials and the oversight committees, a prospect
which threatened the inroads made by the Church and Pike investigations. Senate committee member David Durenberger (R-MN) said,
"we haven't seen much of Bobby [Inman] and we haven't seen much
of Bill [Casey]."[19] Less than a week later, Goldwater reversed his earlier position and publicly called for Casey to step aside as CIA Director. The Senator called a press conference at the Capitol specifically to
deny a CBS News report that he had privately asked Casey to resign,
but after fielding questions about the poor choice in selecting Hugel as
DDO, Goldwater became animated, calling the appointment "dangerous" and "the worst thing Casey has done," bad enough "for either Mr.
Casey to decide to retire or for the president to ask him to retire."[20] Fellow Republican committee members Senator William V. Roth Jr.
(R-DE) and Senator Ted Stevens (R-AK) agreed with Goldwater and
called for Casey's resignation. Roth released a statement saying, "He
should go—NOW." In addition, several other Senators, including
Durenberger and Harrison H. Schmitt (R-NM), indicated they, too,
were upset with Casey's performance and on the verge of calling for
his ouster.[21]

The administration moved quickly to Casey's defense. White
House spokesman David Gergen told the press "the president believes
that Bill [Casey] definitely ought to remain on the job." At the same
time, several of Casey's friends from the intelligence community
launched a public campaign to build support for the Director in Congress.[22] On July 29, Casey appeared before the Senate committee and
offered what many of the members wanted—an apology for the Hugel
appointment. This seemed to satisfy most of the members, particularly
Goldwater, who admitted it was about Hugel, not Multiponics, all
along: "Had he been able to get me on the phone that Saturday before
the [Hugel] story appeared in the *Post*, this probably never would
have come up."[23] He pledged to "get along" and "work hand in glove"
with Casey in the future. Other reports, however, indicated that Goldwater's calls for resignation had been moderated after a *Newsweek*
story reported that his man, Bobby Inman, would not be Casey's replacement even if Casey was fired. Although some members of the
Senate committee said there were still issues to be investigated fur-

ther, Casey's apology essentially ended the row and the committee concluded "there is no basis for concluding Mr. Casey is unfit to serve."[24]

The clash over the Hugel appointment sent an early message to the administration that Congress had serious doubts about Casey's judgment. Fortunately for Casey, and Reagan, Deputy Director Bobby Inman was held in such high esteem by the committees that he was able to dampen much of the displeasure aimed at the Director. In April 1982, Inman resigned as DDCI, removing Congress' only real source of trust and confidence in the CIA and delivering a significant blow to the administration's ability to conduct clandestine operations. Congress was quick to point out the gravity of the circumstances; Senate committee member Richard Lugar (R-IN) called it "a rather traumatic situation" for the agency. During a press conference, Lugar made clear his lack of confidence thus far in Casey and let the White House know that Congress expected consultation before choosing Inman's replacement. Several other committee members expressed their preference for an experienced officer as well. This was an unprecedented invasion into the administration's right to appointment. Nonetheless, the President abided by the request and selected John McMahon, a 31-year veteran of the CIA and the agency's current Executive Director, as Inman's successor.[25]

When McMahon made his first visit to members of the Senate Intelligence Committee, he discovered they were much more distrustful of Casey than he had assumed. They were concerned that Inman's departure deprived them of a reliable source on CIA covert operations—Inman had become the key component of the oversight process. When McMahon met with the Senate panel on May 26 and 27, one by one the Senators repeated their concerns and tried to gain assurances that he would keep them apprised not only of current operations, but also inform them of any of Casey's missteps. McMahon charmed the committee by stressing the need for congressional oversight and pledging to keep it fully informed in the future, and he was approved unanimously by the committee and later by the full Senate. When he returned to CIA headquarters in Langley, he had a simple message to Casey: it's time to make some friends in Congress.[26]

CENTRAL AMERICA

Although Casey was never able to gain the full confidence of Congress, the major source of contention during the Reagan years was not
personnel, but rather the administration's covert policies, particularly
in Central America. Both Casey and Reagan were deeply committed to
preventing the spread of communism in this region. In just his second
month in office, Reagan signed a Presidential Finding affirming the
need to stop the flow of arms to communist rebels in El Salvador. On
November 23, 1981, he signed National Security Decision Directive
17, which offered $19 million in aid to a 500-man Argentine paramil-
itary force aimed at stopping Nicaragua's Sandinista government from
supporting the rebels in El Salvador.[27] Both the House and the Senate
committees reacted with skepticism at this covert alliance with Ar-
gentina, a regime dominated by a corrupt military junta.

Support for the operation eroded quickly in Congress soon after the
"Contra" operation began in Nicaragua in mid-March 1982. House Intelligence Committee Chairman Edward Boland (D-MA) quickly lobbied to eliminate all funding for the operation, seeking to use the
budget as a de facto veto on the administration's agenda. Senator Goldwater wanted it to continue in some capacity, but he knew he would
have to compromise with the House committee, which had a solid majority against the operation. An August 1982 House-Senate conference
agreed to continue the operation, but issued a directive forbidding
funding "for the purpose of overthrowing the Government of
Nicaragua." Boland was satisfied until November when an article appeared in *Newsweek* magazine revealing the breadth of the Nicaragua
operation. It appeared as though the CIA had completely ignored Congress and was actively trying to overthrow the Sandinistas. When
Casey testified before the oversight panels, he admitted that the operation had widened in scope to a 4,000-man force, but he assured the
committees that the goal still remained arms interdiction, not regime
change.

For many members of the intelligence committees, this sounded like
the beginnings of a war, and some felt the only way to prevent this was
to go public with the operation.[28] Representative Tom Harkin (D-IA)
went on the floor of the House and proposed an amendment prohibit-

ing funding for all "military activities in or against Nicaragua." Although this garnered little support, another amendment was introduced by Edward Boland, who pledged to devote his personal attention to the "dirty little war" in Nicaragua. The so-called Boland Amendment, which gave legal standing to the directive passed in the August House-Senate conference, passed by a vote of 411 to 0 in the House.[29] When Reagan signed the amendment later that month, Congress, shrewdly using the power of the purse, scored a major victory in their fight to restrain the administration's agenda.

A few months later, Congress succeeded in halting another covert operation by protesting a plan to topple the government of Suriname. The administration saw a gathering danger in the small South American nation where Marxist-leaning Lieutenant Colonel Desi Bouterse was solidifying his authoritarian regime, raising the prospects of a possible Soviet foothold in South America. Casey wanted to overthrow Bouterse and replace him with a friendly government, so he had McMahon draw up an "enabling finding" which approved a limited covert action to determine whether a full operation was feasible. The Senate committee believed there was no reason for the U.S. to get involved in Suriname and was surprised the administration would even consider the proposal, particularly after the Nicaragua operation met with such strong protest months earlier. The administration eventually abandoned the plan after receiving letters of opposition from both the House and Senate committees, and also from Senator Goldwater, who asked President Reagan if the operation was really worth the political capital.[30]

After restricting Contra support through the Boland Amendment and hindering plans for action in Suriname, the Senate committee believed they had stopped the drive by the administration to reassert executive control over covert operations. Yet in reality the Nicaragua and Suriname debates had no tangible effect aside from causing Casey and other top CIA officials to become even less forthcoming to the oversight committees about ongoing and proposed operations. This became apparent in March 1983 when vivid accounts of Contra activities began to appear in the media, causing some in Congress to question whether the administration had ignored the Boland provisions. Although Congress was on Easter recess, several members made it clear that Nicaragua would be a major issue when they returned. Senate Intelligence Committee Vice Chairman Daniel Patrick Moynihan (D-NY) spoke of a growing "crisis of confidence" many in Congress felt over the apparent disregard of the Boland provisions, and Representative George Miller (D-CA) sent a letter, signed by 37 of his colleagues, to President Reagan urging "strict compliance" with the law.[31]

When Congress returned on April 5, Moynihan and fellow committee member Patrick Leahy (D-VT) went directly to the floor of the Senate and expressed alarm over the operation. Leahy charged the administration with "actively supporting, and perhaps even guiding, a large-scale anti-Sandinista guerrilla movement now involved in open combat inside Nicaragua," a clear breach of the law. There were questions on the Republican side of the aisle as well. Senate Majority Leader Howard Baker said "there is a great concern" about the Nicaraguan operation and Representative Jim Leach (R-IA) questioned the moral foundation of the operation, indicting the CIA as "the financers of anarchy" in Nicaragua.[32] On April 12, Casey, McMahon, and CIA General Counsel Stanley Sporkin met in a closed session with the Senate committee and argued that their actions had not exceeded the scope of the mission. Goldwater, frustrated by his colleagues' charges against the administration, went to the Senate floor after the meeting and defended the CIA, saying it was in compliance with both the letter and the spirit of the law.[33]

The House Intelligence Committee reached a different conclusion when it held a closed session the next day. During the meeting, Representative Wyche Fowler Jr. (D-GA) presented a detailed report on his recent visit to Central America and said that the CIA was not obeying the Boland Amendment. Boland agreed with Fowler and said, "the evidence is very strong . . . that there has been an apparent violation of law." That same day, an eight-member fact-finding group recently back from a trip to Nicaragua and Honduras said the administration was "deeply involved in covert activities aimed at overthrowing the Government of Nicaragua." One member of the mission, Representative Berkley Bedell (D-IA), went as far as to say that Nicaraguan women and children are being "kidnapped, tortured and killed by terrorists financed by the American taxpayers."[34] Unlike the Senate, there was a growing consensus in the House that the administration was breaking the law.

With support for the operation quickly waning, Reagan delivered an impassioned speech to Congress on April 27, 1983, urging them to reject "passivity, resignation, defeatism in the face of this challenge to freedom and security in our own hemisphere," and continue to support the Contras.[35] The address had little effect in the halls of Congress; Edward Boland and Clement Zablocki (D-WI) introduced a measure the next day to cut all funding for the operation and replace it with overt aid to governments willing to assist the U.S. in stopping the illegal arms flow into El Salvador. Boland told a local Massachusetts newspaper that "the covert action in Nicaragua ought to be stopped."[36] On May 3, the House Intelligence Committee voted 9 to 5, along party lines, to cut off all covert funding in Nicaragua, an action criticized by Reagan as "irresponsible."[37]

Meanwhile, the Senate committee, led by Republican David Durenberger, was working on a similar proposal to cut off funding, although support for Contra aid was still strong enough in the Senate to prevent its passage. Senator Goldwater introduced a compromise proposal to keep the operation intact while increasing congressional control over intelligence operations. Approved by a vote of 13 to 2, the measure gave $19 million in Contra aid until October 1, when the administration would have to present a new finding on Central America, and required that each new presidential finding be approved by a majority of the intelligence committee, marking an unprecedented assertion of authority by Congress over the use of clandestine operations. Many in Congress, including Edward Boland, saw this as an unnecessary usurpation of presidential power, but with the future of the operation at stake Casey accepted the vote.[38] The Senate measure, however, had no legal standing and Casey was in little hurry to abide by the vote. To the contrary, in mid-1983 the CIA increased the Contra forces to upwards of 12,000 to 15,000 men, and began to expand the use of economic warfare, most notably mining the harbors in Nicaragua.[39]

The CIA first informed the intelligence communities about the mining operations in early 1984. Casey briefed the House panel on January 31, and the Senate panel on March 8 and 13, and the CIA provided the committee staffers with a detailed account of the operation on April 2.[40] The problem was that Casey's disclosure was a single, 27-word sentence shrouded in 84 pages of testimony, and few, if any, committee members ever even saw the staff reports.[41] When news of the mining became public, Congress was furious with the apparent lack of notification by the CIA. Many of the members who voted to approve $21 million in covert aid to the Contras the previous week said they would have voted against the funding had the mining operation been known to them. On April 9, Goldwater sent a scathing letter to Casey accusing him of keeping the operation from the Senate committee and of making it difficult to defend the administration: "It gets down to one, little, simple phrase: I am pissed off!"[42]

The next day, the Senate overwhelmingly passed a non-binding "sense of the Senate" resolution, with the support of forty-one Republicans, condemning the operation and opposing the use of federal money for further mining. Senator Edward Kennedy (D-MA), the bill's sponsor, said the resolution showed the Senate felt "enough is enough."[43] A senior intelligence officer said, "the whole system of Congressional oversight has broken down. Right now, there's anarchy. Nobody's ever seen it this bad. Frankly, I'm not sure it will recover, at least not under the current leadership on the Hill and in the agency."[44] Senator Durenberger said "on a 0 to 10 scale, Casey rates a 2 on the trust factor."[45]

The CIA reacted with little remorse as it contended that both intelligence committees were properly informed. Members of both sides of the aisle agreed with this, including Senator Leahy and Congressman Boland. Leahy, no admirer of William Casey, observed at the time, "there were Senators who voted one way the week before and a different way the following week who knew about the mining in both instances and I think were influenced by public opinion, and I think that's wrong and that is a lousy job of legislative action."[46] Republican Senator Malcolm Wallop, a staunch supporter of the Nicaraguan operation, agreed with Leahy, telling ABC News that Congress was properly informed "and to claim otherwise is disingenuous."

On April 15, in an interview on "This Week With David Brinkley," Moynihan announced he was resigning his post as Vice Chairman of the Senate committee, saying it was "the most emphatic way I can express my view that the Senate committee was not properly briefed on the mining of Nicaraguan harbors."[47] Fearing a complete breakdown of the oversight process, Senator Lloyd Bentsen (D-TX) said, "I think it's time we had a cease-fire with the committee and the CIA." Bentsen and Senator Richard Lugar brokered a compromise where Casey apologized for failing to keep the committees properly informed about activities in Nicaragua, assured them that the mining operation had been stopped, and agreed to work on new ways to keep Congress better informed about CIA activities. After Casey's apology, Moynihan returned to his position on the Senate committee.[48]

The mining incident convinced the Senate panel that the only way to ensure that the committee would stay fully and clearly informed was through legal change. When Moynihan returned to the committee, he joined with Goldwater to construct a new series of disclosure procedures to prevent the recurrence of the mining controversy. Signed by Casey on June 6, the agreement guaranteed full congressional notification for three areas: (1) any change in an ongoing operation that goes beyond the original presidential finding, (2) any activity that requires approval by either the President or the National Security Council, and (3) any area within CIA jurisdiction that the committee has expressed particular interest or reservation. It also mandated a system of "regular updates" and an annual comprehensive briefing on continuing CIA operations. In *Veil: The Secret Wars of the CIA*, Bob Woodward said this agreement "effectively gave the committee a peephole into his [Casey's] office; they might as well tap his phone and assign someone to sit in his office and travel around with him, taking notes, rummaging through his desk drawers and files."[49]

The fallout from the mining operation become a liability for Reagan's 1984 reelection campaign, forcing Casey to stay under the radar of the intelligence committees and shelve any new proposals until after November. On October 17, a story appeared in the *New York Times* exposing a CIA-authored manual on insurgency and guerrilla warfare given to the Nicaraguan Contras, putting the actions of the CIA back in the headlines. The pamphlet, titled "Psychological Operations in Guerrilla Warfare," contained advice on a variety of rebel techniques, including assassination, a practice forbidden by executive order. Coming just six months after the mining debacle, and less than three weeks before the general election, the release of the manual posed a significant problem for the administration. Although Congress was on recess when the manual surfaced, there were immediate and widespread calls for investigations as to whether the administration was involved in the production of the booklet.

Many in Congress jumped on the apparent hypocrisy of the Reagan administration for condemning tactics used by nations like Libya, Iran and Syria, yet using them to advance their own aims in Central America. Congressman Thomas J. Downey (D-NY) asked, "Is it the position of our Government to hire killers?"[50] Edward Boland called the booklet "repugnant to a nation that condemns such acts by others," and "a disaster for American foreign policy." He said the sponsoring of assassination "embraces the communist revolutionary tactics that the United States is pledged to defeat throughout the world." Boland also pointed to the manual as further proof of CIA complicity in the drive "to overthrow the Sandinista government."[51]

A day after the *Times* story, Reagan ordered two separate investigations into the CIA's involvement in the production of the manual, one by the CIA's Inspector General and the other by the President's Foreign Intelligence Advisory Board. The White House maintained that Reagan knew nothing of the booklet until it surfaced in the news and suggested that it was the product of a low-level intelligence officer in Central America. White House spokesman Larry Speakes said plainly, "This Administration has not advocated or condoned political assassination nor any other attacks on civilians, nor will we." Dissatisfied with the administration's response, the House and Senate oversight committees launched their own probes into the incident. That same day, House Speaker Tip O'Neill called for Casey's resignation: "I say it's time Mr. Casey should leave his job. I want him to get out of there." O'Neill went on to call the CIA investigation a "whitewash" and said that if Casey kept his position "then it shows the President condones his actions."[52]

The Inspector General's investigation, completed shortly after the election, found a group of mid-level CIA officers responsible for the manual's production. The findings were endorsed by Reagan and approved by most members of Congress, including Boland, who said the report was "fair." When the House Intelligence Committee released its report the following month, it was highly critical of both the CIA and the administration for not keeping better track of the manual, which they called "repugnant" and an "embarrassment to the United

States." Some said the mid-level agents held responsible for the manual's release were merely "scapegoats" for a CIA known for its "extremely poor management" record. They also reiterated the notion that the administration was in clear breach of the Boland Amendment as the manual repeatedly offered strategies on how to overthrow the Sandinista government. Casey appeared before the House panel the day the report was released and took responsibility for the manual, pledging also to make changes in the agency's structure to prevent another such incident.[53]

The House report, delivered just four weeks after Reagan captured 59 percent of the popular vote and 49 states in the general election, signaled to the administration that Congress had no intention of giving the President a free pass on clandestine operations during his second term. In fact, with Senators Durenberger and Leahy replacing Goldwater and Moynihan as the committee leaders, greater opposition was virtually guaranteed. Both Leahy and Durenberger had a history of opposing the administration on covert operations, particularly in Central America; Durenberger, a Republican, introduced a proposal in April 1983 to cut off all funding to the Contras. In November 1985, Leahy and Durenberger joined together in opposing a CIA plan to undermine Libya's Muammar al-Qaddafi. Some of the opposition groups designated to receive the aid wanted to kill the Libyan leader, leading many on the oversight committee to charge the administration with tacitly approving assassination, a practice forbidden by U.S. law. Although the proposal had the support of a bare majority in each committee, Durenberger and Leahy drafted a joint letter to Reagan protesting the operation. The White House responded by denying any direct involvement in killing Qaddafi and asked the Senators to remove the word "assassination" from their letter, something that they refused to do.[54]

On November 3, the *Washington Post* revealed the anti-Qaddafi operation to the public along with the protest letter written by Durenberger and Leahy. The White House was furious when the operation became public and Reagan immediately blamed the oversight committees for leaking the information to the press in order to mobilize public opinion against the operation. Casey placed the blame specifically on Durenberger, who he said leaked the operation during "off the cuff" comments at a press luncheon. He then sent a public letter to

Durenberger, saying, "If the oversight process is to work at all, it cannot do so from the front pages of the American newspapers." This was a particularly awkward time for a leak—just weeks earlier, the "re-defection" of Soviet KGB official Vitaly Yurchenko was made public, greatly embarrassing the CIA.[55]

Both Leahy and Durenberger went quickly on the offensive. Durenberger wrote a public letter to the *Washington Post* refuting Casey's charges and affirming the need for a rigorous oversight system. Leahy accused the CIA of "yearning to go back to the good old days" of no oversight, to a time when the agency had made "some of the most colossal failures . . . ever."[56] The dispute between Casey and the Senate leadership was somewhat exaggerated in the press; in his letter, Durenberger made several positive comments about the CIA Director, calling him a "professional" and "a darn good guy in the job."[57] Nonetheless, it further highlighted how far the relationship between the CIA and the congressional oversight panels had deteriorated after nearly five years of Casey's tenure at Langley.

IRAN-CONTRA AND THE COLLAPSE
OF EXECUTIVE AUTHORITY, 1985–1989

In 1985, Congress tacked onto an appropriations bill language prohibiting the CIA or "any other agency or entity of the United States involved in intelligence activities" (Boland II) from spending funds in support of the Contras.[58] President Reagan was confronted with a difficult decision: if he vetoed the appropriations bill the government would be shut down; but signing it could signal the end for the Contras. He chose to sign the bill, but refused to accept this as the death knell for the Contras.

In the wake of Boland II, Reagan's National Security Council staff began to explore alternative methods for sustaining the Contras. While no evidence has ever been produced linking the President to the diversion of the Iranian arms sales funds to the Contras, it is clear that a general edict had been issued to keep Reagan's "freedom fighters" intact. Foreign governments and wealthy conservative Americans were asked to assist in the cause, and many did, including the Sultan of Brunei and

American beer magnate Joseph Coors. While these actions taken may have violated the spirit of the Boland Amendment, they were probably legal. Other elements of the NSC's plan were clearly illegal, most explicitly the diversion of funds from the arms sales to Iran into Swiss bank accounts. The media and many members of Congress immediately focused on William Casey as the likely ringleader in what was quickly dubbed the Iran-Contra Affair. While the operation had many of the hallmarks of the Director's penchant for "off the shelf" operations, it also had an amateurish quality that led others to conclude it was a scheme hatched by National Security Council staff.

No one knew it at the time, but William Casey was entering his final days as CIA Director in the fall of 1986, at the very moment when the confrontation with Congress was about to come to a head. The jousting with intelligence committees over the first six years of the administration had taken its toll on him and everyone involved. Casey was determined to restore some semblance of the old system that dominated from 1947 to 1974, but whatever progress he may have made in that direction was about to unravel. On October 5, 1986, Nicaraguan forces shot down a CIA cargo plane carrying supplies to the Contras, and an American pilot, Eugene Hasenfus, was taken captive. Less than a month later, a story appeared in a Lebanese newspaper, *Al-Shiraa*, which reported that the United States had secretly shipped weapons to Iran. President Reagan flatly denied the story on November 6, 1986, but reversed himself a week later and acknowledged the weapons sales but denied they were sold to secure the release of American hostages held in Lebanon by Iranian-backed militias. The biggest revelation of the story came later that month when the President disclosed that funds from the Iranian arms sales were diverted to Swiss bank accounts for use by the Contras, in an apparent violation of the Boland Amendment.

Various congressional committees were eager to quiz Casey about Iran-Contra, but on December 15, 1986, a day before he was scheduled to testify before Congress about the scandal, he suffered a seizure and was treated for a malignant brain tumor. He resigned his post in January 1987, and died from pneumonia four months later in Long Island, New York. In the interim, there were widespread calls in the media and in Congress for the appointment of an Independent Counsel and for congressional investigations into the affair. President Reagan tried to preempt these actions by announcing the appointment of the Tower Commission on December 1, 1986; the commission, headed by former Senator John Tower, also included former National Security Advisor Brent Scowcroft and former Secretary of State Edmund Muskie. The Tower Commission issued its report on February 26, 1987, which was critical of the President's detached management style and recommended reforms for the NSC, but it in no way deterred the Independent Counsel or the congressional committees from proceeding with their investigations.

Lawrence Walsh was appointed Independent Counsel on December 19, 1986, and he and his staff began a lengthy and costly probe that would stretch well into the 1990s. Walsh's investigation led to a number of convictions, although two of the central figures of the investigation, Oliver North and John Poindexter, had their convictions overturned due in part to the use of immunized testimony. A number of CIA operatives were indicted and convicted, but an attempt to try former Defense Secretary Caspar Weinberger on felony charges of perjury and obstruction of justice was short-circuited when he was pardoned, along with five other figures, by President George H. W. Bush on Christmas Eve 1992.[59]

A joint House-Senate committee began public hearings on May 5, 1987, and once again the old Church Committee canard of a "secret government" growing like "a cancer on the presidency" was raised by members of Congress. Many of the myths promulgated in the mid-1970s were repeated to reinforce the theme of the pernicious effect of the Cold War in warping the American system of government. The Iran-Contra Committee's Majority Report claimed that "peacetime covert action became an instrument of U.S. foreign policy" in response to the Soviet Union, when in fact it had been an instrument of U.S. policy since the 18th century. Proposals were introduced requiring the President to report all covert actions to Congress within forty-eight hours, while another proposal would establish an independent Inspector General's Office within the CIA, subject to Senate confirmation and required to make regular reports to the body. The forty-eight-hour notification proposal passed the Senate but became bogged down in the House, while the Inspector General proposal was signed into law by President George H. W. Bush, despite his reservations that it "could impair the ability of the CIA to collect vitally needed intelligence information." Senator Ernest Hollings agreed, observing that the IG legislation was "another link in the chains that tie down our government and render it passive." The CIA, Hollings added, was in danger of becoming an agency staffed by "cautious bureaucrats who avoid the risks that come with taking action, who fill out every form in triplicate," and put "the emphasis on audit rather than action."[60] Hollings's words were prophetic, but he was one of the few dissenting voices at the time, particularly within the ranks of the Democratic Party.

In retrospect, it is clear that the Iran-Contra Affair was a continuation of a struggle that began in the mid-1970s between Congress and the President over control of the clandestine instruments of American foreign policy. Reagan and Casey wanted to restore presidential discretionary authority in this area. Members of Congress, both Democrats and Republicans, wanted the legislature to play a more assertive role, if not become outright partners, in the management of the American intelligence community. Unfortunately for advocates of executive power and a reinvigorated CIA, the worst was yet to come.

THE CIA AND CONGRESS, 1989–2001: SLOUCHING TOWARD 9/11

During the Presidencies of George H. W. Bush and William Jefferson Clinton, the intelligence committees became more assertive, using both formal and informal methods to increase their leverage over the CIA. A striking example of this was seen in the botched effort to covertly topple Panamanian leader Manuel Noriega. Members of Congress lambasted the Reagan and Bush administrations for their failure to remove Noriega from power, but Congress also resisted plans that might involve violence against the General, or involve the use of corrupt Panamanian officials. Several times prior to the U.S. invasion of Panama in December 1990, the Bush administration presented proposals to overthrow Noriega using disgruntled "assets" inside the Panamanian military and other government agencies. These proposals were subject to lengthy negotiations with the intelligence committees, the latter fearful of CIA entanglement in possible assassination plotting. In one particularly comic incident, Noriega was held at gunpoint by Panamanian officers, while they desperately placed phone calls to CIA officials who ultimately were told to break off the discussions. It was later reported that White House officials were fearful of the congressional reaction if Noriega was harmed in a coup in which the CIA was involved. In the end, after a year and a half of debate over the propriety of harming Manuel Noriega, the U.S. invaded Panama with 22,500 troops, losing 23 American soldiers in the process, and killing at least 220 Panamanians—but Noriega was taken alive.[61]

The CIA became an increasingly demoralized agency as the 1990s evolved. Between 1987 and 1997, the agency had five different Directors: William Webster, Robert Gates, James Woolsey, John Deutch, and George Tenet. While the agency played a prominent role in the presidency of George H. W. Bush (a former DCI), during the Clinton years the CIA became something of a backwater agency. Clinton's first DCI, James Woolsey, was out of the loop; a popular joke around Washington in the mid-1990s concerned a small private plane which landed on the White House lawn and whose misguided pilot was promptly arrested; the punch line had it that it was Jim Woolsey trying to get in to see Bill Clinton. The agency was also rocked by revelations that some of their agents were engaged in acts of espionage against their own country, including Douglas Groat, and most notoriously, Aldrich Ames. While there are a variety of reasons why the agency declined so rapidly in the 1990s, Congress bears much of the responsibility. Shorn of its ability to move quickly, in secret, and if need be with an element of ruthlessness, a new, kinder and gentler agency emerged, encouraged by years of congressional tinkering that transformed the agency into a case study in bureaucratic pathology. CIA employees began filing class action lawsuits seeking redress for their grievances (which on occasion were aired in congressional hearings), pressure was applied from Capitol Hill to remove "bad people" as CIA sources, and agents were required to take ethics courses designed to create honest spies. The agency became top heavy with lawyers between the mid-1970s and the mid-1990s, with some 80 attorneys installed in the agency with broad authority to review its undertakings, while at the same time the agency's management appeared to be equally concerned with day care facilities at Langley as with covert operations.[62]

Congressional Republicans, who had generally opposed the reforms proposed by the Church Committee and Iran-Contra Committee, underwent a conversion during the Clinton years. After capturing control of the Congress in 1994 they took a number of steps to strengthen the intelligence oversight regime. Senate Republicans engaged in a bitter effort to block President Clinton's nominee for DCI, Anthony Lake, demanding raw FBI files on Lake and expressing concern about his approval—while serving as Clinton's National Security Advisor—of a secret Iranian effort to arm Bosnian Muslims. Lake's proclivity for secrecy was apparently deemed an undesirable quality for a Director of Central Intelligence. In another instance, congressional Republicans insisted that the CIA conduct an election-year review of an intelligence estimate, which concluded that ballistic missiles were a remote threat to the U.S. The second study, it was hoped, would produce the desired result—i.e., the U.S. needed to deploy a missile defense system. More high-ranking CIA positions were created and subjected to Senate confirmation, despite the protests of the DCI at the time, John Deutch. Three new assistant directors and a deputy director for community management, along with a general counsel, were added to the layers of management. The Republican Party in modern times has generally opposed top heavy bureaucracies, but in this instance the Party abandoned its principles and thereby accelerated the process of converting the CIA into another sclerotic bureaucracy: a kind of Department of Agriculture with more Ph.D.'s. Pork barrel politics were injected into the intelligence community, as committee members pressured the Agency to buy unwanted technical intelligence collection systems. "Whistleblower" legislation was proposed to protect intelligence community personnel who come forward to members of Congress with information on alleged misconduct. This proposal grew out of a leak of classified information about CIA misdeeds in Guatemala to Representative Robert Torricelli (D-NJ), who, instead of going "privately to the President," as he later admitted was one of his options, proceeded to call a press conference. Mid-level agency officials were subjected to endless briefing requests from Congress (approximately 600 briefings in 1996, along with 5,000 separate intelligence analyses submitted to members) and were sometimes put in the uncomfortable position of choosing between executive branch policymakers and committee inquisitors probing for information to use against the President. The Intelligence Committees frequently requested that the information presented in intelligence briefings be "sanitized" so it could be released to the public for partisan purposes.[63]

Most damaging of all was the flight of talented personnel from the agency throughout the 1990s. Between 1993 and 1999, the agency lost 4,000 of its most skilled employees, or 20 percent of its spies, analysts, scientists, and technological experts. According to a report in the *New York Times*, 7 percent of the agency's spies left the CIA each year during that same period. In 1995, the agency hired 25 covert operations officers, while six times that number were lost to retirement. This hemorrhaging of covert operatives had devastating consequences when the nation entered the new century. Shorn of human operatives around the globe, the United States was ill prepared to confront Osama Bin Laden's Al Qaeda terrorists.[64]

By the mid 1990s, Congress had wrested control of the CIA from the executive branch, in part due to the indifference of President Clinton. One indicator of the depth of this control could be seen in reports that James Woolsey's early retirement as DCI was due in part to his inability to please Senator Dennis DeConcini, the chairman of the Senate Intelligence Committee. One longtime intelligence community official, who knows the CIA from service within the agency and on Capitol Hill, L. Britt Snider, noted in 1997, "Congress has been able to get what it wants from intelligence agencies . . . Some see this compliant posture beginning to take a toll on managers and analysts within the intelligence community. Clearly, it is straining their relationship with the executive branch." Another executive branch official remarked, "Although they would never put it this way, [intelligence agencies] clearly see themselves as working for the Congress rather than the President."[65]

CONCLUSION

The Reagan years marked a significant turning point in the battle between the executive and the legislature over control of America's intelligence community. By 1981, it was clear that an effective intelligence entity could not function while governed by committee, and that elements of spontaneity and risk-taking are the hallmarks of effective intelligence, not a stultifying bureaucratic culture that consults with attorneys before every action and hires technocrats of limited vision and no sense of history. This mediocre culture was encouraged by a congressional oversight system that made few distinctions between the highly sensitive and discreet world of clandestine operations and more routine government functions. Reagan understood how much this new system had "reduced and demoralized" America's intelligence capabilities, and in selecting William Casey as his DCI, he signaled to Congress and the world his determination to reverse this trend and "revitalize" the CIA. Under Casey's leadership, the administration fought for six years to return control of covert operations to the executive branch. Reagan and Casey tried to play by the old rules, and in the end they lost. As a result, William Casey became the last DCI to attempt to wrest power from the congressional oversight system.[66]

Casey is often portrayed as a threat to the Constitution, but he was, at the behest of President Reagan, attempting to restore a system that was in place from 1789 to 1975, when a series of American presidents were given wide latitude to conduct secret operations they deemed to be in the national interest. The nation's founding fathers disagreed on a number of important issues, but they were united in the belief, as Thomas Jefferson put it, that certain functions "should remain known to their executive functionary only." The president was seen by Washington, Hamilton, Madison, and Jefferson as best suited to manage, in the words of *The Federalist Papers*, "the business of intelligence." In our estimation, William Casey did not compromise the Constitution; that description is more appropriately applied to Frank Church, Otis Pike, Edward Boland, and other members of Congress who shifted control of the intelligence community from the executive branch to the legislature. They did so while invoking the legacy of the founding fathers, whose principles and practices they grossly distorted. In so doing, they rendered a once proud intelligence service impotent, setting the stage for intelligence failures with both tragic and fatal results in subsequent decades.

NOTES

1. "Remarks at the Swearing-in Ceremony for William H. Webster as Director of the Central Intelligence Agency," May 26, 1987, *Public Papers of the Presidents of the United States: Ronald Reagan,* Book 1 (Washington, DC: U.S. Government Printing Office, 1989).

2. Stephen F. Knott, *Secret and Sanctioned: Covert Operations and the American Presidency* (New York: Oxford University Press, 1996), 157.

3. Knott, *Secret and Sanctioned,* 160–3.

4. Stephen Knott, "Executive Power and the Control of American Intelligence," *Intelligence and National Security* 13, no. 2 (Summer 1998): 172; Knott, *Secret and Sanctioned,* 174.

5. Kiron M. Skinner, Annelise Anderson, and Martin Anderson, eds., *Reagan: A Life in Letters* (New York: The Free Press, 2003), 546–8.

6. Kiron M. Skinner, Annelise Anderson, and Martin Anderson, eds., *Reagan, In His Own Hand: The Writings of Ronald Reagan That Reveal His Revolutionary Vision for America* (New York: Touchstone, 2002), 121.

7. Skinner, Anderson, and Anderson, *Reagan: A Life in Letters,* 547

8. Skinner, Anderson, and Anderson, *Reagan, In His Own Hand,* 121, 124–6.

9. Lou Cannon, "Reagan Criticizes Carter for Proposing Defense Budget Cuts," *Washington Post,* February 6, 1977.

10. Lou Cannon, "Reagan's Foreign Policy: Scrap 'Weakness, Illusion,' Stress Military Strength," *Washington Post,* February 16, 1980.

11. "Excerpts from Reagan's Televised Speech Rebutting Carter on Foreign Policy," *New York Times,* October 20, 1980.

12. Bob Woodward, *Veil: The Secret Wars of the CIA, 1981–1987* (New York: Simon and Schuster, 1987), 39–41, 46–7.

13. Judith Miller, "Casey, at Senate Hearing, Opposes Shake Up of CIA," *New York Times,* January 14, 1981.

14. Drew Middleton, "For Spying, Old Hands Are Still Better Than the Latest Gadgets," *New York Times,* January 18, 1981.

15. Miller, "Casey, at Senate Hearing, Opposes Shake Up of CIA."

16. Woodward, *Veil,* 83–4.

17. Patrick E. Tyler and Lou Cannon, "Hugel Resigns as Chief of CIA Spy Operations; Career Officer Selected," *Washington Post,* July 15, 1981; Judith Miller, "Director of CIA Asking a Hearing to Answer Critics," *New York Times,* July 27, 1981.

18. George Lardner Jr., "Goldwater Backs CIA Chief, Sees 'Mountain Out of a Molehill'," *Washington Post,* July 18, 1981.

19. Lardner, "Goldwater Backs CIA Chief."

20. George Lardner Jr. and Patrick E. Tyler, "Goldwater, Citing Hugel Scandal, Says CIA's Casey Should Resign," *Washington Post*, July 24, 1981.

21. George Lardner Jr., "Casey Flap: A Short-Lived Summertime Storm," *Washington Post*, July 31, 1981.

22. Patrick E. Tyler, "Friends Lobby to Keep Casey at CIA," *Washington Post,* July 26, 1981; Woodward, *Veil*, 154.

23. Lardner, "Casey Flap."

24. John Prados, *Presidents' Secret Wars: CIA and Pentagon Covert Operations Since World War II* (New York: William Morrow and Company, 1986), 368.

25. Lou Cannon, "CIA Veteran to Be Given Inman's Job," *Washington Post*, April 26, 1982; Philip Taubman, "CIA Expert for Inman Post," *New York Times*, April 26, 1982.

26. Woodward, *Veil*, 210–15.

27. Patrick E. Tyler and Bob Woodward, "U.S. Approves Covert Plan in Nicaragua," *Washington Post,* March 10, 1982; Prados, *Presidents' Secret Wars*, 378–9.

28. Woodward, *Veil*, 173, 176–7, 225–7.

29. Mary McGrory, "SHHHH! Congress Doesn't Want to Wash Our Dirty Little War in Public," *Washington Post*, December 16, 1982.

30. Philip Taubman, "C.I.A. Reportedly Blocked in Plot on Surinamese," *New York Times*, June 1, 1983; Woodward, *Veil*, 240–1.

31. Don Oberdorfer, "Washington's Role Troubles Congress," *Washington Post*, April 3, 1983.

32. Patrick E. Tyler and Don Oberdorfer, "U.S. Role in Nicaragua Arouses Senate Concern," *Washington Post*, April 6, 1983; Philip Taubman and Martin Tolchin, "The Coming Showdown on Central America," *New York Times*, April 10, 1983.

33. Woodward, *Veil*, 243.

34. Martin Tolchin, "Key House Member Fears U.S. Breaks Law on Nicaragua," *New York Times*, April 14, 1983.

35. Ronald Reagan, "Address before a Joint Session of the Congress on Central America," *Public Papers of the President: Ronald Reagan, 1981–1989*, April 27, 1983.

36. Patrick E. Tyler, "Move to End Covert Action against Nicaragua Advances; House Approval Is Predicted," *Washington Post*, April 29, 1983.

37. Patrick E. Tyler, "Senate Panel Compromises on Nicaragua," *Washington Post*, May 7, 1983.

38. Martin Tolchin, "Intelligence Units in Congress at Odds on Covert Latin Aid," *New York Times*, May 18, 1983; Woodward, *Veil*, 252.

39. Prados, *Presidents' Secret Wars*, 389.

40. Philip Taubman, "Central Intelligence Agency; In the Feud with Congress, No Quarter Is Given," *New York Times*, April 13, 1984.

41. Prados, *Presidents' Secret Wars*, 395.

42. "Goldwater Writes CIA Director Scorching Letter," *Washington Post*, April 11, 1984.

43. Martin Tolchin, "Senate, 84–12, Acts to Oppose Mining Nicaragua Ports; Rebuke to Reagan," *New York Times*, April 11, 1984.

44. Taubman, "Central Intelligence Agency."

45. Joanne Omang and Charles R. Babcock, "Moynihan Resigns Intelligence Panel Post, Assails CIA," *Washington Post*, April 16, 1984.

46. Knott, *Secret and Sanctioned*, 179.

47. Omang and Babcock, "Moynihan Resigns Intelligence Panel Post, Assails CIA."

48. Philip Taubman, "Moynihan to Keep Intelligence Post," *New York Times*, April 27, 1984.

49. John M. Goshko and Charles R. Babcock, "Senate Panel and CIA Agree on Notification, *Washington Post*, June 8, 1984; Woodward, *Veil*, 359.

50. Joel Brinkley, "C.I.A. Primer Tells Nicaraguan Rebels How to Kill," *New York Times*, October 17, 1984.

51. John M. Goshko and Margaret Shapiro, "CIA Manual for Guerrillas Denounced by Rep. Boland; Contras Instructed in Assassination," *Washington Post*, October 18, 1984.

52. Joel Brinkley, "President Orders 2 Investigations on C.I.A. Manual," *New York Times*, October 19, 1984; Woodward, *Veil*, 390.

53. Joel Brinkley, "House Panel Calls C.I.A. Manual Illegal," *New York Times*, December 6, 1984.

54. Bob Woodward, "CIA Anti-Qaddafi Plan Backed; Reagan Authorizes Covert Operation to Undermine Libyan Regime," *Washington Post*, November 3, 1985.

55. Warren Richey, "CIA Attempts to Put Finger in Leaking Intelligence Dike," *Christian Science Monitor*, November 21, 1985.

56. David B. Ottaway, "Leahy Joins Durenberger in Criticizing CIA; Agency Accused of 'Yearning' for Days before Hill Oversight," *Washington Post*, November 16, 1985.

57. Sam Zagoria, "Durenberger, Casey, and The Post," *Washington Post*, November 20, 1985.

58. Knott, *Secret and Sanctioned*, 181.

59. *Final Report of the Independent Counsel for Iran-Contra Matters*, vol. 1, *Investigations and Prosecutions*, Lawrence E. Walsh, Independent

Counsel, August 4, 1993, Washington, D.C.; American Federation of Scientists, http://fas.org/irp/offdocs/walsh/chron.htm.

60. Knott, *Secret and Sanctioned*, 182–3.

61. Stephen Engelberg and Susan F. Rasky "White House, Noriega, and Battle in Congress," *New York Times*, October 25, 1989, A10; "Doubts Aired on CIA Policy," *Boston Globe*, April 7, 1990; "CIA Seeks Looser Rules on Killings During Coups," *New York Times*, October 17, 1989, A1. For an example of the congressional sentiment at the time toward coups and assassinations, see Daniel P. Moynihan's op-ed, "Assassinations: Can't We Learn?" *New York Times,* October 20, 1989, A35.

62. "CIA Breaks Links to Agents Abroad," *New York Times*, March 3, 1997, A1; "Why the Senate Loves an Understudy," *Time* (March 31, 1997): 38; "Does America Need the CIA?" *Insight Magazine* (August 17, 1998): 67.

63. Knott, "Executive Power and the Control of American Intelligence," 173–5; Stephen F. Knott, "The Great Republican Transformation on Oversight," *International Journal of Intelligence and Counterintelligence* 13, no. 1, 2000, 53–6.

64. Tim Weiner, "Spies Wanted," *New York Times Magazine*, January 24, 1999, 16; Frederick Hitz, "The Incredible Shrinking Spy Machine," *Washington Post*, September 15, 1998, A21.

65. L. Britt Snider, "Sharing Secrets with Lawmakers: Congress as a User of Intelligence," Center for the Study of Intelligence, February 1997, 50–1.

66. Ronald Reagan, "Remarks at a Dinner for Former Members of the Office of Strategic Services," *Public Papers of the President: Ronald Reagan, 1981–1989,* May 29, 1986; "Remarks at the Swearing-in Ceremony for William H. Webster as Director of the Central Intelligence Agency," May 26, 1987, *Public Papers of the Presidents of the United States.*

Index

About the Contributors

Ryan J. Barilleaux is professor and chair of the department of political science, Miami University, Oxford, Ohio. He is the author or editor of seven books on the presidency and American politics, most recently *Power and Prudence: The Presidency of George H. W. Bush* (with Mark J. Rozell).

Andrew E. Busch is associate professor of government at Claremont McKenna College. He is author or coauthor of a number of books on American politics, including *Red over Blue: The 2004 Elections and American Politics* (with James Ceaser) and *Ronald Reagan and the Politics of Freedom*.

Jeff Chidester is the project assistant for the Ronald Reagan Oral History Project at the University of Virginia's Miller Center of Public Affairs. He earned his B.A. in political science from Grove City College (PA) and his M.A. in international history from the London School of Economics. He is the author of several articles and the coauthor of *The Reagan Years* (with Stephen F. Knott; forthcoming May 2005).

Gary L. Gregg II holds the Mitch McConnell Chair in Leadership at the University of Louisville where he is also director of the McConnell Center for Political Leadership. He is the author or editor of five books including *Considering the Bush Presidency* (with Mark J. Rozell) and *Thinking about the Presidency*.

Wynton C. Hall is assistant professor of speech communication at Bainbridge College. He is the coauthor, along with Dick Wirthlin, of *The Greatest Communicator: What Ronald Reagan Taught Me about Politics, Leadership, and Life* (2004). His written work has also been published in the *New York Times*, *USA Today*, *The Washington Times*, *The Western Journal of Communication*, *Presidential Studies Quarterly*, and elsewhere.

Christopher Kelley is visiting assistant professor of political science at Miami University, Oxford, Ohio. He was a fellow at the Kettering Foundation and is the editor and contributor to *Executing the Constitution: Placing the Presidency in the Constitution*.

Paul Kengor is professor of political science at Grove City College and a visiting fellow with the Hoover Institution on War, Revolution, and Peace at Stanford University. He is author of the bestselling books *God and Ronald Reagan* and *God and George W. Bush*. A former member of the editorial board of *Presidential Studies Quarterly*, his work on Ronald Reagan has been featured in a variety of publications, from *Political Science Quarterly* and the *Chronicle of Higher Education* to *USA Today, The New York Times,* the *Wall Street Journal,* and the *Washington Post*, among many other sources.

Stephen F. Knott is an associate professor and research fellow at the Miller Center of Public Affairs at the University of Virginia. He directed the Miller Center's Ronald Reagan Oral History Project and is the author of *Secret and Sanctioned: Covert operations and the American Presidency* (1996).

Michael Nelson is professor of political science at Rhodes College. His most recent books are *The Elections of 2004* (2005) and *The Presidency and the Political System* (8th ed., 2005). He has written numerous scholarly articles and chapters, more than forty of which have been reprinted in anthologies of history, political science, and English composition. He is senior editor of the American Presidential Elections book series for the University Press of Kansas.

Jack Rossotti is assistant professor in the Washington Semester Program at American University. He has published various articles in the general area of interest groups and the Supreme Court, including "Nonlegal Advice: The Amicusbriefs in *Webster v. Reproductive Health Services*," with Lara Natelson and Raymond Tatalovich in *Judicature*, as well as "Campaigning for the Court: Interest Group Participation in the Bork and Thomas Confirmation Processes," with Christine DeGregorio, in Cigler, Allan J. and Burdett A. Loomis (eds.), *Interest Group Politics* (4th ed.).

Mark J. Rozell is professor of public policy and director of the Master of Public Policy Program at George Mason University. He is the author of numerous studies of the American presidency including, most recently, *Power and Prudence: The Presidency of George H.W. Bush* (2004, coauthor with Ryan Barilleaux) and *Executive Privilege: Presidential Power, Secrecy and Accountability* (2002, 2d edition).

Peter Schweizer is a research fellow at the Hoover Institution on War, Revolution, and Peace at Stanford University. He received his M.Phil. in international affairs from Oxford University and his B.A. from George Washington University. His recent books include *Reagan's War*, *The Bushes*, and *The Fall of the Wall: Reassessing the Causes and Consequences of the End of the Cold War*. His written work has appeared in *Foreign Affairs*, *New York Times*, *Wall Street Journal*, and *Orbis: A Journal of World Affairs*.

Matthew Sitman is a Ph.D. student in political theory at Georgetown University. He received his bachelor's degree from Grove City College. His interests include the American presidency, particularly the Nixon Presidency.

Mitch Sollenberger is a Ph.D. candidate in American politics at The Catholic University of America in Washington, DC.

Elizabeth Edwards Spalding is assistant professor of government at Claremont McKenna College. She is completing a book entitled

The War of Nerves: Harry S. Truman and the Origins of Contain-ment and has been published, among other places, in *Comparative Political Studies*, *Presidential Studies Quarterly*, and the *Claremont Review of Books*.

Shirley Anne Warshaw is professor of political science at Gettysburg College. She received her B.A. from the University of Pennsylvania, MGA from the Wharton School of Finance and Comerce at the University of Pennsylvania, and Ph.D. from Johns Hopkins University. Among her recent books are *The Clinton Years* (2004) and *The Keys to Power: Managing the Presidency* (2004). She specialized in presidential studies, particularly the White House and the Cabinet. She is a frequent guest on National Public Radio and provides commentary in the media on the presidency and elections issues.

DATE DUE

	MAY 04 '10		